KERRY BROWN is Professor of Chinese Studies and Director of the Lau China Institute at King's College London and Associate on the Asia Programme at Chatham House. Prior to this he was Professor of Chinese Politics and Director of the China Studies Centre at the University of Sydney. With 25 years' experience of China, he has worked in education, business and government, including a term as First Secretary at the British Embassy in Beijing. He has written on China for the *London Review of Books*, the *Diplomat* and *Foreign Policy* as well as for many international and Chinese media outlets. He is the bestselling author of *CEO, China* (I.B. Tauris, 2016) and *The New Emperors: Power and the Princelings in China* (I.B. Tauris, 2014). His other books include *Contemporary China* (2012), *Friends and Enemies: The Past, Present and Future of the Communist Party of China* (2009) and *Struggling Giant: China in the 21st Century* (2007).

WHAT DOES
CHINA WANT?

CHINA'S WORLD

KERRY BROWN

I.B. TAURIS
LONDON · NEW YORK

Published in 2017 by
I.B.Tauris & Co. Ltd
London • New York
www.ibtauris.com

Copyright © 2017 Kerry Brown

The right of Kerry Brown to be identified as the author of this work has been asserted by the author in accordance with the Copyright, Designs and Patents Act 1988.

References to websites were correct at the time of writing.

ISBN: 978 1 78453 809 5
eISBN: 978 1 78672 219 5
ePDF: 978 1 78673 219 4

A full CIP record for this book is available from the British Library
A full CIP record is available from the Library of Congress

Library of Congress Catalog Card Number: available

Text designed and typeset by Tetragon, London
Printed and bound in Sweden by ScandBook AB

To Jolita Pons and Rebecca Fabrizi,
for friendship and wise advice

CONTENTS

ACKNOWLEDGEMENTS   IX

LIST OF ABBREVIATIONS   XI

INTRODUCTION   1

1 THE PRINCIPLES OF CHINESE FOREIGN POLICY   11

2 THE WORLD ACCORDING TO XI JINPING   40

3 CHINA AND THE UNITED STATES:
   THE ULTIMATE LOVE–HATE RELATIONSHIP   75

4 ZONE TWO: THE ASIA REGION   112

5 ZONE THREE: THE EU AND CHINA –
   CIVILIZED PARTNERS TALKING PAST EACH OTHER   145

6 ZONE FOUR: THE WIDER WORLD   173

CONCLUSION: TELLING THE CHINA STORY   201

NOTES   217

SUGGESTED READING   231

INDEX   237

ACKNOWLEDGEMENTS

I would like to express my gratitude to the publishers, and in particular Tomasz Hoskins, for commissioning this and the two previous books in this trilogy. Working with I.B.Tauris has been a happy collaboration. I am also thankful for the many people with whom I have discussed ideas drawn on in this work. I would also like to thank Sun Jiabao and Jolita Pons for reading through the first drafts and making many helpful and useful comments. Finally, I would like to thank Sarah Terry for her hard work on the copy-editing.

LIST OF ABBREVIATIONS

AIIB	Asian Infrastructure Investment Bank
APEC	Asia–Pacific Economic Cooperation
ASEAN	Association of Southeast Asian Nations
BRI	Belt Road Initiative
BRICS	Brazil, Russia, India, China and South Africa
CASCF	China–Arab States Cooperation Forum
CCP	Chinese Communist Party
CMC	Central Military Commission
CNOOC	China National Offshore Oil Corporation
DPRK	Democratic People's Republic of Korea
EEC	European Economic Community
IMF	International Monetary Fund
MFA	Ministry of Foreign Affairs
MSS	Ministry of State Security
PLA	People's Liberation Army
PRC	People's Republic of China
RMB	renminbi (the official currency of the PRC)
SCO	Shanghai Cooperation Organization
UNCLOS	UN Convention on the Law of the Sea
WTO	World Trade Organization

INTRODUCTION

On 27 November 2015, the Ministry of Foreign Affairs (MFA) of the People's Republic of China (PRC) declared that it was establishing, for the first time ever, a naval installation beyond its shores, in the impoverished eastern African state of Djibouti. 'These facilities will help Chinese vessels to better carry out Chinese missions like escort and humanitarian operations,' spokesperson Hong Lei declared.[1] In practical terms, the project being envisaged was minuscule, and focused purely on Chinese naval assets. But this did not stop some commentators from reading much more into it. In the British *Daily Telegraph*, one writer stated that

> China's decision earlier this month that it is to build its own naval base in Djibouti, the first time Beijing has sought to establish a permanent military presence beyond the country's borders, has been greeted with deep concern at the [US] Pentagon.[2]

For much of the Western media, this was a tangible sign of Beijing's ambition, its desire to become a new kind of superpower, one with the ability to project far beyond its borders, a force to be reckoned with way beyond its traditional theatre of influence, Asia.

Even with a story as simple as this, however, there are no easy conclusions, and China's new planned facilities can be read as much as a sign of reluctance and weakness as one of assertiveness and strength. That the world's second largest economy had no military assets abroad is the first anomaly. US capability stretches to almost every corner of the earth, with over 640 installations in more than 120 countries.[3] China is the main trading partner for about 130 countries across the globe. And yet, it has one aircraft carrier (an old, retrofitted one bought from Ukraine in the early 2000s). The United States has more than 11, France two. China may well have showed off a lot of new-looking weaponry when it held its grand parade marking the 70th anniversary of the ending of the Sino–Japanese War in September 2015. But, as analysts were quick to point out, almost all of this was untested. In nearly four decades, since the Reform period started in 1978, China has seen only one war, a brief skirmish with Vietnam in 1979 from which it came out badly. It is therefore a vast, important country with a huge military (some 2 million active servicepeople) and almost zero experience.

Djibouti was therefore remarkable because of the amount of interest and speculation such a minor facility drew. In the same tiny country in eastern Africa, the United States has a major site with 4,000 people (almost two and a half times the number of people that China planned to deploy). They have intelligence-gathering assets to hand, and a runway to accommodate aircraft. China simply aimed to have a port. It has a simple reason for this, too, linked not to neo-imperialist designs but to trade. For a country led by a political movement which had made economic development the core pillar of its legitimacy since the death of Mao Zedong in 1976, it was odd that China did not have, at the very least, some local capacity to look after their interests – especially considering its growing reliance on oil imports from the restive Middle East region and the fact that oil transportation along stretches of the Indian Ocean is becoming increasingly vulnerable to US control or piracy. Nor was this situation new. For over a decade, it had been participating in United Nations anti-piracy operations. Within this context, Djibouti made eminent sense. It was strange, in fact, that China had not gone along this route earlier.

China's foreign policy in this era, the era of its material enrichment, has become a battleground. As this book aims to show, there is plenty of disagreement outside the country about who calls the shots over specific policies and issues on international relations, and also within the country over just how to influence and feed into its foreign policy. Outside the country, speculations about Chinese intentions have reached fever pitch. Half the world feels that it is only a matter of time before China controls the whole planet like some modern-day Roman Empire, especially in view of the parlous state of the United States and European Union after their harsh experiences in 2016. But the other half believes that China will remain a low-key, inward-looking, self-interested player who looks more like a mouse than a tiger, timid and cautious in its approach to the world around it and constantly wary of irritating or angering the United States beyond issues that directly relate to it.

This external schizophrenia is exacerbated by two issues. One is the lack of transparency within China over who has real powers, and what the objectives of these power-holders might be. The Chinese Communist Party (CCP) is an organization with a history of privileging covert behaviour and playing its cards close to its chest. But this is only a modern manifestation of a proclivity throughout China's long imperial history to place secrecy on a higher plane than other modes of behaviour. In the third century BC, the great legalist Han Fei declared that trusting others only allowed them to control you. The best attitude was to be remote, hidden, observing unseen, and to never allow others the privilege of quite divining what you were up to. 'Undertakings,' Han Fei declared, 'succeed through secrecy but fail through being found out.'[4] Opacity has remained a strong characteristic of the current leaders of China, modern followers of Han Fei to a man (as of 2017 there are no women in the summit of power, the Standing Committee of the Politburo). This has only been reinforced by the Soviet-style system of governance adopted by the CCP after coming to power in 1949.

Such a style of behaviour is not well suited to making those outside the country feel wholly relaxed and trusting when they interact with it. The lingering feeling that foreigners are not being told the full story – that there is some hidden agenda or some trick they are having played on them – has never entirely been dispelled, no matter how much the People's Republic itself has talked in recent years of being a peace-loving, trustworthy and cooperative actor.

The second issue is not so much China's fault as a result of circumstances. In the Maoist era, from 1949 to 1976, the country had barely any trade with the outside world, and was largely inward-looking. Between the year of its foundation and 1978, there were estimated to have been less than a million individual journeys across the country's borders. This is symbolized by the fact that in 1966, during the opening turmoil brought about by the Cultural Revolution, only one ambassador from Beijing remained in post abroad – Huang Hua, in Egypt.[5] In 2014, the situation had transformed beyond recognition. More than 100 million cross-border journeys were recorded in a single year, with China becoming a major part of global investment, tourist and trade flow figures. In the space of half a century, the country has gone from being an intrinsically parochial, introverted entity to one where every aspect of its new reality has an international dimension. It is a global power, influential in environmental policy (albeit largely because of its own colossal problems), financial issues and global economic developments. The US Treasury has to factor in China's growth projections in order to work out how their own economy is likely to fare. And a slowdown in Shanghai and Beijing from 2013 had an immediate, visible impact in the Australian cities Sydney and Melbourne. A country with an opaque decision-making system is a major global player in most areas, apart from hard military activity. This combination more than any other explains why getting to grips with China's foreign policy attracts so much interest. It is a conundrum that we all need to solve, whether we work in business, government relations or the cultural arena. This remains true today, and will remain true for the next century or more.

In the past, the foreign policy of the PRC was a specialist, under-exposed and under-studied area. That era is well and truly over. In the 1960s, and even into the 1980s, it was more important to put effort into understanding the Soviet Union, and most diplomatic careers tended to be built either by specializing in the United States, Europe or the USSR. China was an exotic sideline. Those sent from Western foreign services to do their time in Beijing (or Peking, as it was called back then) usually did this in order to tick the box saying they had done at least one posting classified as 'hardship', and then could go on to bigger and better things. Being a US or British ambassador to the PRC ranked surprisingly low. China's diplomatic position was either regarded as wholly dictated by its alliance with the USSR (at least up to the late 1950s) or as being bound by narrow definitions of self-interest as it continued its era of inward-looking reconstruction (up to the mid-1980s). It was seen, in US expert on Chinese international relations Robert S. Ross's terms, as predominantly a land power, one with no real interest in projecting its powers in the waters around it, one haunted by a sense of its past greatness but which had had a terrible experience of modernity and was still emerging from the trauma that the modern world had given it. Indeed, through much of the 1990s and 2000s, the challenge was to get China to become involved in issues beyond its borders, rather than trying to contain it and hedge it in.

All of this has now changed. This book will look at the foreign policy of China under its president since 2013, Xi Jinping. It forms the final part of a trilogy of works I have published on the leadership of China since 2014. The first of these, *The New Emperors: Power and the Princelings in China* (2014) looks at the political elite, their backgrounds, networks and the ways in which they managed to reach the summit of decision-making in the country in the period

from 2007 to 2012, when the 18th Party Congress held in Beijing
that year elevated them. The second, *CEO, China: The Rise of Xi
Jinping* (2016), focuses on the eponymous general secretary and
president – the figure at the heart of contemporary political life
in the People's Republic – and the sources of visible and invisible
power around him, from institutions, to ideology, to narratives and
stories. That segues into this work. While *The New Emperors* and
CEO, China place the field of domestic policy in the foreground and
look peripherally at the world beyond China's borders, this work
looks predominantly at China's current view of the outside world,
and how the outside world links to its own internal dynamics and
preoccupations.

There is a simple reason why this deserves special attention. While
showing residual characteristics from an earlier era (strong support
for sovereignty, observance at least rhetorically in the non-interference in others' internal affairs, a desire to keep a low profile and
not opt for unilateral action in issues that do not directly concern
it), China's diplomatic behaviour is undergoing the same kind of
revolution that its economy has seen in the last three and a half
decades. Suddenly, it has become deeply involved in the Middle
East, taking part in the negotiations with Iran over nuclear weapons
in 2015 and, at the end of the year, even hinting at becoming a
mediator over the interminable and terrifying civil war in Syria.
With the United States it has set the global pace in terms of climate-change accords, but it is also creating entities like the Asian
Infrastructure Investment Bank (AIIB) and the Belt Road (new Silk
Road) Initiative (BRI), which seem to be creating a network away
from the United States. This area of greater diplomatic ambition
is striking because it brings to the surface all the ambiguity and
reservations about what sort of power China is. What makes the
country's leaders tick? What do they want to gain? What is their
final vision, and how does the rest of the world fit into this? In the
last few years these questions have become more pressing and more

urgent to answer than they were even in the mid-2000s, or when China entered the World Trade Organization (WTO) in 2002. They have become even more salient with the election of Donald Trump as president of the United States in 2016, pushing China towards taking the lead on even more issues, ranging from climate change to free-trade deals, as the world's remaining superpower looks like it is retrenching and withdrawing from these areas to a more back-seat role.

While focusing on the Xi period, this book will locate current Chinese foreign-policy thinking and behaviour in an historic context, which will predominantly be spelled out in Chapter 1. As with foreign policy everywhere, there are issues that involve emotions, aspirations and moral standing, which run alongside hard-nosed strategic thinking about easily quantified political and economic goals. Beyond these issues, there are nationally constructed narratives of empowerment and victimhood and the ways they betray desires to have status and global standing. These are very hard to quantify and describe. Xi Jinping himself has stated that he wants Chinese leaders to tell the story of their country well, which means that the outside world needs to start listening to this story, and to see what sort of framework they can fit it into. Is China a usurper, a rule-breaker, disruptive and ultimately destructive of the hard-won post-World War II order? Or is it something more benign, a rule-observer, more reliant on the predictability and benign stability of the global political and economic order, rather than one seeking to undo it and remake it in its own image? If it is a usurper, does the world, led by the United States, seek to contain it, thwart it and change it, or is it doomed to see some kind of final conflict, as has happened so often in the past, where a new power seeks to topple the old and create its own form of dominance? If it is power-seeking to defend the status quo, does the current international settlement do justice to the sort of contribution that China could make? Should it be granted more space, more ability to operate in the global financial and political system? And does it offer new models and ideas on how to function as a country in the twenty-first century, a country without a history of colonization, one which comes from different philosophical roots to that of the main players until now – the United States and, before that, Europe?

Answering these questions is important, because once the world knows what sort of China it is dealing with, it can formulate the right policy response. Gearing up on containment policies if China is a rule-keeper and not a rule-breaker would be like fighting with an ally – a waste of energy and opportunity. But ceding space to China would also be wrong if its ultimate plan is to thwart the intentions of the West and remake the world in its own image and for its own purpose; the United States and its allies would be collaborating in something that would be aimed at seeing their demise. Sleepwalking towards a conflict between China and the United States and the latter's allies would also be a needless and terrible tragedy. But trying to stifle and frustrate China's ambition, and the ambition of its 1.4 billion people, would be morally and politically indefensible. It would also prove impossible to restrain such an immense human wave of expectation, creating immense resentment were it to be attempted.

Thinking about modern Chinese foreign policy therefore means considering several vexatious questions that come close to the issue of working out what in essence this country – the People's Republic of China, with its unique 'socialism with Chinese characteristics' political model but its ancient thought, traditions and attitudes – is. The first chapter will therefore outline some of the underpinnings of the Chinese foreign-policy story: the narrative of national humiliation, the strong desire for sovereignty and autonomy, the emphasis on self-determination and the move since 1978 to enjoy relations with the outside world that benefit it while keeping out its less benign forms of influence. These fundamental principles of Chinese diplomatic behaviour will then be brought up to date with the Xi style of foreign relations, showing where they remain the same and where there are differences.

To illustrate the points made above, the rest of the book will look at the zones of influence around China, running from its most important set of relationships with the United States and its regional neighbours, partners it shares a wide range of interests with, to those more peripheral to it where its concerns focus on its need for resources and economic partnership. There will therefore be specific chapters covering the United States, Asia (the world of the 'Belt Road Initiative'), the EU, and finally the Middle East, Latin America and Africa. Surprisingly, very few scholars have attempted to explain the full range of China's relations. While there are superb studies on the various discrete aspects of its currency diplomacy, from Pakistan to North Korea to the United States and the United Kingdom, there are far fewer non-theoretical grand overviews. This book cannot go into minute detail on such a vast subject, but it does attempt to do as Xi Jinping himself said he did in governing China: to rise to a high vantage point and get a good look over the whole terrain, trying to see how it all fits together. Only from this point is it likely to answer the thorny questions posed in this Introduction about what sort of power China is, and how it might behave in the coming decades. This work will hopefully give some suggestions as to how these questions might be answered.

1

THE PRINCIPLES OF CHINESE FOREIGN POLICY

The modern state of the People's Republic of China, for all the protestations of antiquity – its current leaders make much of their 'unbroken' link to an ancient culture – is in fact the result of an extensive period of war, unrest, revolution and change. From 1644 to 1911/12, the Qing dynasty ruled the approximate territory now covered by the PRC. Periods of expansion and external aggression from the late seventeenth to the eighteenth century saw them annex the Tibetan plateau and the area in the north-west now called Xinjiang. Once these campaigns ended, the borders of the Qing empire did not radically change, and they are broadly the territorial limits within which the PRC now sits.[1]

By the nineteenth century, Qing China was a stagnating polity, beset by internal and external threats. Symptomatic of this was the vast Taiping uprising, which ran for almost two decades after 1850 and led to an estimated 20 million deaths. But it was at this time that the Qing came up against the full force of western modernity, in the form of the British imperial navy. The two Opium Wars, in 1839–42 and 1856–60, saw Hong Kong Island ceded to Great Britain and the extraction of vast indemnities from the country, forcing it to open up to forms and modes of foreign trade it had not previously wanted to engage with. By the turn of the twentieth century, successive clashes with neighbours and internal divisions

had significantly debilitated the Qing, and it finally collapsed in
1911/12. Its replacement, the Republican government, saw China
wracked by division and instability, culminating in a calamitous and
tragic descent in the 1930s into international and internecine war.

This history, steeped in blood and suffering, is important to
understand because for modern Chinese political leaders, and
indeed for the general public, it is still alive. In many ways it is
not over. As academic William Callahan has described, the 1990s
saw a reawakening of interest and awareness about the 'century of
humiliation', the label given to the period from 1840 to 1949 when
China suffered so much. 1949 therefore is seen in this narrative
as a double liberation – the first from internal feudalism and old
thinking, and second from external oppression.[2] The creation of
the People's Republic in this historiography is truly a renaissance.
This is best illustrated by the preamble to the official 1982 national
constitutions of the PRC:

> After waging protracted and arduous struggles, armed and
> otherwise, along a zigzag course, the Chinese people of all
> nationalities led by the Communist Party of China with
> Chairman Mao Zedong as its leader ultimately, in 1949,
> overthrew the rule of imperialism, feudalism and bureau-
> crat-capitalism, won a great victory in the New-Democratic
> Revolution and founded the People's Republic of China.
> Since then the Chinese people have taken control of state
> power and become masters of the country.[3]

This idea that the Communist Party acted on behalf of all Chinese
people, and took the lead in their deliverance from all forms of
oppression, is one that gets reiterated to this day. Speaking after
reviewing the military parade marking the seventieth anniversary
of the ending of the Sino–Japanese War and World War II in Asia
in 2015, Xi Jinping stated:

The victory of the Chinese People's War of Resistance Against Japanese Aggression is the first complete victory won by China in its resistance against foreign aggression in modern times. This great triumph crushed the plot of the Japanese militarists to colonize and enslave China and put an end to China's national humiliation of suffering successive defeats at the hands of foreign aggressors in modern times. This great triumph re-established China as a major country in the world and won the Chinese people respect of all peace-loving people around the world. This great triumph opened up bright prospects for the great renewal of the Chinese nation and set our ancient country on a new journey after gaining rebirth.[4]

The themes of national humiliation, struggle, liberation and rebirth have proved rich ones for China's current leaders to mine in order to get public support. This is partly because to some extent these statements are accurate. But as historians continue to show, they are also a gross oversimplification. The key point to observe here is that this historic framework is the primary one within which leaders like Xi Jinping see their country and its role in the world. They are operating within a history where, in their view, a great and glorious civilization was eroded and felled by foreign aggression and internal corruption and weakness. This led to terrible suffering, particularly under the Japanese, until the Chinese people were united by the Communists and the People's Republic was recreated. Since 1949, the country has been on a mission to restore itself to the centre of the world stage. Chinese foreign policy operates within this emotional framework. It is from this framework that issues like the treatment of China's regional role, its relations with Japan, its stand on the South and East China Seas, its attitude towards the United States, and its principles of foreign policy derive.

THE IDEAS

The history of Qing and Republican China had been one of vic-
timization and suffering, and one of the PRC's first promises was
to break with the past by sticking to clear principles of behaviour
in foreign policy matter. In 1949, after all, it was still vulnerable.
It had one major international ally, the USSR, but for Europe and
the United States its choice of political model (Communism) made
it immediately suspect. While the United Kingdom recognized
the PRC diplomatically in January 1950 to preserve its interests in
Hong Kong, the United States resisted. Matters were not helped by
the activities of North Korean leader Kim Il-sung, whose unilateral
launching of an assault on South Korea resulted in a bloody three-
year war which pitted Chinese troops against US ones within a UN
force. The Korean War stalemate in 1953 carried political costs for
China, ensuring that it got locked into the same Cold War environment as the USSR in the eyes of the United States. It also meant
that by the mid-1950s China had become increasingly isolated.

Throughout the 1950s, the new PRC started to articulate what,
by 1955, soon came to be known as the Five Principles of Peaceful
Coexistence. These were: mutual respect for each other's territorial
integrity and sovereignty (at the Asian–African Conference of 1953);
mutual non-aggression; mutual non-interference in each other's
internal affairs; equality and cooperation for mutual benefit (at the
Sino–Indian Joint Statement and Sino–Burmese Joint Statement
in 1954); and peaceful coexistence.[5] There are good arguments to
show that these were derived from ideas originally put forward by
Indian leader Nehru. They were inspired by similar anxieties – a
desire to preserve hard-won autonomy after an extensive period of
colonial interference; the need to safeguard sovereignty; the stress
on cooperation among what were seen as the non-hegemonic and
non-aligned nations; and the desire to demonstrate a peaceable
stance towards the rest of the world – designed to counter all the

fears of a predatory Marxist ideology and world revolution held by many outsiders.

The Five Principles became the mantra on which China's foreign policy and its relations with the outside world have been built ever since, but they have proved controversial. And there are plenty of questions about how fit for purpose they are for a country which is now economically and politically so much stronger and more prominent than the one that adopted these over half a century ago. The principles have been accused of delineating a Chinese attitude which is introspective, self-interested, and, ironically, unprincipled, looking solely after itself and not wishing to have responsibility for others. China has defended its posture on domestic issues like Tibet, Xinjiang and its human rights behaviour by producing the 'non-interference' language taken from the principles, and has similarly desisted from commenting on the affairs of other countries over the same issues. This has sometimes given the country's foreign policy a highly amoral tone. More importantly, critics have also found plenty of evidence that in fact while China has said – and still to some extent continues to say – that it observes the principles, in practice it barely heeds them. This lays it open to accusations of hypocrisy.[6]

TETCHY NEIGHBOUR

Preservation of itself against foreign interference was at the heart of a number of arguments that China had with neighbours over the 1950s and into the 1970s. In this era, when China was not even recognized as a state by the UN (its seat on the General Assembly was occupied by the Republic of China, whose leaders had fled to the island of Taiwan after defeat in the Civil War in 1949), it was engaged in a series of skirmishes, clashes and out-and-out conflicts with its neighbours. Most of these were about contested borders. As US scholar M. Taylor Fravel has pointed out, at its birth the PRC was locked in disputes with over 22 separate parts of its borders. The most contentious of these were with the USSR, Vietnam and India, and over the ensuing three decades it came into actual conflict with each of these – India in 1962, the USSR in 1969 and Vietnam in 1979. Each led to casualties and diplomatic fallout, and the 1969 border clash with the USSR in the depths of the Cultural Revolution alerted the United States in particular to the parlous state of Sino–Soviet relations and the opportunity for a rapprochement. This was achieved in 1972 with the visit by President Richard Nixon.

Remarkably, the PRC was to slowly but decisively address most of these territorial issues, at least as far as land ones were concerned. In the late 1950s and into the early 1960s it resolved some of the disputes with Myanmar and Vietnam. Over three decades later it addressed the Russian issue when then-president Jiang Zemin agreed a huge deal with President Putin. By 2010, all but the two outstanding disputes (those with India) had been resolved. Interestingly, despite its shrill talk in the lead-up to most negotiations about never ceding territory and vehemently protecting Chinese national sovereignty, the PRC was willing to be remarkably pragmatic in the way in which it solved arguments. The case with Russia is illustrative of this, with the PRC relinquishing some 40,000 square kilometres to the USSR in order to reach a deal: something that was never publicly admitted at the time, at least within China.[7]

WHAT'S A BORDER, ANYWAY?

Part of the issue of China's arguments over its own borders was born from the simple lack of an historical Chinese concept within Chinese history of what a border actually was. The idea of sovereignty and of a nation state, after all, was born of the European Westphalian treaty in 1648, and there is no simple Asian equivalent to this. Many would argue that a large number of countries bordering or close to China, from Myanmar to Laos and Cambodia, were creations of colonial interference, their borders the result of historical accident rather than geography, culture or anything remotely approaching diplomatic reason. In addition to this, there was the question of how Chinese rulers, before and after 1949, conceptualized the entity they were in charge of. Historically, it has been argued that Chinese emperors and political leaders saw China more as a cultural or civilizational sphere, rather than occupying a specific geography. There were issues of vassal states around China who had unclear, somewhat contested relations with the 'mother culture'. Through language, religion, art and customs, 'China' operated in this context more as a nebulous concept, something that was able to almost annex and overcome people no matter what territory they were in because of its appeal and civilizing essence.[8]

Beyond this, there were also issues of the way in which the PRC's predecessor entities had operated diplomatically during the long imperial era. They had not supported naval operations – at least not since the Ming dynasty and the famous but brief travels of the eunuch Admiral Zheng He in the early fifteenth century. On the whole, Imperial Chinese dynasties had operated as land entities, creating security from the huge natural bulwark of the Tibetan plateau and the vast, empty steppes of central and north-east Asia. In the era of the Great Khans in the thirteenth and fourteenth centuries, the imperial dynasties of the Song and later the Ming had experienced their greatest threats before the modern era from the land, not from the sea. This therefore created a mindset focused on land issues, one that never looked too deeply into the vast seas and oceans around the eastern and southern coasts. Only in the twentieth century did these really begin to exist for Chinese leaders, and only in the era after Mao did China start to create something approaching a naval strategy.

CHINA AND THE WORLD IN THE TWENTY-FIRST CENTURY: JOINING THE DOTS

The preceding sections offer some context which is important in helping to understand how PRC leaders see the role of the nation they lead in the world of the twenty-first century. History matters to them. The memory of humiliation at the hands of colonizers and aggressors continues to be strong, giving a highly emotional aspect to their foreign policy, a mood Christopher Coker has typified as 'resentful'.[9] It is a foreign-policy attitude which mixes bitter memories of past defeats and humiliations and the desire to be once more a strong, powerful state, along with elements of long-term strategic thinking. It would be simplest to describe it as a hybrid, combining secrecy, resentment, practicality and seriousness.

This idea of Chinese leaders having a long-term, strategic vision for their county, one which is patently clear to them but which they seek to conceal and hide, is a perennial theme of commentary about Chinese attitudes towards the rest of the world and their role in it. In the era since 1978, the most famous statement about this reportedly came from Deng Xiaoping – reportedly, because it is hard to trace the precise time and moment when he used the phrase 'tao guang yan hui'. This is not surprising. The phrase itself is one of the many thousands of 'chengyu', statements usually made up of four Chinese characters, which operate like English proverbs. This one means the same as 'hiding one's light under a bushel'. But rather like Deng's claimed appropriation of the phrase 'it doesn't matter if a cat is black or white, as long as it catches mice', this one had a long history before his supposed use of it. According to one Chinese analysis, Deng deployed it after the rocky period of the 1989 uprising, when he urged fellow cadres to be calm and consider things coolly. In order to have stability, he stated after commanding troops into Tiananmen Square that year, 'we need to be calm, calm and then calm.'[10] Over the following year, he developed it into an edict (known in China as the '24-Character Strategy' due to the number of Chinese characters used), which roughly translates as: 'Observe calmly; secure our position; cope with affairs calmly; hide our capacities and bide our time; be good at maintaining a low profile; and never claim leadership.' This recognized a number of positions China had taken up since the Maoist era – the desire to oppose hegemony in international affairs and observation of the Five Principles – but was also an acknowledgement that China did have aspirations it wished to see fulfilled, even if it was not going to aggressively assert them, thus preventing opponents in its international space, such as the United States, from thwarting its plans.

The edict above, like similar highly general articulations, has been the object of fierce debate inside and outside China. For many, it plots out a unique way for China to avoid the kind of problems that the USSR had experienced in the Cold War, getting lulled into an economically debilitating arms race with the United States, spending huge resources on military kit rather than people's welfare, and ultimately being felled because of the lack of popular support this gave rise to. The Dengist role set for China was to be cooperative, observant of international norms, and a defender of stability and the status quo, but the phrase also implied something that would be achieved beyond this – the idea of biding time and aiming for a grander objective. It was this that made observers uneasy. What was the Chinese vision of its role once it had achieved power, wealth and influence? Could its reassuring language about not aiming for hegemony really be taken at face value?

This sits alongside the idea that Chinese leaders pursue long-term objectives and visions, informed by the ideas and culture of ancient thinkers like Sun Tzu, the author of the great treatise from over two and a half millennia before, *The Art of War*. 'The supreme art of war,' one of the more famous lines in this much quoted and admired work reads, 'is to win battles without fighting them.' The essence of strategic intelligence is simply to outwit, create ruses and clever devices whereby someone's opponent is constantly second-guessing and misunderstanding in the process: 'Be extremely subtle, even to the point of formlessness. Be extremely mysterious, even to the point of soundlessness. Thereby you can be the director of the opponent's fate.'[11] This privileging of deviousness and concealment, almost Machiavellian (millennia before Machiavelli himself), is echoed in the work of the great legalist philosopher, Han Fei, whose advice four centuries before the Christian era was to tell leaders to be almost preternaturally reticent and unknowable, never allowing others to see what they were up to, inside or outside the circles of power: 'Do not let your power be seen,' Han Fei urged; 'be blank and actionless. Government reaches to the four quarters, but its source is in the center.'[12]

For diplomatic practitioners like Henry Kissinger, Chinese strategic thinking on foreign affairs is dominated by the desire to control specific issues that matter to them, to use whatever levers they can in the process, to eliminate areas of uncertainty and to be ruthlessly pragmatic, using an almost intuitive process of confusing, bewildering and subverting the expectations of those they engage with. Kissinger himself compares this to the Asian game of 'Go', a form of chess where the battle is not about control and dominance over lines like international chess is, but about closing down space with the use of strategically placed pieces.[13] For Alastair Iain Johnston of Harvard University, China's behaviour in the Cultural Revolution evinced strong strategic principles – an awareness of what was wanted, a diplomatic plan to achieve this and a strong sense of political commitment backed up by unity among its leaders.[14] This culture of following long-term strategic principles is something that fascinates outside observers. For example, in his massive study of strategy, political scientist Lawrence Freedman devotes a large portion to Chinese principles derived from the time of Sun Tzu and the ways they have informed Chinese politicians' strategic thinking to this day. For him, the key is to make clear the relationship between tactics and strategy; both need to work together. Quoting Sun, Freedman says, 'Strategy without tactics is the slowest route to victory. Tactics without strategy is the noise before defeat.'[15]

RISING PEACEFULLY

There is plenty of evidence that Chinese foreign-policy thinking was – and remains – highly deliberative, perhaps because of the decision-making process in China itself, which is informed by copious amounts of consultation and thinking. According to Xi Jinping's description, the Chinese Communist Party is above all a kind of strategic, evaluative entity, one that is there to assess risks and to consolidate the ideas and practical wisdom that China has accrued since the great Communist experiment started in 1949. It figures almost as a community of knowledge. This is hardly surprising; in terms of its policies and their implementation, the Party made massive mistakes in its early decades, and somehow now has to explain these away and show that they at least served some function.[16] In the twenty-first century, as a mature force, it has reflected on and learned from these errors. That gives it reinforced legitimacy, rather than, as some might imagine, eroding it.

That sense remains in the West too. We all can fall into the trap of believing that (from the time of Deng onwards, at least) China has been pursuing a 'grand strategic vision'. Furthermore, this thinking goes, unlike in multiparty democracies, its leaders are unaffected by the vagaries of short-term electoral cycles and so can pursue long-term domestic and international policy goals unavailable to democratic states. This is married to an 'understanding' that Chinese politicians and leaders embrace opacity and try to keep their intentions buried. These two combined mean that trying to identify what China's grand plan might be has become something akin to the philosopher's gold of modern international relations studies.

Whoever can best describe the real Chinese long-term strategic diplomatic intent will expose one of the most complex but crucial issues in current geopolitics.

This philosopher's gold boils down to a series of simple questions: Is China seeking a kind of hegemony of its own, or is it genuinely a status-quo, cooperative power? Is it a rule-keeper or a rule-breaker? Is it trying to build its economic clout so that it can eventually dictate the global order, making the world in its own image and one day supplanting the United States to be world number one – finally 'ruling the waves' and imposing a 'China model' on the world around it?

In the last decade, the need to find answers to these questions has become more urgent. Now China is the second largest economy worldwide and its influence is much greater now than ever before, knowing its international intent matters far more than when it was a much more modest power. Since 2001, its economy has quadrupled, and while the rest of the world languished in the global economic crisis of 2008, China motored ahead almost faster than people had the chance to notice. Surely this had to translate into something more than simple trade flows? Surely there was a political and diplomatic strategy behind all this?

In the era of Hu Jintao, Chinese leaders stuck rigorously to the template of peaceful coexistence and 'win–win' cooperation. They were keen above all to show that they were biddable members of the world community. In 2005, Zheng Bijian, a spokesperson close to the leadership, authored an article in the influential US journal *Foreign Affairs*, in which he stated:

> Despite widespread fears about China's growing economic clout and political stature, Beijing remains committed to a 'peaceful rise': bringing its people out of poverty by embracing economic globalization and improving relations with the rest of the world. As it emerges as a great power, China knows

that its continued development depends on world peace – a peace that its development will in turn reinforce.[17]

It is true that since 1979 China has not engaged in any international conflicts, beyond the smallest of skirmishes. It has, as US expert on Chinese foreign affairs Bates Gill showed in one study, contributed to many UN peacekeeping missions. And it has joined pretty much any international forum it can.[18] For analysts like Susan Shirk, academic and former deputy assistant Secretary of State in the Bill Clinton administration, it is a fragile, not a strong, pushy entity, one more focused on using the benefits of a benign international environment in order to build up its own domestic stability and power.[19] The priority of its leaders post-Deng has been to make sure the country is rich, strong and successful, and that has meant focusing on the economy. Elite leaders from 1978 onwards have all stated, consistently, that their number one priority is economic. Even the People's Liberation Army (PLA) was situated within this rubric, working with the Communist Party to ensure that the country developed, that its people grew richer, and that it became wealthy.

This strategy has proved very successful. As of 2016, China had raised its per capita GDP from only US$ 300 in 1978 to more than US$ 10,000. It has more billionaires than the United States, and a middle class that is anything from 300 million to 500 million strong. The Party state has to keep this demanding, highly expectant group of people happy, and it is therefore only interested in the outside world in ways that assist in this. But from time to time another narrative creeps in – the idea of an 'historic mission' (as Hu Jintao, the country leader from 2002 to 2012 put it), where it was striving to be a great, strong power again. The efforts the country makes to look at the mistakes others have made is telling in this context. In 2008, for example, the state-run Chinese Central TV (CCTV) ran a 12-part series where it looked at the fall and rise of powers from the era of the Roman Empire onwards. Why pay so much attention to this, and particularly to the cases where such transitions had occurred without conflict? Sun Tzu's words seemed to echo loudly here: *win battles without even fighting them, gain victory before even a shot had been fired.* Was this the real underlying attitude of the Chinese leaders? And wasn't there something ever so slightly ominous about the idea of a 'peaceful rise'? Didn't this hint at a larger ambition to eventually reach the top slot? It is not surprising that US analysts in particular started to find plenty of evidence of Chinese assertiveness, duplicity and ambition concealed as friendliness and protestations of being humble and keeping a low profile.

THE CHINA DREAM

Haunting Chinese official discourse on its global role is the notion of rectifying the unjust deal that modernity has inflicted on it as a culture, country and economy. For all the talk of Chinese strategic long-term thinking and highly rational and deliberative attitudes, this often gets mixed up with high emotions. The key issues are addressing China's honour, pride and sense of worth; the highly emotional nature of Chinese foreign policy is best illustrated through the language by which it is conveyed, the terms used to attack those who are undermining the country's prestige and honour, 'offending,' as the most often used phrase goes, 'the feelings of the Chinese people.' Countries like Japan (as will be shown in Chapter 4) get particular attention here – for their refusal, in the eyes of many Chinese, to apologize properly for the offences committed by the imperial Japanese forces in World War II, and their insensitivity to China's emotional needs and vulnerability thereafter.

Much writing on Chinese foreign policy is blind to this emotional angle. This is perhaps because of the dense network of bureaucratic players who are involved with it (for which see later in this chapter) and the somewhat turgid way in which Chinese spokespeople talk about international issues – except when they are granted the space to wax with indignation over Hong Kong or Taiwan, for instance. There are clear formulae and agreed postures that are trotted out: the repetition ad nauseam of the Five Principles of Peaceful Coexistence, in particular the mantra of non-interference in the affairs of others. This combination gives the impression of a Chinese foreign policy being produced by a coldly calculating and highly rational machine, with its associated language, immune to human emotion.

Politicians have always exploited these emotional historical ties. In China, the ideological appeal of Marxism–Leninism and Mao Zedong Thought has waned, at least for the general public. The Communist Party is searching for new sources of legitimacy, and one of the most powerful, alongside improving people's living standards and economic well-being, is this notion of China restoring its position as central to the world, a new Middle Kingdom as it were, a place at the forefront of modernity, admired, looked up to and followed by others.

This partly lies behind the term Xi Jinping started to use in 2013: the 'China Dream'. As with many of his other statements, this had a pleasing vagueness. Everyone latched onto the phrase. To some it meant cleaner air, better living conditions, more wealth, and for others more freedom to create, innovate, and be independent. For those more interested in China's role in the wider world, the dream had a link to ideas which had appeared throughout the previous century. In the final years of the Qing, when the country that existed then was beset by divisions, foreign oppression and looming economic calamities, a group of young Chinese, many of whom had lived abroad, proposed what they called 'minor reforms'. Two of the most famous were the celebrated modern Chinese thinkers Kang Youwei and Liang Qichao, both of whom had been educated abroad and who brought back ideas about how to modernize the moribund Qing. Their demand was simply that through embracing technology and science, China could once more be great again – a 'rich, strong

country'. The ideal was a potent one, but their announcement was
aborted by a harsh clampdown. The emperor who had sponsored
their initiative was sidelined by his formidable grandmother, the
infamous empress dowager Ci Xi.

The idea did not disappear. The May Fourth Movement, trig-
gered by China regarding itself as the victim of unjust reparations
after World War I (mainly because of concessions which had awarded
the former German-occupied north-east of the country to Japan),
saw this sense of a Chinese-style modernity once again appear, this
time in the form of the twins 'Mr Science' and 'Mr Democracy',
according to a popular slogan at the time. The hopes of that era
were put paid to by the period afterwards in the 1920s when China
fragmented into fiefdoms of warlords and then descended into
the agony of the Sino–Japanese war. But it emerged again when
the Communists won the Civil War, and was announced by Mao
Zedong, whose adaptation simply added the term 'socialist'. The
China Dream over the 1950s and into the 1960s was to be a 'rich,
strong, socialist country'. But after 1978, it reverted once more to its
historic template – being rich and powerful was enough. Socialism,
paradoxically, was a means to that.

The two were closely linked. Without material wealth, China
would always be vulnerable. It needed wealth not just in goods,
though, but in knowledge, capacity and abilities. This hunger to
transform itself impressed anyone who witnessed it. China sent
over a million of its young abroad to study from 1980 onwards.
With the implementation of the Four Modernizations, an idea also
resurrected from China's past (it had first been used in the early
1960s), it saw the reconstruction and development of industries and
areas of technology that had simply been neglected, abandoned, or
unknown in China till then. This process of acquisition, empowerment and modernity is ongoing, but the tantalizing possibility of
the achievement of a great, strong, rich country has never been more

prominent. Once Chinese leaders might have referred to this as an aspiration, an ideal outcome lying far in the future, a future with all the intangibility of a dream. But now it is a looming reality. The Communist Party under Xi Jinping has the very real chance to be in charge of a country that, after a century and a half of suffering and injustice, is truly great once more, especially in view of the disarray in other parts of the world at the time of writing, from the EU to the United States. This is a powerful, compelling source for their appeal, and is offered as an implicit justification for their ruthless attacks on those who are against them. If you tread on the dreams of the Communist Party, the logic goes, you tread on the dreams of the Chinese people, because you threaten the country's best chance to rise once more to its proper and rightful role in the world.

This attitude brings up a number of issues. Was China ever as central in the world as the historic narrative involving it becoming a 'strong, rich power' so often used now implies? That raises questions about what sort of China existed in the past, when its borders increased and then imploded during the era of imperial control. Is this real China of the past, exposed by the painstaking work of Chinese and non-Chinese historians, the same historical China referred to by CCP leaders in popular discourse? Then there is the delicate question of non-Chinese influence on Chinese empires through the ages – from the Mongolians who ruled the Yuan era, to the Manchurians in the Qing. Most intractable of all is this notion of what it even means to be Chinese, what sort of coherence this identity gives across this complex, often fragmented, and confusing history. But all of that counts for little when Chinese politicians in the twenty-first century survey vast ranks of new military kit, and speak to people for the first time living in modern-looking Chinese cities, regarding a future that their parents or grandparents only ever dreamed of – with nice housing, plentiful food, good cars, foreign travel, and a world of opportunity around them. For this aspiring emerging middle class, it is a simple thing. The glorious Chinese past might never have existed. Who cares? But the Chinese present and future can be glorious. This nationalistic trope in Chinese foreign policy will emerge throughout the following chapters.

MORAL RISE

Mao and his successors have been clear about one thing – perhaps the sole thing that they have been unified and consistent on. There is modernity, and then there is the Chinese way of doing modernity. Emulating the rest of the world does not mean becoming like it. It means maintaining your essential quality of, well, being Chinese. The idea is not one that people within China, particularly its leaders, have much interest in becoming reflective and philosophical about. For them being Chinese is a blindingly obvious thing. It needs no dense explanations or analysis.

In the era of the People's Republic, ideas from sources like Marxism, the Soviet Union and, later, US-style capitalism, have been indigenized as soon as they come into the country. It was the nice-sounding 'socialism with Chinese characteristics' that became the dominant state ideology under Deng, even though intellectual interrogation of this idea often proved frustrating. Marxism was meant to uncover universal principles of political and social development; how could it exist in a uniquely local variant? The market became a core issue here. Regarded as anathema in purer socialist systems, in China it was embraced, with the caveat that it had 'Chinese characteristics'. So did that mean it was socialist or non-socialist? No one quite knew. Plenty of other ideas or notions had the prescription 'according to national conditions' attached to justify them. China came across like a world within itself, a universe receptive to those outside of it but utterly insistent that it had a specific set of qualities and defining ingredients which had to be honoured and reflected for any ideas to come in. 'Using the

foreign for Chinese purposes' has become one of the most ubiquitous modern sayings.

With the articulation of a 'peaceful rise' in the early 2000s, a
set of other ideas making this stress on 'Chineseness' even more
pronounced came along. If China was a great power, it needed to
be recognized as such not just through its economic prowess and
its new political prominence, but through appreciation of its 5,000
years (as often stated) of continuous, great civilization, which gave
it not just a political but a moral right to be looked up to. China's
cultural attributes figured in the thinking about soft power. Anxious
not to attract the unwelcome ire and attention of the United States
through being accused of building up hard military assets, the use
of cultural cachet became highly attractive. Confucius Institutes
started to open up across the world, linked to government support.
Chinese music, literature and art started to appear, culminating in a
leader like Xi Jinping whose *The Governance of China*, a book of his
speeches and statements issued in 2014, contained far more references to China's imperial past than it did to Mao Zedong or Marx.

The way that the Communist Party leaders of today talk about
China's traditional culture is contentious. This is particularly the
case because the movement they are now in charge of has historically set itself as the clear enemy of what it labelled as antiquated
thinking, art and philosophy. Confucius was a *persona non grata*
under Mao. He was the figure regarded as the architect of the prison
of Chinese social hierarchy and patriarchal family structures which
Communism wanted to rip apart. Red Guards in the Cultural
Revolution attacked what they saw as vestiges of this feudal history,
labelling them the 'Four Olds' (old customs, old culture, old habits
and old ideas). But it was the bulldozers, cranes and demolition
workers of the post-1978 era which did most to eradicate whatever
historic traces the past may have left in China. A 5,000-year-old
culture is what Chinese leaders claim, but the physical environment
in the country often makes structures just 20 years old seem like

antiquities. Newness reigns everywhere. Only in places like the National Palace Museum in Taipei, Taiwan, which never suffered the political domestic travails of the mainland, is there a world-class collection of artefacts from the Chinese past. In the People's Republic, much of this material heritage risked being smashed to pieces in the era after 1949 if left on the mainland.

The chief propaganda enforcer for Xi Jinping, a former journalist called Liu Yunshan who sat beside him on the Standing Committee of the Politburo from 2012, speaks mellifluously about the glories of Chinese culture. But there is a clear agenda. These 'glorious traditional assets' of the past are made something new, constructed into politically useful resources that can shore up the legitimacy of the modern rulers, contributors to a sense of the country being cohesive, historically strong and built on an age-old cultural structure, however politically and socially unstable it might have been at times. They also allude to a deeper ambition, something which has only been properly articulated by scholars like Yan Xuetong, from the prestigious Tsinghua University in Beijing, who has referred to the need for China to reassert its values and its historic traditions in order to stand not just as a political and military counterweight to the United States, but an ideological, cultural and intellectual one. The ambition in his vision is for China to be the centre not just of its own material world, but more importantly of its spiritual one:

> If China wants to become a state of humane authority, this would be different from the contemporary United States. The goal of our strategy must be not only to reduce the power gap with the United States but also to provide a better model for society than that given by the United States.[20]

There are plenty of counterarguments to this, even in China, where others argue that with a domestic situation so beset by challenges and uncertainty, it would be hubristic to claim that China has the kind of potential role people like Yan are claiming for it. For them, referring back to Deng's 'keep a low profile' suggestion, this is not just a posture of studied humility – it is a necessity for a country that remains vulnerable to attack. The Trump presidency, however, significantly increases the chance for China to achieve this.

Ambitious external visions of Chinese power run parallel to claims (mostly made by non-Chinese) that China has created a new kind of way of operating – a Chinese style, typified by unique diplomacy, one based on the China development model rather than the dominant Washington Consensus. This claim was first made by then-Kissinger Associate Joshua Cooper Ramo in a work in 2004. China offers something new in the way in which it is claiming diplomatic space, he argued:

> China's new development approach is driven by a desire to have equitable, peaceful high-quality growth, critically speaking, it turns traditional ideas like privatisation and free trade on their heads. It is flexible enough that it is barely classifiable as a doctrine. It does not believe in uniform solutions for every situation. It is defined by a ruthless willingness to innovate and experiment, by a lively defense of national borders and interests, and by the increasingly thoughtful accumulation of tools of asymmetric power projection. It is pragmatic and ideological at the same time, a reflection of an ancient Chinese philosophical outlook that makes little distinction between theory and practice.[21]

This notion was subsequently supplemented by Daniel A. Bell, a Beijing-based Canadian academic, whose spirited defence of the Chinese government model involves appreciating its meritocratic base, the ways in which it privileges technocrats in the art of governance rather than Western-style politicians with their expertise at communication, hard sell for policy and often little else. Marking out Singapore as the likeliest future ideal state for China, with the People's Action Party having a monopoly on power despite there being regular universal franchise elections, Bell talks of the ways in which China eschews Western-style liberal democracy, despite its universalizing nature, and has so far shown the real viability of one-party rule.[22]

The theses of both Ramo and Bell have been fiercely criticized.[23] Nor, to be fair, are they that often referred to by Chinese officials themselves, beyond figuring as useful, unsolicited propaganda; even so, they do draw attention to China's unique aspects and put their finger on why these still cause perplexity. China does not figure in a new Cold War in the ways the now defunct USSR once did, a power that could be regarded as a predatory, outright competitor, but nor does it figure as a simple ally; there are many overlapping interests between China and the United States, which will be looked at later. And yet there are clear areas of deep difference and disagreement. The most powerful of these is simple: that China maintains a system where one party has a monopoly on power, something that was not meant to happen after Communist history supposedly ended with the collapse of the Soviet Union in 1991. This anomaly cries out for an explanation. What is it that China has done, what is distinctive about its posture and its strategy that has allowed it to achieve this – economic, capitalist-style transformation which at the same time maintains resolute political stability for a one-party system? How should the outside world relate to this situation? Through some kind of engagement strategy, through containment, or by some other wholly new position?

9/11 AND THE CRASH

There are two final ideas to factor into Chinese foreign-policy thinking before moving to the specifics of Xi Jinping and the era that he dominates. The first of these involves an attitude proposed by Jiang Zemin around the turn of the millennium, when he spoke of a 20-year-long era of strategic opportunity. Jiang was addressing the role of China as it prepared to enter the WTO and undertake a number of difficult domestic reforms. As some commentators have made clear, these depended as much on using foreign competition and involvement to forge change in China as in exploring opportunities for China's benefit outside the country. After the 11 September attacks on the World Trade Center in New York in 2001, an era of contentiousness between the United States and China – which had come to a head on 1 April 2001 after a US spy plane and a Chinese fighter jet collided in mid-air close to the coast of southern China – ended. Washington had a newer, far more pressing priority, and decided to embark upon wars in Iraq and Afghanistan instead. This era of distraction offered unforeseen benefits for China. The ominous language from the United States, which had been portraying China as an ever-increasing threat as the 1990s wore on, died down; George W. Bush, after spending his first year in office excoriating Beijing, started to use a far friendlier tone.

Jiang implied that this era of relative harmoniousness would end. But at least until the start of the third decade of the twenty-first century, the country had the opportunity to pursue its primary objective – to enrich itself, stabilize its domestic situation and ensure that it had a sustainable basis for what the leaders called 'perfecting modernity' in the country. Unsurprisingly, for such a long-term idea, this one was vulnerable to a number of outside forces. Two in particular looked certain to play an important role. The first, the more positive (on the surface, at least) for China, was that its economic ascent had been far quicker than anyone had expected. With entry to the WTO, it unleashed immense forces of productivity which continued throughout the following decade. Far from challenging China, the WTO appeared like a huge motivator, a godsend for those who wanted to see better productivity within the country and knew that the only way to do this was to introduce external companies to turn up the heat on sluggish, underperforming local ones. In this way, far quicker perhaps than even China's most optimistic leaders had predicted, the country was a huge global economic player, with new markets, business contacts, links and an associated importance far beyond its shores.

But there was the second, less positive issue – the calamity the outside world visited on itself during and after the global economic crisis of 2008. As China became more successful, therefore, the economies of the United States and the EU weakened. The era of strategic opportunity, of China maintaining a low profile, focusing on its own issues and simply biding its time, ended well before the 2020 deadline. The dominant mindset in Beijing was to focus on issues directly in the country's national interest – whether they were diplomatic, economic or military. China, therefore, did not on the whole initiate much through the UN that did not directly relate to it, and it tended to follow the leadership of others (since taking up its seat in 1971, China has deployed its veto only seven times, while the United States has deployed it more than 40. Of those seven times, it only acted unilaterally on four).[24] Through this apparent passivity, it garnered a reputation as a freeloader to such an extent that in 2005, Robert Zoellick, a US official, demanded in a talk to the National Committee on United States–China Relations that it become a 'responsible stakeholder' and involve itself much more in international affairs, taking up a position not just on matters close to home like North Korea and governance of the international finance sector, but also on more global issues:

> China is big, it is growing, and it will influence the world in the years ahead. For the United States and the world, the essential question is – how will China use its influence?
>
> To answer that question, it is time to take our policy beyond opening doors to China's membership into the

international system: We need to urge China to become
a *responsible stakeholder* in that system.[25]

Like it or not, China was now a global power. Being enticed into
this exposed position was something that Chinese leaders had done
all they could to resist: witness the fierce rebuttals of a suggested
G2 (the United States and China) that started to appear in 2009.
But it was impossible from 2010 onwards, when it became the
world's second largest economy, to continue presenting itself as a
weak, vulnerable player best left in the anteroom of global action.
The decision by the United Kingdom to leave the European Union,
creating space for increasing disunity there, and the Trump presidency in the United States heralding an era of more mercantilist,
isolationist behaviour by the world's supposedly sole remaining
superpower, only underlined this sense that China was being forced
into a position of responsibility and prominence far sooner than it
ever wanted, solely because of the irresponsibility of other, previously
dominant partners.

In 2009, as a partial response to this, Dai Bingguo, a state councillor and at that time the most prominent foreign-policy official in
China, set out the country's 'core interests' for the first time. These
were threefold: 'number one [...] is to maintain its fundamental
system and state security; next is state sovereignty and territorial
integrity; and third is the continued stable development of the
economy and society.'[26]

This was hugely general, but the message was clear. Engagement
that was aimed at undermining China's own choice of political
model, and carried some attempt to reform or change it, was posited
as fundamentally against its interests. In the ensuing years, even
more shrill statements were made condemning Western attempts
to challenge, or seduce or otherwise attempt to change China's
domestic political choices; state sovereignty and territorial integrity
related to the issues of Taiwan, Tibet, Xinjiang, and the contested

South and East China Seas. The third covered its burgeoning overseas economic interests. Even a charitable observer could not but
regard this as a somewhat self-interested menu of requirements.
Remarkably, however, this is the closest that an elite leader in recent
times has come to outlining in one framework a holistic Chinese
philosophy of engagement with the outside world.

THE TOOLS

There is one final issue to pay attention to in this overview. Having
mapped out the background of its posture on foreign policy, and the
core ideas in its diplomatic mindset, it would be best to conclude
with an attempt to describe the practical tools that China has – or
any country, for that matter – in its foreign-policy strategy. Whereas
governments have a high degree of control and powers of initiative
over domestic issues (and even with this advantage often struggle),
their powers inevitably reduce quickly with matters that lie beyond
their shores: the levers of control diminish. It then becomes a choice
between moral suasion, economic inducements, or, in the worst
cases, military force to get one's way, all of which carry high degrees
of uncertainty and risk.[27]

In the era of Maoist enclosure, China had few diplomatic allies.
It had few connections to the outside world in terms of logistics,
movement of people, and trade. This has now changed. In the
following areas it has its own distinctive interests, as well as ways
in which it is vulnerable to forces and issues beyond its borders
but can also exercise influence over them in new ways. These have
given it tangible interests it needs to protect, and new modes of
engagement with the wider world:

· **INWARD AND OUTWARD INVESTMENT:** Since 1978, China has
allowed foreign capital into the country, and, since the

2000s, has promoted a 'going out' campaign that sees its own state and non-state companies working in the rest of the world. In 2014, China was the largest global recipient of foreign direct investment. But it also, more remarkably, started to figure as a major international outward investor, with stock of more than US$ 100 billion. It invested in Europe, the United States and Australia, buying companies like Weetabix in the United Kingdom, Volvo in Sweden and Standard Bank in South Africa. It took shares in companies as diverse as BP and Tesco, but also through Huawei and ZTC became a major player in technology – and, because of security concerns, a highly contentious one. It became a large investor in the resources and agribusiness sector in Australia and Latin America, and in the energy sector in the Middle East. Investments were an important part of China's economy, and a new aspect of its influence.

- **MOVEMENT OF PEOPLE:** As already mentioned, between 1949 and 1978, very few people travelled into and outside China. It was in many ways a closed country. Access was very difficult, meaning only a few Europeans or North Americans got in, and even fewer Chinese travelled outside of it. In 2014 alone, though, 100 million individual journeys were made by Chinese people, embracing tourists, academics, business people and officials. They became the largest spenders in luxury shops in Paris and New York, and the source of immense tourism opportunity – so much so that whole retail centres were established for them in places like Bicester in the United Kingdom. People from China also figured as workers in Africa, students in the United Kingdom, United States and Australia, and as highly skilled migrant labourers. People-to-people links took on a dynamic of their own, with Chinese appearing visibly in people's lives as students, customers and visitors in ways they never had before. But it also meant that the Chinese government had become responsible for the same demands for care of its people abroad as Western governments: 36,000 Chinese had to be repatriated from Libya during the uprising there in 2011, and a Chinese man was tragically murdered by the Daesh group in the Middle East in late 2015 after being taken hostage. In the last decade, China has had to arrange 15 major rescue operations – including ones in Yemen, Iraq, Libya and Syria.

· **MILITARY ASSETS:** Chinese expenditure on its military went up exponentially from the year 2000 onwards, with a process of modernization that meant by 2015 and the military parade to celebrate the 70th anniversary of the end of the Sino–Japanese war mentioned in the Introduction, more than 80 per cent of the kit on display was new. China started to innovate, with its own stealth fighter jet, the J-20, and its own aircraft carrier. It built its first overseas military asset in Djibouti off the east coast of Africa, and developed a credible naval capacity for the first time ever, in order to protect its overseas citizens and its crucial trade routes.

· **CULTURAL ASSETS:** millions are starting to learn Chinese, trying to visit and understand China and be exposed to different forms of its culture. Chinese cultural assets, its history, language, literature and people have partly become a means by which the Chinese government (and other actors from China) is able to promote more benign and useful images of the country abroad, one that blunts the negative impressions given by its political system. There has been fierce argument about just how deliberate and strategically thought through this has been. What is

indisputable is that China's soft-power assets and govern-
ment-led messaging did impact on international images
and imaginations about the role of China in the world,
its importance and its potential.

These issues are a source of hard and soft influence arising from
within China, but they are also a new means by which outsiders can
influence the country. The situation now is very dynamic. Many
of the issues above will figure in the following story of Chinese
foreign policy in the second decade of the twenty-first century.
They show that in many ways, for all the talk of grand strategy
and frameworks, Chinese foreign policy has often had to tie itself
to protecting or supporting very practical issues. First, therefore,
it is important to look at the network and the people at the heart
of this system of protection, influence and influencing, and try to
answer the question of how they view the outside world, how they
develop policies towards it, and how they regard the future role of
their country within it. Right at the centre of this sits the figure
of the current general secretary of the CCP and president of the
PRC – Xi Jinping.

2

THE WORLD ACCORDING
TO XI JINPING

Foreign policy might seem very remote to the daily lives of most people, whatever country they are in. Taxes, housing, living costs, transport, their immediate environment – this is the currency of everyday life, what really matters and directly relates to people, and on which they judge the performance of their leaders and governments. On the surface, at least, remote foreign places, especially ones that speak different languages, have different cultures and follow different customs and habits, seem to have little impact on the domestic issues that people are concerned about. But as shown by the impact on other economies of rising and falling energy and resource prices, or the ways local natural disasters can disrupt global food and supply chains, foreign issues and challenges are part of anyone's daily life, no matter how insular they appear on the surface.

The great sociologist Fei Xiaotong described Chinese society in the middle of the twentieth century as one which was agrarian in its roots, and where people predominantly lived in tight-knit communities where overlapping links through kinship and networks bound people together. Ideas of contract and judicial enforcement had no real necessity or meaning in this context. People lived with others, and did deals with others who were personally known to them, and because of their daily proximity the costs of deceiving or alienating others was high.[1] But with the modernization of the Chinese economy since 1978, society has been transformed, becoming more liquid and mobile. In cities like Shanghai, with over 500,000 new arrivals each year, everyone is a stranger. The problem is that China has so far lacked the social, legal and community infrastructure to be able to cope with this kind of rapid change. In many ways, it lacks the basic infrastructure of trust.

Now, in the second decade of the twenty-first century, through size alone, China is an intrinsically global player. The daily choices of its citizens, in terms of whether they eat more meat, use more cars or live in larger houses, have a huge impact on the world's natural environment and its economy, not just China's. A collapse in the Chinese housing market remains the most likely precipitator for a global recession, such is its domestic and therefore international importance. For that reason, a country which until the last decades of the twentieth century showed evidence that it had only the most loose notion of foreign affairs and diplomacy has, since 1949, and particularly since 1978, needed to build the diplomatic architecture of a modern state.

At the heart of this are the organizations, politicians, leaders, bureaucrats, business people, soldiers, academics and ministries that have clear stakes in China's global role and in the ways it relates to the outside world and that world relates to it. In Maoist China, the people who had any clear role to play in China's foreign affairs numbered no more than a few dozen. Mao Zedong set the parameters of China's international role, and he had elite leaders around him like Zhou Enlai, who interpreted and then religiously implemented his precious imperial words. The management of the rapprochement with the United States was the classic case. Mao made the decision, it seems, sometime after the start of the Cultural Revolution to consider closer links with the United States, despite over a decade of coldness and antagonism. Through his premier, Zhou Enlai, he mandated a group of PLA generals who were, in fact, detained at the time for political reasons and labelled as class enemies, to brainstorm about what a détente with Washington might look like. Their report filtered through to the central Zhongnanhai compound around the time that clashes with the USSR on the northern border in 1969 added a note of urgency. In 1970 and 1971, the embassy in Warsaw and then US and Chinese officials in Pakistan started to have more contact. This led in late 1971 to then US Secretary of State Henry Kissinger's secret trip to Beijing from Pakistan, and his direct meetings first with Zhou Enlai and then with Mao himself. It was clear when Nixon finally visited in 1972 that foreign policy was wholly under Mao's control, and that if he desired something to happen, it happened – no matter how contentious. And contrariwise, if he vetoed something, it didn't happen.[2]

The terrain of power now is more complex. In *CEO, China*, my book on Xi Jinping, I set out the different locations of power in modern China – from the Communist Party and its various organizations and subgroups, to ministries, state enterprises, social groups, right down to grass-roots entities.[3] This largely concerned domestic issues and sources of control, influence and power over them. For foreign policy, there is a parallel world of 'movers and shakers'. The one most striking characteristic they share with each other is that real power seldom sits in the most obvious place, but is diffracted in different ways to different organizations and personnel. The only commonality is that many of these have clear links with the Communist Party.

WHERE IS FOREIGN POLICY DECIDED IN XI'S CHINA?

Ministries of foreign affairs always attract bad press domestically, no matter how much prestige they accrue abroad. In the United Kingdom, the accusation is that they are stuffed with people who are overly sympathetic to foreigners. The famous *Yes Minister* satirical TV show from the 1980s contained lines about how the British Foreign Office was busy representing the objectives and views of outsiders within the United Kingdom. Despite this, the Foreign Office is very typical of ministries dealing with external issues in other multiparty democracies. It enjoys high visibility and status, but has only a tiny number of personnel compared to interior ministries, usually has minuscule budgets (in the United Kingdom's case, less than 1 per cent of all government spending), and more often than not has to fight daily to try to get its voice heard.

Interestingly, despite the different political model that China has, the same situation exists in Beijing. In many ways, the Chinese Ministry of Foreign Affairs (MFA) has an even worse deal. Foreign Secretaries in the United Kingdom, on paper at least, rank among the top four great offices of state, next to the prime minister, the Chancellor of the Exchequer (in effect the minister of finance) and the Home Secretary (the minister of the interior). In the United States, the Secretary of State is similarly high ranking, and enjoys huge profile and visibility. In China, the head of the MFA, at least at the time of writing in early 2017, does not sit on either the full Politburo, or its Standing Committee. The best they can manage is to be a relatively junior-ranking member of the Central Committee (a Party body of about 200 full and 150 alternate members) and have a place on the State Council, China's version of a government cabinet. In terms of budget and personnel, the MFA barely registers – with 2,500 full-time professional diplomats, less than that of the Australians (despite China having more than 20 times its population), and a budget that would barely cover the costs of a small town in the western region of China. It is remarkable that it manages to promote China to the outside world as effectively as it does.

The MFA suffers from the same personal attacks and arouses the same public irritation as organizations elsewhere. When there are tensions with the Japanese, or the United States, Chinese 'netizens' – Chinese citizens empowered by a burgeoning online community – routinely accuse the diplomats representing them of being spineless, even sending them calcium tablets to suggest they strengthen their backbones. This is ironic, because the MFA has very little power to articulate fresh positions on foreign-policy issues. All of that comes from higher up, from Party bodies like the Leading Small Group on Foreign Affairs, currently chaired by Xi Jinping. This is one of a number of elite-level bodies, coordinating policy in specific areas. But its operations, how often it meets and what kind of decisions it makes are shrouded in secrecy.[4] It is suspected (though not known for certain) that alongside Xi as chair, the current group consists of Foreign Minister Wang Yi, State Councillor Yang Jiechi, the minister for finance, minister for commerce and then a representative of the PLA and security forces. Politburo member Wang Huning may also sit on it, because of his very clear importance in issues of foreign affairs.

Institutionally, the membership of the leading group, however speculative, does show clearly the sort of ministries with the clearest vested interest in having a voice in articulating and implementing Chinese foreign policy. The Ministry of Foreign Commerce is clear enough, but so is the Ministry of Finance, or, for that matter, any other of the central ministries with a role in economic issues. Through inward and outward investment, and through import and export, technology transfer, currency and a host of other links, China's economic interests are global: they have a tangible connection with the world beyond its borders. So all of these ministries would have views on China's role, for instance, in Africa, Latin America or the Middle East, or its posture on issues that impact on global trade flows, the composition of international finance entities, and the internationalization of China's domestic finance and services sector.

One of the unique issues about China is that while it has a centralized fiscal and political system, provinces are still hugely influential economic actors, and for this reason they also have an international role. Places like the coastal provinces and cities of Zhejiang, Shanghai, Guangdong and Fujian have vast logistics, trade and investment links with the rest of the world. Even a province as ostensibly remote as Yunnan in the south-west is involved through its state enterprises in resource investment and cooperation in Australia, and has a role in Chinese security due to its borders with Myanmar and Vietnam. Border Autonomous Regions like Inner Mongolia have important business, cultural and social links with Russia and the Mongolian People's Republic. Even the most landlocked of provinces, from Shanxi to Shaanxi and Henan, have been seeking international partners for trade and educational cooperation in the last four decades. All of them might work in the national articulation of foreign policy, but they would be operating from local calibrations of this. And this runs from provincial level down to China's cities, counties, prefectures and even into its townships. They too have different national foreign-policy priorities they pursue, mostly in the economic realm, but increasingly diversifying into more complex and sophisticated areas. Cities like Suzhou, for instance, advertised their tourist assets on London buses in 2015; Xi'an has been twinned with Edinburgh for the last three decades; and the city of Zhuhai took out adverts in the United States, Australia and the EU to showcase its investment attractions. All of these places would be seeking ways to optimize their influence on national policy. China is, under its centralized surface, a hugely competitive place.

This is more than simply about economic links, however. Fujian Province, where Xi Jinping spent almost 16 years of his career as a leader, has deep links with Taiwan, separated from it by 100 kilometres of water but sharing many linguistic and cultural commonalities. In the era of Taiwanese settlement, from the sixteenth century onwards, it was predominantly people from the Fujian area who took part, and Taiwanese dialect is similar to that used in Fujian.[5] The views of the local government in Fujian therefore are regarded as being particularly sympathetic towards Taiwan because of these close links and the deep interconnectivity of their economies. Beijing officials and academics use the dismissive and mocking label 'capitulationists' over their colleagues in Fujian because of what they regard as their overly understanding and sympathetic attitude towards the island.

MAINTAINING SECURITY: THE ARMY AND THE SPIES

Alongside Party and government organizations with an interest and role in foreign policy, there are the security actors – the PLA in particular, but also the Ministry of State Security (MSS), the People's Armed Police and other entities. Their role in terms of operational foreign policy, and the framing and articulation of threats with strategies to deal with them, is self-evident. But there are perennial arguments about just how much influence they have.

The People's Liberation Army, founded as the Red Army in 1927, has always been answerable to the Communist Party, and the Communist Party alone. This remains true. Its supreme tasking and organizational entity is the Central Military Commission (CMC), on which sit a number of civilians, the most important of whom is the chair of the body, the Communist Party general secretary, Xi Jinping (another source of his power). In the Maoist era, the PLA was a significant source of control and influence, and China's early generation of leaders all came from military backgrounds. Even as late as the 1980s, Deng Xiaoping relinquished all his formal roles except that of chair of the CMC (he only served as vice premier till 1982), a position he maintained until 1989. The army, like armies elsewhere across the world, was a lobby group for its own interests, able to influence industrial policy, security issues and domestic politics. In China, as in the Soviet Union, it operated in ways which resembled a huge state company, involved in factories producing not just military but civilian kit and running enterprises that got involved in almost every sector. It was natural that the PLA would run nightclubs, hotels, shops and other companies given just how huge the army was up until the 1980s, with over five million personnel. Around this core staff were any number of dependents and associates. If the Communist Party often seemed like it looked like a state within a state, the PLA was a mini-state in its own right running alongside the Party like an internal vassal kingdom, even enjoying its own parallel appointment system which the Party could only rubber stamp rather than veto.

Chinese leaders observed the problems that an overmighty and disloyal military gave to leaders of the Soviet Union before its demise in 1991, and drew important lessons from it. The PLA had put in a mixed performance in quelling the disturbances of 1989 in Tiananmen Square and elsewhere. Loyalist troops from outside Beijing had eventually been summoned to 'pacify' the situation in the capital, as the euphemism used in the official press for the firing of live ammunition on students put it. In the mid-1990s, there was a strategic rethink about the kind of modernized military China needed, one which had undergone the same kind of transformation as the economic realm. The result of this was a move in 1998–9 to simply remove the PLA from all areas of commercial activity, to slim it down, upgrade its equipment and improve its doctrines. It became, from that time, an organization closely aligned with the Party's mission of raising the economic status of China, ensuring that it had regional offensive and defensive capacities, and upgrading its technical capacity, particularly in the area of what was somewhat clumsily called 'informationalization' (espionage and the use of high-tech equipment).

Over the years since then, according to some the PLA's influence has been huge, and according to others largely focused in specific areas. Military figures ranging from retired generals like Xiong Guangkai and active ones like Lieutenant Colonel Liu Yuan have

articulated blood-curdlingly fierce ideas about how China needs
to be more assertive and aggressive with the outside world. Xiong
famously threatened West Coast US cities with Chinese nuclear
warheads in one of his more fanciful outbursts in the late 1990s.
Liu took a more cerebral approach, writing a book on the China
Dream which merely mapped out a position for China where it was
able to be more autonomous and no longer had to endure being
pushed around by the United States in its own backyard. It is hard
to assess how influential some of these figures are. Some, like Liu
Yuan, son of Liu Shaoqi, Chinese president until his fall during the
Cultural Revolution in 1967, did have clear links with Xi Jinping
through attending the same kindergarten and primary schools,
though it was hard to work out how these translated precisely into
any specific influence on Xi's policy position and thinking. Others,
like Ma Xiaotian, sat on the CMC and were regarded as being
spokespeople for more purely military viewpoints. These could be
broadly categorized as highly assertive on regional issues, but less so
on issues further from China's shores. Like retired military anywhere,
China had plenty of grand old soldiers who were free and loose
with their comments – and offered entertainment if nothing else.

Clearly, through the CMC, the military does have a say over
foreign-policy issues. But this is more as a supportive participant
rather than an initiator of bold new lines. Under Xi, from 2013,
the anti-corruption struggle targeted a range of military figures,
showing just how clearly it was the servant of the politicians,
not an autonomous centre of power in its own right. Xu Caihou
was among the most senior: a member of the CMC before his
retirement in 2012, he was figured as a target for the graft busters
fighting against corruption in 2014, but his case was complicated
by his having terminal cancer. This did not, however, prevent the
Party from expelling him in 2015. Over a dozen other military
figures received the same treatment. Once regarded as a place of
protection and privilege, the army and navy were now ostensibly

being held up to the same standards as the CCP, state enterprises and the non-state-sector actors. Tellingly, when a matter which had a high degree of military significance arose – the deployment of a destroyer by the United States through an area of the South China Seas in October 2015, despite shrill threats emanating from the PLA personnel – the Chinese Ministry of Defence issued a rather tepid response: 'China strongly urges the US side to conscientiously handle China's serious representations [and] immediately correct its mistake.' This was some distance from the threat to 'deliver a head-on blow' which the PLA's rear admiral Yang Yi had said would be the consequences a few weeks before at an international security conference in Singapore.[6]

Over issues like Taiwan, the South and East China Seas, and the border dispute with India, the PLA obviously does have a voice. And because of its importance in these areas, it has secured consistent double-digit budget increases since the 1990s. But the PLA rarely initiates foreign-policy positions, and like most military, it is often keener to prevent wars than see them start, particularly as its real experience of conflict since 1979 has been next to zero, something that weighs on the confidence of the military top echelon.

The Chinese security services inevitably have a less clear-cut role. For those that are involved in espionage activities against foreigners, either inside or outside China, their function is clear enough. They are no different to the CIA in the United States, or the Secret Intelligence Service of the United Kingdom. Domestically, the MSS, like the PLA, articulates and analyses threats, and then lobbies for resources to address these. The MSS is mandated by the Communist Party leadership to keep an eye on potential sources of challenge and trouble, domestically and externally. Its lack of transparency means that its real influence is hard to assess. But once more it certainly has insights, and capacity, to feed into the formulation of foreign policy, and a clear vested interest. After all, for these organizations, a mishap involving China abroad will be something they will have to become immediately involved with. The reportedly Chinese cyberespionage spies from an intelligence arm of the PLA were named as wanted criminals by the US FBI in 2015, becoming a bilateral international issue between the two countries. This will be dealt with in more detail in the chapter on United States–China affairs.

As with intelligence agencies anywhere, the cachet of slapping a 'top secret' strapline on even the most asinine material means it stands a better chance of reaching the desks of senior leaders and getting their attention. But at the time of writing in early 2017, with its six military districts and various provincial and sub-provincial entities, China has what appears to be a thriving, highly competitive market in the production of classified material. Such a large number of intelligence reports risks degrading how seriously they are taken, and how much attention leaders pay to them. The creation in 2014 under Xi of a National Security Commission has been one way of trying to coordinate this vast industry manufacturing secret reports. Like any other government entities, the Chinese secret services have been eager to ratchet up a sense of threat because it can be used to justify their budgets. Even so, the investigation, arrest and detention of a high-level MSS leader in 2014 was a sign that even this previously almost untouchable part of the state firmament was no longer safe. Unlike in the era of Hu Jintao, therefore, rampant state-security activism and a culture almost of complete impunity has come to an end. Spies are hard to tame, but it seems Xi is making a bold (and so far successful) attempt.

STATE ENTERPRISES:
THE SHARP END OF INTERNATIONAL AFFAIRS

There is one significant difference between China in 2017 and the China that existed 60 years before, beyond the obvious issues of the size of the country's GDP and the increase in its domestic prosperity. Up to the 2000s, China had historically never deployed capital abroad. Its mercantilist behaviour meant that it accrued capital – to such an extent that in the middle of the nineteenth century there was a global shortage of silver bullion because of Qing China's demand that its silk, spice and other exports be paid for with silver coins. Once it earned these coins, it did not use them for imports. When the emperor Qianlong rebuffed the Macartney delegation in 1793, he had at least been honest; China really did think it neither needed nor desired European manufactures. It just wanted to stockpile large amounts of wealth in its coffers in Beijing.

In the era of early capitalism, Chinese companies were small artisans, family-based traders. They did not figure as international players. While foreign companies like Standard Chartered and Royal Dutch Shell went to work in China in the late nineteenth century, setting up offices in the concessions there and creating supply and sales networks, there was no reciprocal movement of Chinese companies abroad. China simply did not have entities that would be able to deploy capital internationally. Massive state-run companies were established with the simple understanding that they operated on the Soviet model, employing huge numbers of people to produce goods, based on centrally decided plans, which were either sold domestically or sent abroad, largely to fellow Communist partners, with the central state keeping the revenue raised and redistributing some of the profits back to the enterprises as parts of its mandated central subvention.

These SOEs were vast enterprises, operating as work units (the famous *danwei*), with huge social as well as economic functions, employing, educating and supporting people from birth to death. They figured like mini states within states, and were as much a means of social control as they were of material reconstruction and economic development. Employees enjoyed cradle-to-grave welfare and lifelong employment, with work units even figuring in permissions for them to marry, to have children, in their choice of subject to study if they went to university, and in career plans afterwards.[7] State enterprises were not direct actors outside of China. They did not figure as investors, or as customers. Only in the era after 1978 did they start to appear as potential partners for multinational companies, which were allowed for the first time to go into China. And then, gradually, those that focused on resources started to make tiny international appearances, investing small amounts, usually via Hong Kong. Minuscule amounts grew incrementally up until the late 1990s, when state enterprises underwent dramatic reforms, reduced their huge workforce, got out of much of the social welfare provision they had historically been involved in, and were increasingly exposed to market forces. A parallel but initially far smaller process of non-state companies emerging also took place, so that by 2005, according to an Organization for Economic Co-operation and Development (OECD) report, over half of all GDP came from this source – a remarkable result for an economy that was still ostensibly state-run and under a Communist system.[8]

After China joined the WTO in 2001, its external investments started to increase. They remained small as a proportion of global foreign direct investment flows, but in the areas of resources, commodities, raw materials and energy, they were noticeable. Companies like PetroChina, Sinopec and the China National Offshore Oil Corporation (CNOOC) in particular emerged as players in markets like Africa and Latin America. The sheer novelty of Chinese state companies suddenly playing this role caused a great deal of commentary and heated argument. In 2005, a small US energy company, Unocal, became the target of CNOOC interest. But before a formal bid was even announced, the Chinese company withdrew, struck by the fierce response from politicians in Washington, particularly in Congress, who threatened to overrule any attempt to proceed. With the global financial crisis in 2007–8, there were loud proclamations that China would be 'buying up the world'. But as more sanguine voices made clear, the oddity was not so much that Chinese direct outward investment was becoming noticeable, but that one of the world's largest economies remained such a small player in this area.

One company that represented all the complex issues of Chinese outward investment was the telecoms provider Huawei. This company combined the good, the bad and the ugly in perceptions of Chinese money abroad. In Africa it was regarded as a technical partner, a bringer of new collaboration opportunities, a positive force. In the United Kingdom, there was initially neutrality towards its role, with the company taking on a major contract supplying British Telecom. Huawei worked in Germany, and started to figure in the United States and Latin America. But fears about the links between it and the People's Liberation Army and security services persisted – largely because its founder, Ren Zhenfei, had started off as a PLA officer.

The 'good' side of Huawei in terms of perception was that it was an authentically Chinese company which was modern, outward looking, and working in a fast-developing area of technology, away from the stereotype of a resource-focused, asset-stripping, domestic-prioritizing entity. *Financial Times* journalist James Kynge described this model in a book in 2006 – the purchase of a steel plant by a Chinese company in Germany had ended up with wholesale relocation of the purchased corporation's equipment back into China. Chinese companies using this model were seen as simply asset stripping in order to carry technology they badly needed back home, failing to create local employment, to work as long-term external partners and to play a positive role.[9] Huawei was different – a more collaborative partner, one that really did, on the surface, look just like Apple, or Deutsche Telekom, or AT&T.

But as the company developed, the fears about its links to the Chinese state began to increase. The *Sunday Times* in 2009 claimed Huawei had been blocked from growing its share of the UK market because of security concerns.[10] Things did not improve when it was effectively banned from bidding for an Australian national broadband project a couple of years later.[11] And despite spending more than US$ 200 million on a lobbying effort in the United States, the company was not permitted to invest there, or to bid for major contracts. Huawei employed highly regarded international figures to sit on its international board and had foreign senior executives. But the fear that it is a Trojan horse, sucking up information in the telecoms sector which it is duty bound to report back to its political overlords in Beijing, will not easily disappear. The idea is fixed that there are costs of Chinese outward investment that go beyond simple issues of job creation, profit and loss.

In 2017, therefore, Chinese state companies have a significant role in Chinese foreign policy. They have assets, employees and interests abroad that need to be safeguarded. Chinese nationalists and military figures might get strident about attacking the Japanese, North Americans or Europeans, but Chinese companies have different priorities, especially when their profits and prosperity are involved. Chinese state companies have presidents who sit on the Chinese Communist Party (CCP) Central Committee. Senior Chinese leaders like Zhang Gaoli, vice premier and Standing Committee member since 2012, came from the state energy sector. Many others have accrued networks and strong links with state companies during their provincial careers, and these have been instrumental in producing economic growth, allowing them to deliver their targets for promotion. An increasingly large part of this growth is coming either from exports to foreign markets, or from direct investment into those markets. For this reason alone, their voice matters, and this feeds into the development of foreign policy. They have significant vested interest in ensuring that China

has positive relations with the outside world. It is not just domestically, therefore, that business figures in China see sources of profit.
The outside world increasingly matters to them too, and that makes
them key stakeholders in China's development and articulation of
foreign policy.

Similarly, non-state companies have started appearing in this context. With their role as innovators, employers and generators of GDP
outputs, having good supplies networks abroad, markets to export
to and technology partners has become increasingly important to
them. As economist and academic Yasheng Huang made clear in the
mid-2000s, the simple fact is that for many Chinese entrepreneurs,
with the favours from the state granted to state-owned companies
giving them unfair advantages internally, working outside China
is often easier than trying to do things domestically.[12] Figures like
Jack Ma (Ma Yun), the former English teacher from Hangzhou in
the highly entrepreneurial province of Zhejiang who founded the
internet company Alibaba, are poster boys for the Chinese non-state
sector. Through the listings of their companies on foreign markets in
London or New York, or through creating sales markets or networks
internationally, these figures have a profile which often exceeds that
of Chinese political leaders. Ma Yun regales audiences at places like
Davos with his punchy, fast-talking business wisdom. Chinese private companies had mattered far less than the large state ones in (for
instance) Australia – until, with the resource crash from 2014, they
started to become much more important, working in agribusiness,
finance or other areas of technology which showed much brighter
growth prospects than copper, iron ore or steel.

Chinese non-state companies, unlike their state equivalents, do
have one issue with getting their views and interests looked after:
in the way the Chinese government promotes the country's interests abroad. While state company senior leaders are appointments
mandated and put in place by the Organization Department of
the CCP (and therefore in effect political appointments), non-state

leaders were not even allowed to join the Party until 2002. Even after this point, it was hard to see how they were represented in the political system, despite their willingness to become Party members. The one place where they might be able to have a say is on the Chinese People's Consultative Congress (CPCC), a body which combines social, artistic and non-Party figures and derived from the United Front that the Party had established in the 1940s to lay claim to being truly representative across Chinese society. Crucially, however, for this body, the clue is in the title – it is a *consultative* entity. It does not have real executive power. Very occasionally, ostensibly entrepreneurial figures like Zhang Ruimin of the hybrid-owned electrical white appliances company Haier have had a place as an alternate on the Central Committee. But the puzzle is why, despite the rise of private companies' importance to the economy and the rhetoric the government devotes to this sector's cultivation and importance (because of its far superior record of generating intellectual property and high profit levels), so few of its members are enfranchised in the system and have a visible voice on areas of relevant policy interest, particularly those involving foreign policy. All that can be said is that issues important to them are a consideration for politicians when they devise Chinese international relations strategy, though precisely how this indirect power works is less easy to spell out.

THE THINKING INDUSTRIES: UNIVERSITIES, INTELLECTUALS AND THINK TANKS

In the world around the central leadership compound in Zhongnanhai in Beijing, and its various satellites across the country at provincial level, people in government are too busy reacting to day-to-day local events to ever properly have the time to think about the wider world. The Politburo, with its so-called 'study days', equivalents of awaydays where the members go on a retreat and focus on one particular set of policy challenges, gives an air of sedate calm. But more often than not, Chinese officials, military figures or state enterprise leaders above a certain level are overwhelmed with immediate issues. This is part of the problem of a system where so little is actually delegated. The core 3,000 or so people who run China, the high-level cadres, barely have time to breathe and eat, let alone contemplate the role of their country in the world or devise new principles and practices for how China should act in the coming decade or so. Nor is this group likely to be particularly original in their thinking. They are, by nature, risk-averse. Slight mishaps and mistakes can precipitate the collapse of their career and, they believe, the country they run, so their appetite for innovation beyond purely rhetorical support is limited.

That being the case, where do new ideas or decent analyses come from, particularly on foreign affairs? Working in this area is a constellation of intellectual influencers, public opinion-formers, located in places like Qinghua University and Beijing University in the capital, elite educational organizations with strong links to the outside world, good networks among their leadership (many of whom, like Xi, are their alumni) and well-regarded international relations departments. The then dean of Beijing University's School of International Studies, Wang Jisi, formed the idea of China opening up more to its western-facing geography than its eastern. This has had a direct influence on the evolution of the Belt Road Initiative since 2014 – the largest infrastructure project in history – and his thinking was the driving force behind the desire to create a vast zone of common economic interest centred on China, throughout Central and South Asia and into the Middle East. At Tsinghua University, Yan Xuetong, also a professor of international relations, is a significant, more nationalist commentator, writing about China's need for more leadership and, in recent years, the need to take a harder line on Taiwan.

There are more directly mandated entities in the intellectual sphere, too – the Central Party School, for instance, think tank to the Communist Party itself and host to foreign figures whose ideas are of interest to the leadership. In the past, this has held events involving figures as diverse as Peter Mandelson, Britain's architect of the Third Way, Jürgen Habermas, the great German philosopher who created the concept of civic society, and even more esoteric figures like the late Jacques Derrida, French thinker. It was the Party School that served as the home of Zheng Bijian, the original proponent of the idea of China's 'peaceful rise' and its renaissance in the mid-2000s.

Beijing has been called the lobby capital of the world. And at the heart of this lobbying there is the myriad of government think tanks, running from the Chinese Academy of Social Sciences to the more foreign-affairs-centred Chinese Institute of International Studies (CIIS) and the Chinese People's Institute of Foreign Affairs. Some, like the China Institutes [sic] of Contemporary International Relations (CICIR), are closely linked to the Ministry of State Security. But others, like the Charhar Institute, appear as semi-private endeavours, even though they clearly enjoy friendly, close links with the government. The question of whether any think tank in China, no matter what area it is in, can truly be independent and contemplate a world where the Party does not have a role, is a moot point. The political system that China currently has, and the ways that system remains off the menu for open discussion and debate, means that think tanks with Chinese characteristics often operate more as organs of justification than ones of challenge. The more critical might say that of their many functions, thinking does not count among them.

One way in which new perspectives do make their way into China's ideological system is not directly through think tanks and universities, but more because of how these organizations allow access to ideas from other countries. In the 2000s, journalist

Thomas Friedman's *The World is Flat* (2005) enjoyed its moment of vogue among the Communist Party elite, with officials at the Central Party School and in the Chongqing government reportedly reading it. Plenty of other visiting figures are able through these organizations to talk to the leadership, directly or indirectly. A plethora of voices, perspectives and provocations on Chinese foreign-affairs issues is constantly doing the rounds throughout the country. Some of these are used as intellectual justification of events like the large-scale Chinese conferences the Chinese Party state has an endless appetite for organizing – from the Boao Forum on the southern island of Hainan, held mostly in April each year and usually addressed by the president or premier, to the Chinese summer World Economic Forum, in the latter part of the year, held occasionally in the north-east in Dalian, or Tianjin. Again, though, these gatherings tend to be vast networking and media scrums where elite political figures perform in front of a benign audience of mostly retired foreign leaders rather than places for detailed and thoughtful deliberation and consideration of new ideas. As with the Chinese political elite in general, there is little tolerance for allowing those to attend who might subvert, challenge or simply refute the dominant Chinese government foreign-affairs narratives. One requirement is that attendees are vetted beforehand to ensure they are 'qinhua' – that they have a friendly attitude or feeling towards China. This does not mean that they are enslaved lackeys who are constantly on the Party state's side, but it does mean they must have a sense of politeness and sensitivity and not choose to confront or upbraid their hosts. Ideas do matter in this area in China; it is just that there are surprisingly few methods of access to elite political leaders for good or interesting ideas to easily get through, and little real sense that China is a receptive, open-minded environment for full, robust debate about foreign-policy issues except on its own terms.

POWER TO THE PEOPLE?

The final major group to consider is the people. 100 million Chinese people travelled abroad as tourists in 2014 alone, and a million plus have been abroad as students either at undergraduate or postgraduate level since the first tranche in the 1980s. To this can be added the million who lived and worked across Africa, and the many more who went overseas to be business people in Latin America, Australia or remote parts of the Pacific. Then there is the general Chinese population, whose lives are all touched in some way in the era of global China by links to the outside world.

Coming across travellers or tourists who came from the People's Republic of China was once a rarity. So too was being able to freely meet people if you were actually granted access into the PRC. Before 1978, it was hard to get in and out of the country. The French philosopher Roland Barthes wrote *Travels in China*, a hilarious account of a tightly controlled visit to the country with a group of other intellectuals including Julia Kristeva, which typified foreign experiences from this era in the early 1970s. It sounds at times like a tour of another planet, with the great *penseur* either commenting on the quality of the food or the latent sexuality of the waitresses serving them as they made their way across the country.[13] Direct interaction, except with their chosen minders, was rare to non-existent. The late, great Pierre Ryckmans (otherwise known by his pseudonym Simon Leys) complained that most non-Chinese accounts of Chinese people at the time of the Cultural Revolution made them sound like fish from the depths of an ocean who spoke, thought and experienced things differently to 'us' – people from Europe, North America and the outside world.

By 2017 this has changed. Chinese people figure as customers, sources of tourist dollars, aid workers, students, teachers and marriage partners. Chinese expenditure in capitalist headquarters like London's Oxford Street or Paris's Champs-Elysées is critical to our consumer economies – the highest per capita of any group. Chinese student fees make up to a fifth of the revenue of universities from Australia to South America. Chinese economists sit on the board of the International Monetary Fund (IMF), Chinese soccer players play in the English Premier League (despite the dismal record of China's own national team) and Chinese comedians have even started finding fame in the United States.

This is a significant trend – the face of what diplomats somewhat sniffily call 'people-to-people diplomacy'. The EU made 2014 the year of people-to-people contact. Events presided over by high-level politicians sang the praises of links that now existed between schools inside and outside China and of cultural entities like orchestras, sports organizations and non-government associations. Chinese visiting scholars have appeared in almost every university in the West. Such contact became a major part of United States–China relations too, when the annual Strategic Economic and Security Dialogue held in 2015 announced the hope that 100,000 US students might follow in the steps of the Chinese who had come out of their country and go to China to study its language, culture and customs.

Chinese people, ordinary, working people, matter in international relations. They matter in a practical sense – during the first Libyan Civil War in 2011, 36,000 Chinese citizens had to be rescued by the Chinese government when order and security broke down. They also mattered when a Chinese citizen tragically became a victim of the abhorrent extremist Daesh group in late 2015. But Chinese citizens who have stayed at home also matter, and their ideas and expectations have to be figured into the articulation and messaging of foreign-affairs issues, perhaps even into its formulation. The Chinese government must consider public reactions particularly intensely when it deals with Japan, for example, because of the high emotions and tensions Chinese people have inherited from history. The opinion of the people matters when dealing with the East and South China Sea disputes, where complainants are often highly vociferous. Some of the most visceral of these come from bloggers like Wang Xiaodong and his colleagues, who in works such as *China Can Say No* in 1996 and *Unhappy China* in 2009, rage about offences and slights against their country by neighbours like Japan, or powers like the United States.[14]

It is clear in the language that Xi has used about the 'China Dream' from 2013 onwards that he and the people around him are aware of the importance of factoring in the dynamics of public opinion to diplomacy. There have also been times when Chinese behaviour abroad has become a huge problem – rude and ungracious manners for instance by Chinese tourists, particularly in places like Hong Kong, where the case of a mainland mother allowing her child to defecate in public aroused fury, or when an elderly Chinese man was mocked worldwide for trying to open the door of a plane while in flight. The Taiwanese poet, essayist and historian Bo Yang, some years before, wrote of the phenomenon of the 'ugly Chinaman', a notion modelled on that of the 'ugly American' of uncouth, selfish, boorish behaviour abroad and defensive bigotry at home.[15] In the twenty-first century, a level of perceived insensitivity and arrogance by first-time Chinese travellers abroad has developed that risks damaging China's reputation so much the government has produced educational material requesting that people behave appropriately. Even so, Chinese people, despite the lack of any democratic power through voting, do have an interest in foreign policy and a role to play. They do this through indirect lobbying, by manipulating the desire of the Chinese government to keep them happy and compliant, and through the impact of their tourist and investment money. They are therefore a major constituency in the making of Chinese foreign policy, albeit one whose real influence is very hard to quantify precisely.

JOINING THE DOTS:
THE MAKERS OF FOREIGN POLICY

Between all these various constituencies and groups, how is foreign policy developed? How are people's voices factored in? How does a leader like Xi, sitting at the centre of all this, make everyone feel like they are being listened to and their needs being attended to? Is there some immense process of negotiation or consultation, so that they all get to feel Chinese foreign policy fairly reflects their views, or at least gives them a chance to convey what they feel?

For Xi Jinping's generation of leadership, the country they are in charge of is intrinsically global. Even when they are considering domestic issues like the construction of new cities, changing the country's energy profile to reduce dependence on fossil fuels and focus more on renewable or nuclear sources, or liberalizing their currency, the size of China and its role in the global economic and security system means there are external repercussions, some of which can be considerable. Falling Chinese demand for iron ore led to a slowdown in the Australian economy from 2014. And Chinese stock market volatility in Shanghai and Shenzhen in July 2015, and then again in January 2016, meant that London, New York, Frankfurt and other markets witnessed knock-on effects.

Are Chinese leaders now comfortable with this prominent role? As the rest of this book will show, they often adopt a position of strategic ambiguity. When it suits them, they do want influence and a strong voice. They need this for their own legitimacy and to demonstrate to nationalistic groups back in China that they are worthy custodians of their country's historic mission to be rich and strong again. But they also need it for the simple reason that solving their severe domestic issues almost always involves calculations about outsiders and how they can help. However, it is also clear that they want this influence on their own terms. Notions of getting heavily embroiled in issues in the Middle East, as the somewhat tepid government White Paper in January 2016 issued by China on relations with Arabic countries made clear, has limited appeal (see the final chapter for more on this issue). Notions of creating a 'G2', where China sits beside the United States in some new 'superpower club', have been rebuffed in Beijing. For some of China's foreign-policy thinkers, getting seduced and flattered into becoming a new global policeman is against the country's interests, exposing it to burdensome and distracting new responsibilities it cannot attend to during its present phase, a phase where its priority is to continue developing and emerging from poverty and weakness. This lies behind its very cautious initial response to Donald Trump's election success. It was an opportunity, but also a threat, placing China far outside its comfort zone by pushing it to the foreground on issues of trade and climate change.

Xi's predecessor, Hu Jintao, maintained a low profile, barely figuring in international affairs. His silence, even over issues that mattered directly to China, was infamous. The more talkative Xi has certainly raised the profile of the Chinese presidency and the Party leadership. He has travelled more since becoming president, and his book, *The Governance of China*, contains many statements about foreign partners and the role of China in the outside world. The fact that this sort of book was issued so early in his projected period in power is itself telling; Hu did not issue a collection of speeches and ideas in this way, and Jiang Zemin before took ten years to come out with his collected statements. For the Xi leadership, messaging is clearly important. And it is hoped that the simple fact that this is a leadership more willing to speak openly about external issues will in itself solve some of the problems China has – often being criticized for sitting on the fence, being opaque, freeloading and avoiding taking responsibility.

For all the voices, influences and interests listed above, however, the heart of this system of decision-making is remarkably small. On foreign-affairs issues, every single one of China's 1.4 billion people has an interest. So too does the rest of the world's population. And yet, beyond the military, state enterprises, security services, the people themselves, the National People's Congress (NPC), think tanks and intellectual influences, and into the Party itself and the Central Committee, the Politburo, the Standing Committee of the Politburo – even into the Leading Group on Foreign Affairs – there sits at the heart of this a startlingly small number of people for such a vast country, who somehow are expected to pull all of these strands together and make this thing called foreign policy. The key figures here are Xi himself, Wang Huning, the fellow Politburo member who has been the architect of many of the key ideas, and then economists like Liu He and figures who work as bureaucratic enablers like Ding Xuexiang and Zhu Guofeng.[16] This highly personal network is the ultimate 'black box' – the life and heart of the system, sucking in what all the others provide and then producing the final distillation – the great guiding narrative frameworks on which foreign policy is constructed. This sort of set-up means it is important to get a handle on the personal outlook of a leader like Xi. It is his personal interest, and his ambition, that is now the core driving force of Chinese foreign policy. Perhaps one of the most remarkable diplomatic facts of the second decade of the twentieth century is that a matter as significant and important to so many people as Chinese foreign policy should still remain in the hands of such a tiny group of people, and be a reflection of their ideas. In this area, China has not moved much further than the era of Mao Zedong when, once again, only a handful of people really mattered, and only one, Mao himself, was truly decisive. China under Xi is only a little better.

XI AND FOREIGNERS

What does Xi think of the outside world? As far as his career is concerned, he has never lived abroad for any length of time. His famous first trip to the USA in 1985 on a trade delegation, when he stayed in Iowa, only lasted a matter of days. And since then, his forays abroad have been measurable in hours and days, rather than months. Certainly, as a provincial leader in Fujian he had the chance to travel, and went to almost every state in Australia and a number in Europe. But he got to become a leader largely because of his abilities in the domestic realm – lobbying, delivering things locally, and dealing with internal issues – rather than his performance on the international stage. Focusing on issues abroad would not have helped his chances, unless it was linked to getting investment or benefits from foreigners into China.

In 2010, Xi did seem to let slip his somewhat ambiguous attitude to the outside world, when during the fallout from the international financial crisis he was overheard on a visit to Mexico complaining about foreigners with full bellies pointing the finger at China and blaming it for ills that were down to their own ineptness and incompetence. In that sense (and assuming Xi meant these comments) his views towards the outside world are not much different to many of his compatriots' – it is interesting and intriguing, its culture and technology sometimes admirable, but it is also often frustrating, ignorant about and unsympathetic towards China, and a little unsubtle and inferior. This cultural hauteur and sense of superiority works well for Xi domestically. His key audience when he travels is not foreigners he is spending time among, but his people back home – and for them, seeing a leader with confidence, and any sort of swagger, is appealing after the years of China being almost invisible on the global stage.

Xi certainly has had plenty of experience dealing with foreign companies and visiting foreign leaders in provinces where he once worked. When he left Fujian and moved to Zhejiang, which is one of the most open and entrepreneurial of the great coastal economies, he worked to get US companies like Microsoft and McDonald's to invest in China more heavily. He approved marketing campaigns for Zhejiang abroad in order to raise the profile of the province's economic attributes and attract more foreign investment. He even took part in some trips abroad. But he saw the outside world in pretty much the same terms as all Communist Party leaders of his generation – a place which was there to be of use to China, supply China with things it needed, and, where it suited the Communist Party, to be emulated. But there were clear limits. The outside world was as much a source of threats and unwanted changes as desirable ones. Whereas its prowess in producing new technology, establishing global companies and nurturing innovation was embraced, other countries' political models and ideas about law, civil society, freedom of speech and other political matters were rejected – labelled as 'unsuitable for China's national conditions', to use the standard term.

Since his elevation in 2012 to Party leader, and then to the presidency in 2013, Xi Jinping has done nothing to change this assumption about the wider world. Under him, the Party's ideological arm has issued commands against adopting Western models of multiparty democracy or Western-style legal reform, where courts would be able to hold the political authorities to ultimate accountability. Ideas that suit the continuation of stable, one-party rule have been embraced – the development of rule by law (rather than the more extensive 'of law') and improvements in commercial and economic reforms, for instance. But political reforms of any sort remain tightly circumscribed. In many ways, with harsh crackdowns on dissent and rights lawyers, things have deteriorated even further since the era of Hu. For example, restrictions remain firmly in place over the internet and China's connectivity with the outside world. Xi's mindset can best be typified by the phrase used in the time of Deng: 'when one opens a window to let in a little air, flies also enter'. Xi's view of the outside world therefore is a strategic, hard-nosed one. He must be open enough to the world to allow the good things to come in that the Party state wants, prevent the bad things from entering, and ensure the boundaries between the two are clearly delineated. This attitude is positive towards outside companies who want to invest in and transfer new technologies to China, but far less positive about allowing multinationals to make vast profits domestically. For commercial lawyers whose work is seen to be creating a stronger, more predictable economic environment, the Chinese government under Xi has been supportive. But for those lawyers dealing with political and social issues, the attitude is not so warm. Their work is seen as challenging the legitimacy of the Party state and constituting a threat to it. Many of these have been harassed and victimized since 2014. That principle of making clear choices between the desired and undesired elements of the outside world, and dealing with them accordingly, lies at the heart of the foreign policy he has sponsored. Its accompanying strategy is to use the inducements China now has in terms of opportunities that come from its growing domestic market and its appeal to foreigners, and its increasing interests in international issues, to bring in the kind of foreign ideas, partnerships and actors that the Communist Party around him believes China needs, ones that deliver tangible benefits for the country in its historic mission to gain great-power status. This is best summarized by a single sentence: Xi wants relations with the outside world that are on China's terms.

THE WORLD OF ZONES

As the People's Republic proceeds in 2017 towards great-power status, and increases its links to the outside world, Xi Jinping has clearly articulated – far more than any previous Chinese leader – the sort of role his country occupies in the world, and China's aspirations for itself. Since becoming Chinese leader, he has mapped out a world of zones: areas of interest guided partly by the principles of Chinese foreign policy he has inherited from the era of Mao onwards and shaped by the drivers of that policy, which I outlined in Chapter 1.

All of this is influenced by sources of advice and input described above. All this together has created a contemporary world vision in which China sits as a new kind of middle kingdom, with spokes emanating out from it, binding it to the affairs of others through the identification of common threats, common interests, and common issues. Some of these are tangible ones, such as investment levels, the existence of strong diasporic links, or political commonalities. For the last of these issues, China's situation is unusual; it has no full treaty alliances with others, apart from North Korea, and only four other countries share its political model – Laos, Vietnam, North Korea and Cuba. With almost all of these 'allies' its relationship is often tetchy; ironically, the worst of these is with the country that (on paper, at least) China has the most common links with: the Democratic People's Republic of Korea (DPRK). We will return later to this issue of the view China takes of alliances and the benefits and burdens they offer.

To Beijing, at least from listening to the words of Xi Jinping and the people around him, there are four clear zones. Nowhere on earth can truly say it does not matter to China. Even the remote Arctic and Antarctica have started to figure in Chinese strategic thinking, as will be subsequently explained. But there are levels of intensity in these relationships. These depend on the depth and diversity of economic links, the extent of security interests and potential conflicts, and the ways in which other partners can supply China with things it needs – from resources, to technology, to diplomatic support at the UN over matters like the South and East China Sea disputes or Taiwan. Finally, there is the simple issue of geographical distance. Those countries located physically closer to China will inevitably matter more to it than those further away, due to logistical or territorial issues.

Put simply, a country which has high levels of trade with China, common, overlapping security interests in terms of the power of its armed forces and extent of its alliances, strong technology and intellectual assets and geographical closeness, will matter more to it than somewhere which has low trade levels, few common security interests or issues, limited technology or intellectual assets, and is geographically distant. Of course, no single country occupies these extremes; nowhere has everything China wants, and everywhere figures to some degree in China's list of wants and requirements – even a place as remote from it as Iceland. But most countries can be located along a spectrum where each factor spelled out above can be tallied and a rough measure of its importance to China given.

In Zone One, the key area, the sole occupant is the United States. The United States is by far and away China's greatest foreign policy priority, and has been since the 1970s. Deng Xiaoping's advice in 1978 was to constantly keep the most powerful country in the world onside, and to ensure China never came into direct confrontation with it. The United States is that country. Its economic power is important to China, and it is its largest export market. But it is also its greatest security rival, with a military that is technically far ahead of China's and which spends from three to four times more than China annually. It has treaty allies surrounding China, from Japan to the Philippines, to Indonesia, and down to Australia. It also has many of the technological and intellectual assets that China most desires – whether it be through companies like Apple, or through its dominance as producer of intellectual property. As a fellow Pacific power, the United States is, as Xi Jinping made clear when meeting with President Obama in 2014 at Sunnylands in California, part of the same neighbourhood as China, despite their coasts being separated by a vast stretch of water.

Zone Two is occupied by a combination of regional powers, some of whom are in the Association of Southeast Asian Nations (ASEAN), some in the China-instigated Shanghai Cooperation Organization (SCO), and some which fall under the new 'Belt Road Initiative' (BRI) rubric. For these countries, totalling about 60, most are geographically within what China might call its 'zone of strategic interest'. They almost all have China as their largest or second largest trading partner, and they operate as important markets – at least when regarded together – for Chinese exported goods. But they are also suppliers of resources, from energy to minerals. For many countries in this zone, such as Singapore, Malaysia and Indonesia, there are also strong ethnic links with a diaspora tracing their family origins back to China, many members of which have been asked since 1978 to assist in the process of reform and opening up through investment, supplying intellectual property, and being a source of links with outside countries.

In Zone Three is the European Union (EU). A combination of (currently) 28 member states, with a population approaching 450 million and some of the highest per capita income levels in the world, the EU matters to China as a market and its largest trading partner, and is the destination for the second largest amount of its exports after the United States. But beyond this economic link there is also perhaps a more significant one – the fact that the EU is by far and away the largest partner for transfer of technologies, through companies like Volkswagen and Siemens and through the immense number of university linkages across Europe. China has sent tens of thousands of students to the EU, particularly to the United Kingdom, and it has in recent years made large investments within the region which, compared to the USA, is less politically contentious for it to operate in. The EU's cultural assets are also hugely admired. But it does not, however, figure greatly in China's security thinking, relegating it to third position, below the regional partners referred to above.

In Zone Four, there are regions like the Middle East, Latin America and Africa. For these places, China's primary interest is the supply of resources it needs and the opportunity it has to make investments, along with some diplomatic support (over Taiwan, for instance, or on issues that matter to China, like being condemned for human rights abuses at the UN). Brazil, Saudi Arabia and Iran are all core suppliers of iron ore, oil or precious metals. For these countries, there might be one specific thing that China has an interest in getting from them, and on the back of this it is willing to construct a narrative of engagement. Sometimes this has been through ideas imported from outside, for example via the BRICS (Brazil, Russia, India, China, South Africa) collective. Or it might be divined from high-level visits, in which China confers the accolade of 'strategic relationship' on countries across the world (there are currently more than 50 of these). For the fourth zone, China's interests are combined with a clear desire to avoid political commitments. In the Middle East, as we will see in Chapter 4, but also across Africa and to some extent in Latin America, it operates in terms of desiring 'win–win benefits' and the fiction of non-commitment in other areas. Xi Jinping's China is not interested in binding alliances, or being pushed into the position of world policeman-in-waiting – though, as will be shown in Chapter 3, its commitments are likely to become more complex under a Trump presidency from 2017 that threatens to be more isolationist and more expectant towards China to play a stronger security role in areas where it is currently regarded as a freeloader.

Under Xi Jinping, the strategy has been to attach a specific label to each of these relationship 'zones'. The one with the United States has been referred to as a new model of major power relations. The second, encompassing the highly diverse series of countries around China's borders, has been embraced in the idea of the Belt Road Initiative. The third, with the EU, Xi has accorded the status of 'civilizational powers'. And for the last, Xi has yet to articulate an overarching description, although some areas do get included as part of the BRI (the Middle East, for instance). While in the past China was happy to present itself as leader of the Third World, the term for developing countries which it created in the 1960s to oppose itself to the First World (which was aligned with the United States), and the Second World (aligned with the former

USSR and some eastern European countries), in a reversal of this it is now the United States, EU and regional countries that it ties into a narrative structure, summarized above. The rest of the world has now been left in a slightly less certain place regarding China's views of it.

CHIEF FLATTERER-IN-CHIEF

Just as domestic politics is often guided by emotion and feeling, so too is the realm of foreign relations. For Xi Jinping, the main task has been to convey to the world two different messages. The first is that China is getting stronger, has the right to be taken more seriously, and deserves a place at the main table for any economic, security or governance discussions. But the second is that China's power is for the good of everyone; that it appreciates and seeks out mutually beneficial relations with the rest of the world, and is a threat to no one. There are times when China's message slides from the first to the second and then back again. This makes it a highly ambiguous power, and its message is often hard to accurately interpret.

Yet Xi's grand foreign-policy narratives have always placed reciprocity at their heart. Harking back to the demands for multipolarity in the world from the 1990s onwards, China has stressed its humility and focused only on things that matter to it. For Xi's China, the message of great-power relations or civilizational partnerships are important ones to convey, because they carry the idea that China is the equal of its main interlocutors, not better, not worse. This friendly tone, however, has been interpreted in some places as insincere, as we shall see later in this book. Many feel it conceals Chinese ambitions to assert its values and interests even more on the world stage.

In many ways, talking about a uniform 'China view' of the outside world is a fiction. There are instead multiple views, and they are spread across all of the groups talked about earlier in this chapter. The rest of this book will look in detail at specific areas, trying to unpack what relationships with these groups might mean to China. Xi Jinping urged his officials and fellow leaders to 'tell the China story, and tell it well' soon after his appointment as general secretary. This telling of the China story, of what China means to the world and the world means to China, will be the subject of the rest of this book. The first part of that story, which I will cover in the next chapter, is to work out the way the United States figures in the minds, and the hearts, of modern Chinese people and their leaders.

3

CHINA AND THE UNITED STATES
THE ULTIMATE LOVE–HATE RELATIONSHIP

Walking almost arm in arm like best buddies, Xi Jinping and President Obama spent over nine hours in conversation at the June 2013 summit at Sunnylands, on the US West Coast. That the new leader of China should, against protocol, have given up time to go across the Pacific in order to build a relationship with the leader of the United States was only one of many clear pieces of evidence that if there truly was a 'special relationship' in the twenty-first century, it was not between the United Kingdom and United States (a coupling that has borne this description for decades, despite no one in London or Washington knowing precisely what it means), but between the United States and China. Talked of as a G2 in the previous decade, they are the essential partners in future global prosperity and security. Various issues – from climate change to reforming international finance governances to sorting out developing world debt and poverty, even doing a 'nuclear freeze' deal with Iran – had to involve them both in order to succeed. The absence of one or the other (and sometimes both) almost immediately reduces the relevance of any international agreement.

Yet, as many point out, the United States–China relationship is one contaminated by distrust, fractiousness and tension. Only a year after the cordial meeting between Xi and Obama, the Federal Bureau of Investigations (FBI) issued an unprecedented formal accusation against five officials in the Chinese PLA, accusing them of cyberespionage crimes. The language used in the official press release announcing the accusations came from another planet than the warm words which had characterized the two presidents' relationship as they walked together over golf courses in California, as this quote from the former FBI director James B. Comey illustrates:

> For too long, the Chinese government has blatantly sought to use cyber espionage to obtain economic advantage for its state-owned industries [...] The indictment announced today is an important step. But there are many more victims, and there is much more to be done. With our unique criminal and national security authorities, we will continue to use all legal tools at our disposal to counter cyber espionage from all sources.[1]

These two events, which took place in the space of just 12 months, illustrate the spectrum of United States–China relations and its complexity. The roots of that complexity arise partly from clear political and cultural differences between the two countries, but also from their often torturous and difficult history. Even before Donald Trump was inaugurated in January 2017, that complexity resurfaced with his taking of a phone call from Tsai Ing-wen, the president of the Republic of China on Taiwan – a place the United States has not even recognized since 1979. This caused shock waves in China and across the world, illustrating, almost half a century after the Nixon rapprochement, how much potential there still is in the relationship for tension and clashes.

THE ERA OF MUTUAL SILENCE

Sometime in 1969, just as the most violent phase of the Cultural Revolution was coming to an end, a group of PLA leaders who had been victims of the movement and ended up in prison in the north-east of China were summoned to a meeting where they were tasked with thinking through something which, had it been spoken aloud at the time, would have risked a death sentence – how China could forge closer relations with the United States. In the topsy-turvy world of the late Mao era, people could think – and even say – the unthinkable. Whether they survived was dependent on where the order had come from (if Mao mandated it, they were safe. If not, then they were often exposed and could find themselves in deep trouble). In this case, the command for their ruminations had come from the very top. Mao Zedong himself wanted to know how to give his country (and at that time, it literally was his country) security and space from the USSR. A closer relationship with the United States was the most logical choice, despite all the barriers.

The USA and the PRC's relationship had been extremely frosty since 1949. In the 1950s, they had as good as been at war with each other due to the Korean confrontation, even though this was mainly driven by the UN. Right to the bitter end of the civil war that had begun in 1946, the United States had provided Chiang Kai-shek's Nationalist forces with equipment and funding in their struggle with the Communists. With the Nationalists' flight to Taiwan, the United States became the island's chief patron – a situation that prevails to this day. Red China, as Washington labelled it then, was part of the Soviet-dominated world, politically alien and in effect an enemy on the wrong side of the Cold War.

Through the 1950s and into the 1960s, the United States figured in Chinese propaganda as the great imperialist, the new colonizer, its war in Vietnam evidence of its desire to set up client states throughout the Asia region. The United States had troops in South Korea, the Philippines and Japan, and alliances (after the 1952 Treaty of San Francisco) that reached down to Australia, Indonesia and New Zealand. Very few US citizens ever visited China, apart from a few who were politically favoured. Access was restricted on both sides; through China's internal *Reference News*, a digest of translated material from Western newspapers and journals circulated to the Party elite leaders, those in the upper echelons got some idea of what was being reported in US papers, but most Chinese people were not allowed access to this material. For Americans, their main conduit of information was via Hong Kong. The nadir of the relationship was the highly charged moment when Premier Zhou Enlai was attending an international peace conference in Geneva in 1954, and came into contact with the US Secretary of State John Forster Dulles. There is no clear account of their encounter, but the reported refusal of Dulles to shake Zhou's hand has entered international political mythology.[2] It has come to typify the way in which the United States was regarded as 'losing' China in this era.

The disagreement between China and the Soviet Union in the late 1950s started to change the dynamics of geopolitics. China did not fit easily into the Cold War bloc of countries. For example, it was the only country in the Communist world to maintain friendly relations with Albania, despite the fact that Moscow had labelled the tiny European country a maverick, and a socialist traitor. Under Mao, the PRC became an increasingly idiosyncratic actor, but it was regarded as being predominantly introspective, never attempting to export its political values beyond its borders. There was a brief phase at the high point of Maoism when voices abroad calling for more support for the Maoist revolutionary struggle became more strident, irritating the United States and Europe. But this proved short-lived, and its impact negligible. The simple fact was that Maoism, beyond being an exotic marginal force, never had much impact on even the radical fringes of cultures in democracies, and had limited traction even in developing countries.[3] Chinese Marxism was far too esoteric.

Mao's anxiety about the Soviet Union and its intentions was long-standing. But in 1969 this was exacerbated by the clashes with the Red Army that the PRC had suffered on its vast shared north-eastern border with the USSR (known as the Sino-Soviet border conflict). Concentrated on Zhenbao Island on the Ussuri River, it involved skirmishes throughout March of that year, resulting in up to 1,000 casualties on both sides. Chinese media at the time portrayed the event exhaustively as an indication of the USSR's ill intentions and aggression towards its neighbour. Battles continued throughout the rest of the year. For the political leaders of the PRC in Beijing, however, with their memories formed during an era where war and conflict was the norm, they assumed the worst-case scenario about where matters were heading. For them, the USSR was almost certain to use its nuclear weapons against them. From this period, therefore, Russia figured as a far greater and more immediate threat to the PRC than the more remote United States.

Contemplating détente in some form with the United States flowed from the simple logic – as the old Arabic adage states – that 'my enemy's enemy is my friend'. The three high-level, detained PLA officials mentioned earlier in this chapter had to run through the various options of how an improved relationship with the United States might work. They were operating, in effect, as a deeply secretive, unorthodox think tank – one with a single client: Mao Zedong.[4] Their conclusion was that moves towards a rapprochement that triangulated the USSR into a situation where it was on its own against the two other powers, China and the United States, made sense. Their advice appealed to Mao. After all, his paranoia towards the Soviet Union was not new: it had inspired his Third Front policy, relocating much of the country's heavy industry, including its aerospace engineering and aviation factories, to provincial places like Xi'an, Shenyang, Harbin and Chengdu (where they remain to this day). But the 1969 attacks had added a real element of urgency that something even more dramatic had to be tried in order to preserve the PRC's security.

SNOW IN AUTUMN

The first attempt to reach out to the United States fell on deaf ears, though more by mistake than through deliberate intent. US journalist Edgar Snow, who back in the 1930s had been one of the first foreigners ever to interview Mao, and whose book *Red Star Over China* had introduced the Chinese Communist movement to the outside world, was invited to participate in the National Day celebrations and stand beside the Chairman himself in 1970. There were two audiences this was intended to reach. One was Washington, which Mao hoped would heed his friendly gesture and start responding; the other was domestic, the hardliners around Lin Biao, his heir apparent at the time, and his wife Jiang Qing, who were resolutely set against seeing the United States as anything but a wholesale enemy. Both audiences failed to understand what this gesture was trying to tell them. For the United States, Snow was regarded as a long-standing left-wing sympathizer, now resident in Switzerland and almost *persona non grata*. There were no surprises to them in seeing him cosy up to left-wing leaders. For the Chinese radicals, rapprochement with the United States was simply unthinkable – another scheme to weaken the country cooked up by enemies within, and one that they needed to destroy by lobbying the Chairman. Snow was simply there as an old friend of Mao. They thought nothing more of it.

Mao proved resolute, however, his fear of the USSR trumping all other considerations. In 1970–1, first via Chinese representatives in Poland and then through their own diplomats in New York once the People's Republic had been readmitted to the UN in 1971, China began direct talks with US officials. The presiding genius behind these was President Nixon's Machiavellian national security advisor Henry Kissinger. It was Kissinger's secret mission to Beijing from Pakistan in 1971, during which he met both Zhou Enlai and Mao Zedong himself, which paved the way for the ensuing presidential visit and the start of normalization of ties in the September of the following year. When Nixon landed on the tarmac on a cold day in Beijing to be met by Zhou Enlai, something which would have been hard to imagine even a few months before was seen playing across TV stations around the United States.[5]

The 1972 visit still casts a resplendent shadow across US–Chinese relations to this day. Its anniversaries, particularly significant ones like the 30th and 40th, figure large in diplomatic calendars between the two countries. This is probably because it showed a confluence of two highly unorthodox political imaginations – those of Mao and of Nixon. It is unlikely that other more sanguine, risk-averse leaders would have taken the plunge in the way these two did. For Nixon, too, his credibility in the United States as a fierce critic of the left wing and of Communism meant that he was trusted to do deals with China which were seen to be in the United States' interests in a way a Democrat might have found hard. Nixon's fate, being to all intents and purposes removed from power during the Watergate scandal, also provided some education to Chinese leaders about the vagaries of democratic multiparty systems. Mao was simply bewildered by how the main leader of a country could be summarily thrown out of office in this way. And for Nixon, he was famously deeply impressed by the ways in which Zhou, in front of his eyes, was able to decide the front-page layout of the *People's Daily*, the party-controlled national newspaper.

Under President Carter at the end of the decade relations were normalized completely, with diplomatic recognition shifting from Taipei to Beijing. This was in line with comments Nixon himself had made a decade earlier in the journal *Foreign Affairs* just before becoming president, when he had asked rhetorically how it was possible for a country of almost 800 million people (as the population stood back then) to simply have no recognition on the United Nations, disenfranchising a fifth of humanity. Once full diplomatic links existed between the two countries, a new era of engagement started.

SHARING THE SAME BED, DREAMING DIFFERENT DREAMS

For all the bright words at the start, this was never going to be a straightforward relationship. The 1980s typified the good years, an era characterized by US journalist Jim Mann in *Beijing Jeep: A Case Study of Western Business in China* as economically wild and freewheeling, one in which Deng Xiaoping appeared for the second time on *Time* magazine's cover as Man of the Year. The countries almost enjoyed a love affair, with US brands like Coca-Cola and Kentucky Fried Chicken finding a vast new market hungry for its products, and figures like the legendary comedian Bob Hope doing shows from the capital, Beijing, telling the 'folks' back home about how wonderful China was.

With the economic reforms promoted by the Deng leadership, China did need US markets, capital and, in particular, its technology. For them, at least, it was a relationship built on clear strategic need. For the United States, however, there was always, even in this period, a slight asymmetry. China was strategically important in the Cold War, as a means of needling the Russians. But under reformist Mikhail Gorbachev, the man that British prime minister Margaret Thatcher said the West 'could do business with', the USSR became less problematic. Questions about what the strategic attitude towards relations with Communist China should be revolved largely around the idea that through engagement, China would move towards not just economic liberalization but also political reform. It would, in effect, become just like the USA, and yet another major hurdle would have fallen in the global march towards freedom, democracy and human rights.

THE 1989 MASSACRE AND THE BIG UNANSWERED QUESTION

The 1989 student uprising, which was brutally put down by the Chinese military, has been exhaustively discussed in other sources. As far as Deng Xiaoping was concerned, it was the end of the United States' idealism towards him as a man who wanted to transform China into a democracy. On the night of 3 June, he proved where his real loyalty lay; he was to the end a believer in one-party Leninist rule. His own words reported after the event, when speaking to the loyalist military units that had taken the lead in suppressing the rebels, was to blame the 'complex' international context. The role of the United States, the suggestion it was lurking in the background, was never explicitly stated, but the ideas the United States represented – zealously promoting different values, the adoption of which at the very least would lead to political competition for the Communist Party – was not hard to divine. The two powers had been, in the words of one famous saying of the time, sleeping in the same bed but having different dreams.

There is a more serious question about the 1989 events and their impact on United States–China relations, and one that is not often asked. According to analysts like US academic Robert S. Ross, the attitude of the George H. W. Bush presidency at the time was that China needed stability.[6] The world was entering a period in which not only the USSR but also the Middle East was in turmoil, and the United States did not want to add China to this equation. Bush was to prove in his final response to the war against Iraq a highly cautious figure. He had served in Beijing as head of the Liaison Office there in the mid-1970s. He knew the Chinese leaders well. His view was clearly that there was no value in enforcing change on them. So while there was initial coldness, and the imposition of trade and travel embargoes, the remarkable thing about the US response to 1989 was how quickly United States–China relations were normalized again.

Did the United States have the opportunity to put more pressure on China at this time, when it was clearly weak and divided? Could it have encouraged more radical political change, forced China into making concessions to democratic reform? The United States is often accused of having lost China and forced it into isolation from the early 1950s onwards. There are heated arguments about whose fault this was, with some stating that the United States pushed it into this position because of its campaign of ostracization, and others advocating that the United States had zero influence and that China was always likely to occupy this sort of position. Following the events in 1989, there was the possibility that a US president with more grit might have placed pressure on China and seen change, correcting this prior history of failed attempts to get closer to Beijing.

In the end the Communist Party at the time had the space to make this decision, partly because of the slack it had been cut by the United States. It did understand its primary focus had to be on economic development (something that in many ways the 1989 protests had been about, with rising inflation and Party corruption). It knew that better economic performance would form the core pillar of its legitimacy into the future. Eventually, the main thrust of its response in recovering from the 1989 turbulence was to ensure that economic growth continued and the prosperity of Chinese citizens kept increasing. But this was not accompanied by any political reforms. Within two years, with the 1992 'southern tour' of Deng Xiaoping, this commitment had clearly been made – to continue to change the economy, but never the one-party governance model. Deng had stated that without reform there was only the road to perdition. But reform in this context meant accepting the core role of the Party, and the Party alone, as the best way to achieve this without chaos returning. The irony was that in this way 1989 served in some ways to strengthen one-party rule in China rather than weaken it, something most people in the United States and other democratic countries assumed at the time would not be the case. It made the Party more aware of its mortality, more cautious, and more resolute than ever to hold power by whatever means necessary.

Deng had talked directly in 1990 about the risks, saying:

> Last year there was some unrest in China. As was necessary, we brought the situation under control. I asked others to tell President Bush that if the political situation in China became unstable, the trouble would spread to the rest of the world, with consequences that would be hard to imagine. Stability is essential to economic development, and only under the leadership of the Communist Party can there be a stable socialist China.[7]

Throughout 1990, Deng's comments focused on the need to oppose foreign interference in internal affairs and to develop the economy. From this point onwards, then, his logic was set in stone: economic improvements would make China strong and powerful again, but that could only happen under the Chinese Communist Party. We can call this the Dengist paradigm, and it continues to be the chief basis of political life in China to this day.

The United States, however, may have missed a strategic opportunity. For all the tough talk from Beijing, the CCP had suffered a moment of existential crisis. 1989 had shaken it profoundly. There was plenty of division within the political elite. And if the United States had really believed in the necessity for democratization and reform, there could never have been a better moment to promote this. For all its calculations of risk and potential instability, the pursuit of a strategy which eventually proved supportive to the regime in Beijing showed that the United States, despite its zealotry about promotion of values, democracy and rule of law, remained a hard-nosed realpolitik player in the Kissinger mould. Its core calculation was based on self-interest, and the potential for the collapse of Communist rule in Beijing created the sort of unpredictability and instability that the United States didn't want to deal with. The price it paid for its hesitations, however, was to see a China eventually emerge which was economically far stronger but also politically resolute in the conviction that the Communist Party was central to the preservation, and delivery, of great-power status. A quarter of a century later, that prognostication has proved correct. And now some in Washington, faced with a China they see as more assertive and more confident by the day, must have wondered if they missed the Thucydides moment back in 1989, the time when they could have truly thwarted the Communist Party's grand ambitions before it became too strong.

THE CORE DRIVERS OF UNITED STATES–CHINA MODERN RELATIONS

The United States and China have had more dialogue than any other two nations in modern diplomatic history with such major differences in their political views. A simple look at the statement issued by the United States after the 2015 high-level Strategic and Economic Dialogue (the annual bilateral meeting that for every year since 2008 has managed the relationship on a government-to-government level) is an illustration of this. The dialogue encompasses military matters, disability rights, disaster response capacity, and the larger strategic issues of safeguarding security. But it reaches down to immensely detailed and specialist areas: boiler efficiency and fuel switching; green ports and vessels; management of chemicals; forest health management; fisheries and marine litter; clean cookstoves; satellite collision cooperation and severe weather monitoring. In all, the 2015 statement covered 127 separate areas of dialogue and cooperation. And this was just on the strategic track.[8]

It was this profusion of interests that made Xi Jinping's statement during his Sunnylands visit in 2013 seem fitting. Standing beside Obama, Xi stated, somewhat boldly, 'The vast Pacific Ocean has enough space for two large countries like the United States and China.'[9] He went on to respond to a reporter from Chinese Central TV who asked what precisely Xi had been referring to when he had spoken before of building a 'new model of major power relations' by stating that it was something largely motivated by consensus between the two countries to

find a new path – one that is different from the inevitable confrontation and conflict between the major countries of the past. And that is to say the two sides must work together to build a new model of major country relationship based on mutual respect and win–win cooperation for the benefit of the Chinese and American peoples, and people elsewhere in the world.[10]

Obama's response to this bold vision was an interesting example of what some have described as 'hedging':

[I]t is very much in the interest of the United States for China to continue its peaceful rise, because if China is successful, that helps to drive the world economy and it puts China in the position to work with us as equal partners in dealing with many of the global challenges that no single nation can address by itself.

DEVIL'S GAMBIT

'The test of a first-rate intelligence is the ability to hold two opposed ideas in mind at the same time, and still retain the ability to function.' This famous quote from US novelist F. Scott Fitzgerald illustrates the difficulty faced in recent years by US presidents coming to speak about China: they have to demonstrate their 'first-rate' intelligence. On the one hand, they have to embrace the idea that a country with a wholly alien political system and values which are so different to its own can, daily, prove that it is no longer necessary to be a democracy in order to practice what (on the surface, at least) looks like vibrant, freewheeling capitalism. On the other, they have to hope, despite this situation having been the status quo for an increasingly long time, that China will ultimately succumb to the practice of multiparty democracy like every other economy of its size. By early 2017, the Party in China was living, gargantuan proof that the congratulatory moment after the fall of the Soviet Union in 1991, when there had been brave talk of the 'end of history' and the ultimate victory of liberal democracy over one-party Communist systems, had been overly hasty. Perhaps it had even been wrong. As long as the Chinese Communist Party continues enjoying a monopoly on power, it can be said at least that the 'end of history' has been put on hold.

The United States is pragmatic about this paradox. Americans have become better off, able to buy consumer goods by the tonne from Walmart and similar places and seen their living standards rise because of cheap labour costs in China. Apple products, including iPhones, along with toys such as Barbie dolls, are produced for tiny sums of money in Chinese factories and then exported, largely to markets in developed countries. Former Premier Zhu Rongji boasted in the 1990s that China had become the factory of the world. But it has also seen plenty of companies spring up which look remarkably like sweatshops. This is not considered a good thing, and provokes the ire of plenty of people in China.

So Americans do half-want to see the peaceful rise of China and to see Chinese people prosper, to work with them to solve global environmental and resource issues, stand alongside them when they face terrorists in Central Asia, the Middle East or elsewhere, and help them solve global financial crises (including the one in 2008). But signs that China has another agenda, and is promoting another set of values which go against the freedoms of the individual, are at the expense of freedom of speech and belief, and are often targeted at Christian and other religious groups, can trigger difficulties in communication, and often cause it to break down entirely. Americans and their leaders certainly do not want this side of China. But how can they extricate themselves from their involvement in the one side but not the other; how can they invest in and export from a China they detest the political values of and want to see fundamentally change? Surely their economic links are one of the key means by which the single-party system they so dislike remains in power? And yet the United States has become unable to walk away from something it feels it has half created, and yet also half detests.

For this reason, the relationship between China and the United States in the twenty-first century suffers from immense cognitive dissonance. The United States likes China's ability to support its economy and work with it when it suits it, but deeply dislikes China stretching out to take up more strategic space in the region around it, in the East and South China Sea in particular. As the 2016 Trump campaign rhetoric about China proved too, there is a large market of people in the United States who also believe that trade policy has favoured Beijing and taken jobs and opportunities from blue-collar workers at home. For the Chinese, there is the irrefutable fact that they both admire and also dislike the United States. The United States remains the destination of choice for Chinese students. It is the place where most Chinese manufactured goods end up. Chinese cinemas would be permanently full of US blockbusters was there not a government-imposed annual limit to the number that can be shown domestically. American English rules the world of print and the world of TV in China. In many ways, when Xi Jinping talks of the China Dream, it is the American dream he is emulating.

The Chinese do want to see their culture admired and better known, and they take national pride in their achievements since 1978. But the United States still remains an object of both fascination and resentment, particularly to the elite. Xi Jinping and Li Keqiang sent their daughters to US, not Chinese, universities, raising all sorts of questions about how they had been able to afford this on their modest salaries and why they hadn't had enough faith in their own system to have their children stay back at home. Chinese officials put immense efforts into understanding the United States, with legions of US study centres across the country and huge amounts of scholarly engagement. Most telling of all, of the core advisors around Xi, his most trusted lieutenants on foreign affairs are most knowledgeable about the United States. Liu He, deputy director of the National Development and Reform Commission, an all-important macroeconomic planning body, had spent a year in the United States, at Seton Hall University and Harvard University. Wang Huning, the Politburo member with the most influence over international affairs and ideology, had been influenced by a visit to the United States in the 1980s. And Xi himself had enjoyed his first visit there as early as 1985, when he had briefly stayed in Iowa. All this proves that if there is a country officials want to know about and spend precious time on, the United States is it. Other places are sideshows.

Such attention might be viewed as profoundly flattering. And were China to have pursued its admiration for the United States even up to the point of adopting its political values, then things would have been straightforward. That was partly behind the engagement strategy pursued from the 1990s onwards, particularly under President Bill Clinton. This culminated in China's entry into the WTO in 2001, a moment which was meant to see the United States and the rest of the world start to enjoy increasing linkages with and involvement in the Chinese economy. Behind this, however, lurked another agenda: the idea of a 'peaceful evolution', something Chinese strategic thinkers were aware of from early on – the belief that as with most gifts, the United States' largesse and generosity in terms of openness to China carried a price tag, the attempt to subtly change and influence it. To make it, in the end, more like the United States, in effect to see the Communist Party either accept political competition or fall from power and be replaced by a democratic system. In their hearts, this was the attitude of the US political elite in their engagement with Beijing.

HEDGING, CONTAINMENT AND THREAT

When it became clear that China's implementation of WTO standards had not led to the sort of political changes expected, some constituencies in the United States were inevitably disappointed. This perhaps came to the fore most sharply during the Beijing 2008 Summer Olympics, at which the country was due to open its internet as never before, allow unfettered access to journalists and create a space for peaceful protestors in the capital. Never before had the Chinese government allowed this sort of liberality within its own country. But the results were initially underwhelming, and soon proved to have been short-lived in terms of positive impact. No sooner had it been opened up than the internet was rapidly closed down again, with Facebook and other social media platforms blocked again by 2010.

More worrying than this was an incremental attack on civil society and other actors, especially those linked to international groups. Legal scholar and academic Xu Zhiyong of the Open Constitution Initiative was detained in 2009 (and subsequently given a suspended jail sentence in 2015), largely due to his links with the Paul Tsai China Center, the home for activities related to China at Yale Law School. The National Endowment for Democracy and other US-supported groups became anathema in Beijing, blamed for their funding to Uighur and Tibetan groups, areas which had become very restive in 2008. China's brief dalliance with liberalism had not ended well; instability seemed to have risen. The world outside, with the 2010 Jasmine Resolution in the Middle East and other uprisings, had become more precarious and turbulent. From 2009, a clampdown on rights activists and others grew, with figures like intellectual and writer Liu Xiaobo, awarded the Nobel Peace Prize in 2009, sent to jail for 11 years.

For US ambassador Jon Huntsman, serving in China from 2009 to 2011 under Barack Obama, things became more complicated. Obama's own experiences during his visit in late 2009 seemed to typify this. His visits to Beijing and Shanghai were carefully controlled by his hosts: he was allowed almost no access to Chinese people directly, except one meeting with students during which he held a question-and-answer session in a remote suburb of Shanghai, and the city was in virtual lockdown during his time there. There were no press conferences, and it seemed at the time like a deliberate attempt to belittle the newly elected US leader by limiting his access to Chinese people and seeking to control almost every aspect of his visit so that it looked like he was from a weaker country visiting a stronger one. Despite this, the two sides managed to issue a long, comprehensive joint statement. But the sense of a relationship that was becoming increasingly complicated and unmanageable for both sides intensified, as did the idea that the United States was hedging, still hoping that through engagement China would change. This notion was put most forcefully by Aaron Friedberg, who argued in a 2010 book that the United States and China were almost fated to some kind of battle in the Asian region as they tried to assert hegemony.[11] This harked back to the earlier work of international relations specialist John Mearsheimer, who described relations between great powers as being 'tragic' – doomed despite accommodation to brutal power struggles, leading to war, conflict and the final prevalence of one over the other.[12]

Hearing Americans talk of China as a potential threat gave rise to a parallel narrative – that of containment. The idea of a United States which was ubiquitous was something that was referred to for instance in the work of Beijing academic Wang Hui, who complained in one essay that the borders of the United States came right up to those of China.[13] There was no space left where it could get away from the world's sole remaining superpower, a superpower that seemed to regard itself as the only essential country on the planet. This was not just about geographical space, but also about cultural, moral and intellectual zones. Referring back to Yan Xuetong's argument (cited in Chapter 1) about China needing to represent a different kind of power and a different approach to the current world order, for intellectuals like Wang the whole Western discourse – with its tendency to universalize, imposing its own frameworks and Enlightenment values – was an expression of control, an attempt to rob China of its voice and its autonomous culture where things were centred more on the person and on the calibration of social relationships, something that lay at the heart of Confucius' teachings. At heart, it was a campaign revolving around a form of cultural theft and reduction no less brutal than the colonial humiliations China had suffered in the past. But this time, under the CCP, the country was strong, unified, wealthy and at last in a position to resist.

Containment is also a physical reality. Chinese leaders like Xi look out from their government compound in Zhongnanhai, Beijing, and see a world around them infected and interlinked with the United States. The United States has a huge wall of treaty alliances, running from Japan, down to South Korea, the Philippines, Malaysia, to Indonesia, right down to Australia and New Zealand. It also has, under the Taiwan Relations Act of 1979, a commitment to security with the island the PRC still regards as nothing more than a renegade province of the mainland. But even more alarming are the ways in which the United States is also involving itself in Mongolia, increasing its activities on the economy and security front in Myanmar, and, even more distressingly, developing closer links with Vietnam, a country it has been at war with within living memory. It seems only North Korea is immune to US influence – but even the leaders in Pyongyang seem to spend their lives plotting how best to capture Washington's attention and bring the two countries back into direct dialogue.

Containment has weighed on the psychology of Chinese leaders for a generation. The Deng framework supplied a temporary solution to this – working in the economic dimension in ways which clearly benefited the United States and which it chose not to oppose. But in a 2009 book by several writers, including nationalist blogger Wang Xiaodong, the complaint following the 2008 Summer Olympics was bitter and heartfelt. Why had the elites in Beijing simply sold Chinese people out to an economic model where their sweat and hard graft had been responsible for maintaining the comfortable living standards in the United States and other developed countries? Wang and his co-authors made a particularly sharp attack on their government in *Unhappy China* by asking how it was that Chinese people could not even trust the food they ate, let alone rely on their leaders to start pushing back at the world and not requesting but demanding more status and space.[14]

Ironically, writers like Wang Xiaodong were far more scathing about the people they labelled as their 'elites' than were figures like Liu Xiaobo, the Nobel Prize-winning dissident, who never issued anything quite as contemptuous of Chinese leaders as the nationalist bloggers. And yet, at least up to the time of writing, they remained at liberty. In many ways, they were perceived as having a strong influence on government – though a fierce debate has continued to rage over the years of whether ardent Chinese nationalism provokes the Chinese government, or whether nationalism is provoked by the government; in fact, it is probably a combination of both. There is plenty of evidence in blogs and different statements by academics, intellectuals and other figures that the United States is regarded with deep ambivalence – admired for its power, its hard assets, its global reach and wealth, but also loathed for its proselytizing nature, the ways in which it seems to want a world in its own image, one where its engagement and attention are motivated by the desire to see partners change to follow its ways and ultimately become more similar to it. All of this was well illustrated by commentary about the election campaign of Donald Trump where, despite his fierce rhetoric over 2015 and into 2016 of China being an unfair trade partner and thief of US jobs, Chinese newspapers like the nationalistic *Global Times* expressed some admiration for his aggressive attitude, and begrudging admiration for the fact that a complete outsider could be elected to the supreme position of power in the country.

Underneath Chinese notions of US containment is the reality that, out of all the current nations, the United States is the only one that remains feared. In 1991, Chinese military figures watched as the US army invaded Iraq, obliterating its army in a matter of days with hardly any casualties. The immediate images carried by CNN of this shock and awe campaign brought the immense gap between Chinese and US capacity into the open. As things stand in early 2017, the Chinese military has seen no active combat since 1979, whereas the United States and its allies have been almost continuously engaged with military actions (for example in the Balkans in the 1990s, and later in Afghanistan, Iraq and then, through NATO, in Libya). The deployment of US destroyers in the South and East China Seas – sailing through waters that China lays claim to and declaring that these are international and that it has right of free passage – is a potent sign of how much the United States remains dominant, even in China's backyard. The United States is able to send spy planes flying close to and even into Chinese territory (one of which collided with a Chinese plane over Hainan in 2001, killing its pilot and bringing the two powers into an ugly confrontation, something only dispelled by the tragedy of 11 September that year), yet China is unable to operate outside its region, and certainly not deep into the Pacific towards the United States. The United States maintains over 600 military installations across more than 120 countries, whereas China has established just one, a naval refitting entity, in Djibouti, east Africa, which was set up in 2016 (and which I referred to in the Introduction). The United States has over a dozen aircraft carriers, effectively policing the world's waterways; China, a very late arrival to naval power, has only one, bought from Ukraine, with a second planned in 2017. It is questionable whether it will even be able to properly deploy these.

Then there are even larger issues. The United States, which only shares borders with Canada and Mexico, lives in a kind of dream neighbourhood where its greatest problem is illegal migration from the latter. China shares its immediate geography, its border, with 14 countries, four of which (Russia, India, Pakistan, and now North Korea) are nuclear states, one of which (Afghanistan) has been riven by war, and another (Vietnam) with which it enjoys fractious relations and has been at war in living memory. With India, it continues to dispute its land border. Would anyone in the United States want to swap their location with China? The answer will most likely always be no. If the function of strategy in international relations is to create predictability and some sense of stability (Henry Kissinger's argument in *On China*), then it is unsurprising that something as important as geographical location and the nature of its neighbours has made China's strategic thinking highly cautious and circumspect. It lives with too much unpredictability within itself, and with its closest neighbours. It would gladly swap these issues for those faced by the United States inside and outside its borders.

US INSECURITY

The mystery is not so much that as China has grown in economic power in the period since 2000 it has sounded more confident and assertive, but that a sizeable constituency in the United States has viewed its emergence as a real threat, sign of an inevitable long-term conflict. Christopher Coker, a UK academic, referred to the 'preponderance of resentment' in China, some of it derived from the narrative promoted from the 'century of humiliation' and World War II.[15] This victim mentality grates in the United States when they see a country which seems to excel in concealment, in playing the international system while refusing to step up to its own responsibilities and using covert rather than overt means to subvert and contest the United States' primacy.

Cyberespionage is a particular area of contention. By nature it is hard to detect, but has a visible effect on people's perceptions of those involved, and a report issued in 2013 by US-based consultancy Mandiant added fuel to this by giving granular detail on the places where China's cyberespionage units were, the main actors, and the things they got up to. The core message of this impressively documented report was that the Chinese state was the key actor, and that for all the Chinese leaders' declarations of ignorance when confronted about this issue, it was clear that at some level they must have sanctioned it, so widespread and well-funded as it was. Chinese actors, it stated, were 'able to wage such a long-running and extensive cyber espionage campaign in large part because [they receive] direct government support.'[16] The PLA are behind this, funding, directing, managing and collating information, particularly about commercial targets. But there are also suspected political targets, with the White House, the office of the German Chancellor and the internet network of London's government headquarters in Whitehall all attacked by actors, some of whom seem to have originated from China.

Strategically, some Chinese see cyberespionage as fair game because the virtual space puts them on an equal footing with the United States: the dice are not loaded against China, as they clearly are in other areas of contention. Chinese leaders are realistic.

Whatever ambitions they might harbour about one day taking their country to be the world's great and most central power, they also assume that this is decades away. And provoking a direct military clash with the United States when they are doomed to lose is senseless. In cyberspace, there is a golden opportunity to put up a fight in a place where there are no agreed international conventions and where confusion and obfuscation can reign. It is the only true frontier territory left, and one that China feels it has every right to try to colonize.

It is highly fitting, therefore, that when renegade US security operative Edward Snowden fled with huge amounts of data on US surveillance (of its own citizens, among others) through a 'dark web' scanning process involving providers like Gmail and Facebook, his initial port of call was Hong Kong before eventually going to Moscow. More interesting, however, was the suggestion that while he was holed up in Hong Kong for a few weeks in 2013 his application to seek refuge in China was not positively received. Beijing simply didn't want the trouble of accommodating a person who would inevitably prove to be a bugbear in their relationship with their main international partner. The service that Snowden did provide, however, was to knock some of the sheen off the US government's attitude that it occupies the moral high ground in the realm of electronic surveillance. It is, in fact, up to the same dirty tricks and availing itself of the same wonderful opportunities to get information as everyone else. That at least was the jubilant claim of some of the commentators in China.

Cyberespionage is more symbolic of a sense of amorphous threat. To some Americans who subscribe to the China challenge, it seems to revolve around a feeling reminiscent of that felt by the great English poet Samuel Taylor Coleridge in the early nineteenth century, who referred to being afflicted most of his life by a sense of a nameless dread always pursuing him. China encapsulates these fears for the United States – its alien political system in particular, and the fact that for a country where religion, and specifically Christianity, are still such strong forces, China's official adherence to atheism is clearly distressing, particularly to those who are members of the right wing. A powerful discussion of this 'threat' thesis appeared in a special report issued for the Council on Foreign Relations in Washington DC in 2015, where former diplomats Ashley J. Tellis and Robert D. Blackwill painted China as a place of looming and imminent danger, somewhere driven by values that were not just different to the United States', but inimical and often downright threatening.

This grew out of the broader 'pivot to Asia' moves from 2009, during President Obama's period in power. This had been heralded in statements made by his first Secretary of State Hillary Clinton while attending the ASEAN Regional Forum in July 2010. She had stated that 'The United States has a national interest in freedom of navigation, open access to Asia's maritime commons and respect for international law in the South China Sea.'[17] The phrase 'national interest' raised particular concerns in Beijing, implying a heavier US security presence in its own backyard. Such worries were exacerbated by President Obama himself, who used the phrase 'pivot' and, more frequently, 'rebalancing', with regard to Asia, as a central part of his foreign policy approach. Speaking in the Australian parliament during his visit there in 2011, he stated that the United States was a Pacific nation, and that 'as a Pacific nation, the United States will play a larger and long-term role in shaping this region and its future, by upholding core principles and in close partnership with our allies and friends.' He developed this theme further when it came to security: 'As we plan and budget for the future, we will allocate the resources necessary to maintain our strong military presence in this region.' While seeking a 'cooperative relationship with China', the United States, Obama stated, would 'continue to speak candidly to Beijing about the importance of upholding international norms and respecting the universal human rights of the Chinese people'.[18]

Just over four years on, Tellis and Blackwill's argument had a brutal simplicity about it. Things needed to go beyond pivoting and rebalancing. Two decades of 'engagement', in which China has been allowed more access to the international community and benefited from deepening links with it, had to be reviewed. Those who did undertake this review could only reach one conclusion: that there had been a failure of reciprocity. Engagement, at least on these terms, had failed.

> Because the American effort to 'integrate' China into the liberal international order has now generated new threats to US primacy in Asia – and could eventually result in a consequential challenge to American power globally – Washington needs a new grand strategy toward China that centers on balancing the rise of Chinese power rather than continuing to assist its ascendancy.[19]

Preserving US centrality has to be the prime objective of Washington in international relations, as the report puts it:

> Sustaining this status in the face of rising Chinese power requires, among other things, revitalizing the US economy to nurture those disruptive innovations that bestow on the United States asymmetric economic advantages over others; creating new preferential trading arrangements among US friends and allies to increase their mutual gains through instruments that consciously exclude China; recreating a technology-control regime involving US allies that prevents China from acquiring military and strategic capabilities enabling it to inflict 'high-leverage strategic harm' on the United States and its partners; concertedly building up the power-political capacities of US friends and allies on China's periphery; and improving the capability of US military forces

to effectively project power along the Asian rimlands despite any Chinese opposition – all while continuing to work with China in the diverse ways that befit its importance to US national interests.[20]

There is nothing ambiguous about this red-blooded approach to dealing with China. Indeed, in the closing words of the report, the authors categorically state that 'there is no real prospect of building fundamental trust, "peaceful coexistence", "mutual understanding", a strategic partnership, or a "new type of major country relations" with China.'[21] And yet despite this, their policy proposals are remarkably tepid, consisting of expanding US trade relations in the region, increasing measures on cybersecurity, creating deeper links with India and other neighbouring countries (shadows of containment here), and, most specific of all, increasing expenditure on the military.

SHADOW-BOXING

If China is to be configured as an adversary by some constituencies in the United States, then these people might do well to take heed of the words of Sun Tzu in *The Art of War*, written two and a half millennia before: 'If you know the enemy and know yourself, you need not fear the result of a hundred battles. If you know yourself but not the enemy, for every victory gained you will also suffer a defeat.' The quote finishes with the most disastrous of all outcomes: 'If you know neither the enemy nor yourself, you will succumb in every battle.'[22] The fear of US containment within China and the language of 'Chinese threat' in the United States indicates a conflict involving distortions both in conceptualizations of the self and of others. In conferences throughout the world focusing on the China–United States relationship, there often seems to be

a huge act of therapy going on, with supporters of the Chinese
threat theory bemoaning the weakness of the world's sole remaining
superpower and its need to remain dominant, and those supporting
China's position stressing its internal challenges, its lack of wealth
per capita, its huge environmental and diplomatic issues, and the
simple fact that as an international player it is bereft of the rich
global network of support and alliances that the United States has.
On the one hand, the United States is being belittled by this China
fear, and on the other it is flattering a China that is a long way from
being powerful enough to challenge it, even in the Pacific region.

At one conference I attended in the city of Changsha, Hunan
Province in the early 2010s, I listened to two iterations of this. On
the one hand, a US speaker stated that despite all the challenges in
recent years, particularly during the George W. Bush presidency and
the debacles in the Middle East, the United States would reclaim its
moral mantle and continue indefinitely to be the dominant power.
But this speaker's words were followed by a Chinese speaker who
protested that China could – and would – never want to be dominant. They gave an impressive list of reasons why: lack of its own
resources; the continuation of entrenched poverty, including even
a lack of stable water supplies; environmental problems that would
take decades, if not longer, to address; and finally the simple fact
that, in their words, no one supports China's rise. When America
rose, they continued, its ascendancy was welcomed. But for China,
it is isolated and alone. Its political model alienates people outside.
And that is not going to change.

The clash of these two radically different perceptions was again
demonstrated when, in 2014, Chinese premier Li Keqiang started
to unpack some of the ideas flowing from the notion that China
was now a 'major power' by announcing the establishment of the
Asian Infrastructure Investment Bank (AIIB). China's irritation –
particularly since 2008 and the Great Financial Crisis – at its lack
of voting rights on bodies like the IMF, which had resulted from the

post-World War II US-dominated international financial order, are well known. The World Bank and Asian Development Bank were little better, with the latter headed by a Japanese national (Japan and the United States between them control 26 per cent of the voting rights). As China was the world's second biggest economy, this seemed unfair, but efforts by China to lobby for increased rights have been addressed at a glacial pace.

The AIIB is a response to this, and represents the ambiguity of China's position perfectly. On the positive side, it does seem to be a response to Robert Zoellick's 2005 demand when he spoke of wanting to see a 'stakeholder' nation, one willing to take some responsibility. Since 1978, China has accrued a huge amount of knowledge about building infrastructure, developing cities and lifting people from poverty. All of this has been recognized by entities like the World Bank and others. It would seem natural therefore that in its own region, where demand for new infrastructure on some estimates ran into the trillions of US dollars, it could play a powerful and positive role. But the United States' response to the idea was initially tepid, and then hostile. The White House and State Department felt that there were questions about China's capacity, its ability to observe international norms and rules, and its motives. For some of the critics, there was the clear sense that the AIIB was yet more evidence of China seeking a greater role, attaching clear political conditions to its activity and using the Bank to find ways to influence and, with its new-found collective wealth, 'buy' others.

When the United Kingdom, a faithful ally of the United States, applied to become a member of the new proposed bank in 2015, the response in the United States was dismissive, complaining of the British 'constant accommodation' of China. The application by Germany, Italy, Australia and others to join by the summer, however, leading to 55 foundation partners when the Bank was formally launched later in the year, showed that many among the United States' closest allies felt that in the economic realm, at least,

China did have space internationally to initiate and develop things. In many ways, the AIIB is likely to prove a litmus test of China's ability to work in a leadership role with others and show that it can be a more normative actor, rather than one always seeking to demonstrate its exceptionalism. The simple fact is that by the start of 2016, the Bank was in a position to make loans, and it would be on the quality and performance of these that it would be judged. There are huge risks to China in this endeavour, but also clear opportunities and benefits.

The narrative of China constructing a new hegemony away from the United States and its influence does have some evidentiary foundation, however. The Shanghai Cooperation Organization, which will be discussed later, has never involved the United States since its initial establishment in the late 1990s. With the Association of South East Asian Nations China has developed a separate dialogue, once more without the United States being in the room. In the realm of economics, this 'parallel' world of Chinese activity and interest existing away from the United States has proved strong, with bilateral trade deals starting to emerge between China and countries like Switzerland, Iceland and, more significantly because of its size and security importance to the United States, Australia. The US counterproposal to have a Trans-Pacific Partnership with 11 countries has been striking because it, too, attempts to create a Pacific zone where economic interests are the commonality, and where the missing partner is China. Was this an attempt to shadow China's own strenuous efforts to build a non-US-dominated world?

FRIENDS IN NEED

Mutual dependency has always been a theme of China–United States relations. In the early era, the United States' attitude was often that it was gifting or granting China attention, space and cooperation. US leaders still speak of the ways in which without their collaboration or support China would never have achieved what some call its 'economic miracle' since 1979. US capital, technology, export markets and, above all, the security that the United States has provided in the region, have all been beneficial to China in this account. But, as the anthropologist Marcel Mauss showed in his classic work about the meaning of gifts, there are some forms of assistance and granting of aid that carry a high price tag.[23] The issue of the United States' concealed expectations, and the likelihood that it has really been driving towards a 'peaceful evolution' of China becoming a democracy, lurks near the surface. It is the principal reason, analysts in Beijing and elsewhere argue, why the Chinese need to be clear-headed and circumspect about the ways they listen to and interpret US talk of how much the country has helped and assisted China.

Xi's rhetoric of a 'new model of major power relations', like many of the grand ideas he has articulated, does beg the question of what this sort of conceptualization of the relationship between the world's largest and second largest economy might practically achieve. Where, as one candidate in an election in the United States' recent past demanded of an opponent long on talk and short on specific ideas, is the 'beef'? In what ways can the United States and China buck the trend of the past and the 'tragedy of great power relations' outlined by analysts such as Mearsheimer in his influential book?[24]

The US–China Strategic and Economic Dialogue referred to above was striking because of its stress on process. There were plenty of dialogues and a great deal of talk. But on the core outputs, the solid things both sides were working in concert with each other on, there was less to speak about. The United States and China certainly were loquacious partners. The famous motto of the BBC is that 'nation shall speak peace unto nation', but in the case of Beijing and Washington they had taken this outpouring of words towards and with each other, at almost every conceivable rank of government and society, to a new level. Where were they really working for a common cause, however? Military to military cooperation was minimal. China did not (and, indeed, could not easily have) involve its military in any meaningful way in conflict in Afghanistan, Iraq or elsewhere beside US troops. The United States and China did not share a common vision of the global finance system, and they disagreed even about the rate that the Chinese renminbi (RMB) should be set at, with US economists constantly complaining about Chinese manipulation of the figure set in order to favour its exports.

Under Obama, however, a theme emerged where, simply because it clearly suited China, there was the promise of much deeper cooperation. The reality of climate change and the need for environmentalism are things that have been accepted by the Chinese political elite for most of the last two decades. And China's blighted cities, smothered by terrible smog and polluted air since 2013, are a powerful, and unavoidable, testament to the physical impact of rapid and often unsustainable industrialization on its water, air quality and natural resources. This issue matters profoundly to the all-important emerging middle class in the country – the sort of aspiring, service-sector-orientated, high-consuming, home-owning stakeholders that Xi and his government need to maintain the support of. This group's anger and a collapse of its faith would deliver a killer blow to the Communist Party in Beijing. Addressing environmental issues, therefore, has become a matter of critical importance over the last decade.

For this reason, under Xi, the discourse of environmentalism has strengthened and the means by which China speaks with the United States has changed. In the past, bickering about how the United States, along with other developed countries, has been polluting more per capita and for a longer period than China, and that they need to do more to address the problem, becomes less important when considering that the environment within China's most important cities has deteriorated so badly in the second decade of the twenty-first century. Having a stand-off with the West will not solve this problem, however satisfying it might be to eventually win it. This logic was behind the bilateral climate-change deal announced between the United States and China at the Asia–Pacific Economic Cooperation (APEC) meeting in November 2014. Much to the surprise of many, China committed itself for the first time to capping its emissions by 2030. For the world's largest and second largest emitters to agree in principle to tacking climate change together showed one way in which, when they do identify an area they can agree on, things can really start to happen. It is unlikely that the Paris meeting a year later, in which more than 180 countries came to an agreement on environmental protection, would have happened without the clear sign that China and the United States were largely speaking from the same page. This proved a more fruitful and happy experience than the Copenhagen summit of 2009 in which Chinese negotiators were accused of wrecking a potential deal.

FOLLOW THE MONEY

Outside observers sometimes have to be forgiven for regarding Chinese–US relations as something akin to a clash of vanities. The way in which Chinese leaders seem keen whenever the opportunity arises to boast about their ancient, glorious and rich cultural traditions stands alongside the United States' self-professed prowess at modernity, it being the most successful template of a wealthy, powerful, rich country. This cocktail of emotions is striking. But, to use the words originally provided to journalists Bernstein and Woodward by 'Deep Throat', their source for the Watergate story in the early 1970s, the key means we have of clarifying the relationship is to 'follow the money'.

Like it or not, for all the complexity of United States–China relations, there is one immense tangible symbol of their deep interrelationship. As China's economy grew in the 2000s, so did its foreign-currency reserves. By 2007, these reserves already stood as the world's largest. Coming close to two trillion US dollars, they proceeded to rise to over three and a half trillion by 2014, before stabilizing and then dipping. Never before had so much capital been accrued. China's foreign exchange reserves fueled the arguments of those who accused it of mercantilism, taking advantage of a favourable and weak currency level to export goods and then sucking in money from across the world through the enormous trade surpluses other countries had with it, exporting far more from China than they ever managed to import.

The composition of Chinese foreign exchange is a secret. However, the estimate is that perhaps half is in US treasuries, with the rest in Eurobonds and a basket of other currencies. This means that China is exposed to the fortunes of the US economy as its largest single stakeholder. It possesses more US debt than any other country or entity. More remarkably still, it means that a US downturn – or worse, a full-blown sustained US recession – would be a disaster for China. China is the greatest stakeholder in US prosperity. It was for this reason that, according to documents leaked from the United States and placed on the WikiLeaks website, the then US Secretary of State Hillary Clinton complained that for the United States, it was 'hard to argue with your banker'.[25]

Due to the colossal amounts involved, it is not easy to see how China would be able to walk away from the United States. There are no other large, reliable investment vehicles to put their money in; it is by far and away the best bet for fiscally cautious Beijing. Using the money to invest in the outside word, or opening the country's current account overnight and making the RMB fully convertible, would be unconscionable; they would lead to global economic meltdown and immense structural uncertainty.

The United States and China, therefore, are locked in tight mutual dependency for the foreseeable future. Neither seems happy with this, and both are working in the long term towards a world and a time when they will be liberated from each other. For China, that would be a world where they have strategic freedom over their region, the ability to control their own logistic supply routes, and dominance (at least in the economic realm) without needing to be beholden or answerable to the United States. For the United States, their dream would be to see China peacefully evolve, as soon as possible, to a country with a multiparty democratic system, one where Christianity would be more dominant, where values would be shared with the United States, and, most important of all, where there would be an acceptance of future US dominance.

The election of Donald Trump may well shift the emphasis of the relationship in new, unexpected directions. His economic hawkishness towards China and desire to charge China as a currency manipulator, claiming it keeps its own currency weak in order to produce cheaper exports to the detriment of other countries it sends goods to, thereby destroying jobs there, has to be countered by the fact that cheap Chinese imports have maintained at least some of the living standards in the United States over the last decade. A more likely approach under Trump will be to attempt to place fierce pressure on China to open up some of its investment and finance sectors to foreign ownership and cooperation. Market access in China remains a bugbear for many. Far less certain is the nature of the opportunity Trump provides for a retrenchment from the rebalancing to Asia under Obama and the spaces this opens up for Beijing. Despite the surprise there of his success in the 2016 election, the assumption was that as a businessman he would pursue pragmatic, transactional strategies – a style that suits China. This would then raise the possibility of some grand 'deal' whereby China might cede ground in economic spaces in order to get what they want in the realms of security or territory – more influence over Taiwan, for instance. The unprecedented phone call between Taiwan's President Tsai and Trump in early December 2016 figured in some interpretations as

the president-elect going for an issue he knew would matter a lot
to China, in order to unsettle it. The problem with this approach
was that it raised the stakes considerably in an area where China
has no real wiggle room. Its commitment to seeing off any moves
by Taiwan to creep towards independence are even enshrined in a
2005 law which commits Beijing to taking military action should
the island unilaterally declare independence.

Trump's presidency also potentially pushes China towards a
more exposed position. On climate change, as mentioned above,
through self-interest as much as anything else, China has become
a committed supporter of international action to cut down man-
made emissions. But Trump's scepticism about this issue provoked
China to make a very unusual statement about the need for the
incoming administration to stand by the convention it had signed
and passed into law only a few weeks before. Even more remarkable is the way in which China now has to survey an international
terrain where it is regarded as being the more stable, and reliable,
partner of the two major economies. Exploiting the United States'
potential retrenchment and isolationism in order to secure concessions and gain advantage in its hunt for dominance in Asia is one
thing. But having others expect the country to step in where the
United States has said it will no longer provide security or support
is quite another. China therefore strongly resists the desire by Trump
to unpick the nuclear deal with Iran, and, for that matter, to get
more involved in the Middle East generally, despite its resource
interests. More quickly than it had ever wanted, it is now looking
at a world where its position is becoming increasingly dominant
and exposed – a position that it regards as more threatening than
welcoming. Like the United States and the rest of the world, too,
China has had to factor in the immense unpredictability that Trump
has brought with him.

Whether under Trump or any other US president in recent times,
when a Chinese leader invites people to dream, as Xi Jinping has

since 2013, starkly different visions rise up in the collective imagination of Washington political elites and those in Beijing. This truly is a story of starkly contrasting dreams. The issue at the heart of this is the entity that the United States has to deal with most of the time – the Chinese Communist Party. Its role in China proves a constant sticking point for the United States, and is the subject about which there is most consternation. For the CCP, there would be no united, peacefully rising China were it not in power. In their view a China without the Party would revert to turmoil, unpredictability and anarchy. The US dream for the People's Republic, on the other hand, is to see the country freed from the shackles of its one-party system. And the CCP's dream for the United States – for the country to realize it needs to share power with or cede it to China – is also a nightmare, despite Trump's rise. For both, therefore, the current default is to strive for an uneasy status quo, leading into a future where these profound differences might one day prove resolvable. That day is unlikely to come any time soon. Until then they truly will be sleeping in one bed, but having very different dreams.

4

ZONE TWO
THE ASIA REGION

Chinese elite leaders are prone to bouts of nostalgia and harking back to a golden age when life was simpler, the sunshine nicer, the food better and people happier – just like the leaders of any other country. Perhaps it was for this reason that China started to make references to the 'Silk Road' around 2013, a usage that some historians had queried. On the outskirts of Xi'an (the location of Chang'an, meaning 'eternal peace', which was the capital of central China in ancient times), through the myriad of old and new streets and the chaos of busy crossings, alleys and lorries jostling with old tractors for space on the roads, is a sign declaring 'Start of the Ancient Silk Road'. The sign includes a painting of a statue of a group of people dressed in old-fashioned merchants' clothes, with camels laden with goods, and is almost bucolic in its nature.

Those standing to gaze at the sign (if they can find a safe place among the chaotic traffic) have to occupy two worlds – the one in their head, and the one in which they are standing. With its frequent pollution and a population of close to seven million people, most of them currently working in heavy industry and with moderate per capita wealth levels, Xi'an is an unlikely place to start growing ruminative and sentimental. Frequently blighted either by searing heat in the summer or bitter cold in the winter, this is hardly the field of dreams. And yet, over a millennium ago, Xi'an was almost certainly the world's most advanced and populous metropolis during the high era of the great Tang, one of the most glorious and fondly remembered of the dynasties of ancient China.

It is certainly true that there were trade links between the city and the outside world then, some reaching deep into what is currently the Middle East, with spices and silk being traded as far afield as modern-day Europe. Marco Polo reached the city in the thirteenth century, recording details of it in his travels. Even at this late date, it was an impressive place. But its decline afterwards was long and painful, and its only reappearance in the course of modern history is as the place where, briefly, Nationalist leader Chiang Kai-shek was kidnapped in 1936.

The phrase 'Silk Road' conjures up an image of a unified thoroughfare, neatly running from Imperial China up through Central Asia, through the vast nomadic lands and into the deserts of Arabia and the land of the *Thousand and One Nights*. The reality, as uncovered by archaeologists in modern times, is more complex. A historian of Imperial China, Mark Edward Lewis, referred to the genealogy of the idea in his book on the ancient Qin and Han era. 'There is no evidence of substantial trade between China and the western region prior to the first century BC,' he writes, adding, 'the term "Silk Road" itself was coined by a German geographer in the late nineteenth century.'[1]

Aware of this complicated history but also evidently intrigued and tempted by the resonances and symbolic resources that the Silk Road concept offered, almost out of the blue Xi Jinping started referring more often to the concept closely related to it: 'One Belt, One Road'. He first used this term in 2013 while travelling through South East Asia, only months after becoming the country's president. Mentioning the 'shared destiny' of the region while addressing the Indonesian parliament, he went on to say that China was ready to open itself up to ASEAN countries and to enable them to benefit

more from its development.[2] This stress on commonality and a
shared regional vision between China and the countries around
it was the key. It exposed China's aspirations to become a fully
regional power with more autonomy and strategic space around it
and greater security, but it also raised tough questions about what
precisely China had in mind for the era of new pre-eminence it
was enjoying with partners like Japan, Vietnam, Thailand, India,
Pakistan, North Korea, and further afield down to Australia and
New Zealand. Beyond the rosy optimism of the Belt Road Initiative
rubric, with its epic ambition and its invitation for all and sundry
to enjoy greater links and better relations with China, there were
thorny questions – some from history, some from current squabbles
over land and sea borders, and some arising from areas of distrust
between neighbouring countries and China – about its long-term
intentions. The 'One Belt, One Road' had its name changed in
2015 to the more official-sounding 'Belt Road Initiative' (BRI).

Geographical closeness alone means that China's imprint on the
Asian region, across into South and Central Asia, is immense – and
increasing. And this alone poses one of the greatest modern conun-
drums. Almost every country in the region clearly has very strong
reasons for pursuing positive economic and trade relations with
China. A glance at figures across the different countries involved
shows that for almost all of them, China is their largest trading
partner. China's market of urban, emerging middle-class potential
customers is the greatest engine of prospective growth for the foreseeable future, not just for its regional partners but for the rest of
the world. It is difficult – for some, perhaps, impossible – not to
engage with this opportunity. Despite this, there is a low level of
trust among the same countries when it comes to security; China's
ambitions make many uneasy, and there is some outright opposition.
All of this uncertainty is focused on the South and East China Seas,
the periphery immediately around China's vast south and eastern
coastal region.

XI ALL AT SEA: THE MARITIME DISPUTES

The South and East China Seas are the ultimate geopolitical head-ache, involving a constellation of issues. These include notions of international law and competing rights; claims of one historical narrative having pre-eminence over another; the residue of colonial interference; and the potential clash between the world's current superpower, the United States, and the other that is most keenly seeking to contest its role, at least in this region. Added to this is the involvement of international arbitration, the possible location of highly lucrative and important natural resources within the area, and the endlessly complex relationship between the People's Republic and the Republic of China on Taiwan. The Taiwanese have a saying: 'A bad soap opera never ends,' and on this issue, each week the plot simply thickens. This is the closest analogy to the story of China's maritime borders.

The South and East China Sea clashes are best seen as a space in which there is a clear collision of mentalities and world views. For China, its claims are epitomized by the infamous 'nine-dash line', which strikes down deep into maritime territory so that at its farthest extent it reaches the coast of Malaysia and sweeps down to Indonesia, 2,000 miles from the furthest shores of China's southern island of Hainan. Xi himself has articulated the idea that China's claims are immemorial, stating that 'islands in the South China Sea since ancient times are China's territory.'[3] This sense of history and longev-ity is meant to trump all other claims, particularly those which have arisen from colonial meddling in the era after 1840 and the century of humiliation. The framework within which this area is conceptu-alized in Beijing, therefore, is from the position of a large country, and behind this lurks the sense of other partners in the region being akin to vassal states, a throwback once more to the imperial era.

Scattered around the South and East China Seas are various small islets, shoals, tiny promontories and submerged features.

Depending on how these are defined, they can either give rise to claims over 12 nautical miles of space around them (a submerged feature which is sometimes above water) or 200 nautical miles for a whole island that is regarded as being permanently above sea level. That, at least, is the ruling of the UN Convention on the Law of the Sea (UNCLOS). For some of these entities, China risks a conflict with Vietnam; for others with the Philippines or Malaysia, in one small area with Indonesia, and in the East China Sea over the Senkaku/Diaoyu islands with Japan. The Republic of China on Taiwan, as the signatory of the San Francisco Treaty of 1952 which granted ownership of some of these areas, is also a highly active and important partner, bringing it sometimes into unusual alliances with the PRC, and sometimes creating clashes.

For decades, this area was sleepy and largely unnoticed, with only sporadic bursts of tension.[4] But as China has grown more powerful and its military and economic resources have increased, so too has its interest in developing naval capacity. In the 1980s, the most influential figure was Liu Huaqing, commander of the Chinese navy in that era and deputy of the powerful and important Central Military Commission, the final authority over all China's military strategy. Liu articulated the idea that China needed a 'blue water' capacity. For a nation which had not shown interest in developing any naval capacity to speak of in the five centuries prior to this, Liu's ideas were revolutionary. But over the next two decades, China was to acquire its first aircraft carrier, and to modernize and build up its navy as an integral part of the reconstruction and improvement of the PLA generally. Liu was to die at the age of 94 in 2011, just as his ideas were starting to have real global impact.

The South China Sea is predominantly a major logistics route. Most of the trade to and from Chinese ports goes through these waters, as do the energy resources that China needs, imported from the Middle East but also (in smaller quantities) from Africa and elsewhere in Asia. In the boom years, enormous amounts of iron ore came from Australia in the south, as did liquid natural gas from Indonesia. Chinese worries about their inability to control this area have been long-standing. The possibility that the United States and its allies could simply blockade the country in times of conflict figures regularly in disaster planning scenarios. The natural response has been to increase Chinese capacity in the region, and start a process of pushing back incrementally. This, in effect, started before Xi Jinping came to power, but it has only increased since 2013.

The most tangible sign of this is the construction of huge new facilities on some of the most minor of maritime features – protruding rocks, reefs and sandbanks – so that they now figure as substantial islands, some of them with their own airstrips and quasi-military bases. This in particular has infuriated the United States, causing it in late 2015 to send a destroyer out to some of the features, demonstrating the importance of freedom of navigation and showing that it did not regard Chinese claims over this territory as legitimate. Things are complicated by the fact that the United States has yet to ratify UNCLOS, which makes the appeal to usual arbitration through international law difficult. The other problem is that it has proved impossible for those countries contesting this territory with China to reach a unified position. As of 2016, therefore, the whole region had become subject to a mishmash of different claims, on different historic and legal bases, by half a dozen different countries, none of whom show any appetite to back down.

When the US destroyer came out to do its exercises in 2015, the interesting issue was not so much the United States' actions, but the Chinese response to them. Weeks before, China's military leaders had issued blood-curdling threats about what might happen if areas regarded as its strategic space were violated by foreign powers (and particularly the United States). When the United States did precisely this, the MFA resorted to further stern-sounding rhetoric but did nothing else. There is a very good reason for this. At the moment, China simply does not have the capacity to oppose the United States even in its own backyard; if things really did escalate to out-and-out conflict between itself and its neighbours, it would be the ultimate case of lose–lose. The South and East China Sea issues, therefore, have so far been dealt with by proxy players like coastguard vessels and fishing boats acting as provocateurs and defendants, with varying amounts of evidence about how much they have been sanctioned by the state. In this way, the seaways around the region have become like a vast aquatic version of Chinese-style chess, with tiny incremental moves, slight assertions of superiority, and tactical advances and withdrawals.

A major development occurred in July 2016 when a case brought by the Philippines to the International Court of Arbitration in The Hague, Holland, received judgement. While the court's decision had no prescriptive force, it did carry great moral authority. And when its judges stated that the Chinese claims on the disputed islands had no historic basis, and that some of the installations and activities undertaken by the PRC or their agents were illegal under the UNCLOS convention, Beijing responded immediately with a powerful rebuttal. Despite this, it was significant that there had now been a decision made by an international body largely regarded as neutral. However, the Philippines, under their newly elected president Dutarte, started to row back from their more aggressive position prior to the judgement. During a visit to Beijing in late 2016, Dutarte expressed the view that the US alliance was no longer as important as it had been for his country, and that China now mattered more. There is every possibility that this sort of rhetoric will play into the hands of President Trump and make it clear why they need to expect Asian partners to deliver more of their own security.

Does Chinese behaviour in this region reveal anything profound about Chinese long-term strategy? It is natural enough that it should want security and greater predictability around its borders. We might expect greater wealth and resources to lead to more assertive behaviour, too. In many ways, Beijing has no desire for this tit-for-tat uncertainty. The lives of their leaders would be easier if there was a negotiated settlement and they could concentrate on other issues. But the other partners involved share their stubbornness, with no one wishing to talk about sovereignty and final resolutions through fear of being seen to lose all credibility among domestic constituencies in their home countries. The South and East China Sea is the ultimate 'Asian face-off', with everyone making shrill denunciations but also knowing that any solution will involve compromise and that things can't continue this way forever. In its land border negotiations, China has often shown flexibility and finally made concessions. Why are its maritime borders so much more contentious? The ongoing dispute with Japan, with the shadow of history looming over them, perhaps illustrates why they are so intractable.

JAPAN: THE WEIGHT OF HISTORY

The maritime Belt Road Initiative would, in a perfect world, include Japan. But since the mid-2000s, Sino–Japanese relations have been a political minefield, lurching from sporadic tepid expressions of unity to snarling mutual aggression. This relationship is the ultimate geopolitical version of Go, the ancient chess game that Kissinger refers to as typifying Chinese strategic thinking, involving tiny incremental moves and barely a flicker of compromise on the surface. The great burden China carries is its memory of the war from 1937 onwards, pitting imperial Japan's industrialized might against the agrarian vulnerability of China. Around 20 million died, and many more were made homeless by the onslaught. These memories keep resurfacing, particularly because – in Chinese eyes, at least – Japan has refused to adequately apologize. For many Chinese, no matter what apology might one day be given, nothing can eradicate the humiliation and suffering of this event, perhaps the most pitiless and vicious war of modern times. As the late Lee Kuan Yew, founding leader of Singapore, was to acerbically comment, the essential problem in the modern relationship between the two is that China forgets nothing, and Japan seems to remember nothing. This causes endless bad feeling and clashes.

Anniversaries like the celebrations of the 70th year since the ending of the war in Asia, held in early September 2015, bring out the complexities of the memories of the conflict, and its residual meaning and influence in regional politics. Hardly any people survive from this era, and yet the CCP held a massive event in Beijing, at which Xi Jinping inspected serried ranks of troops and, more importantly, advertised China's new combat assets to the outside world, some 70 per cent of which were supposedly new. World leaders (Americans and Europeans conspicuous by their absence) were present to watch this symbolic display. But there were plenty of questions a more sceptical onlooker might start asking – for example, who exactly is the audience for this sort of mass event? Elite leaders need these performances to bolster their legitimacy, for sure, and there are core parts of the public that are impressed (and need) these shows of national might. But for the outside world, such jingoistic Soviet-style parades are either interpreted as a sign of China's latent aggressive intent, or as indications that its language about 'peaceful rise' is empty rhetoric. Why would a peaceful rise need so much state-of-the-art military kit to support it?

Beyond these questions are more specific ones about what Japan and China truly mean to each other in the twenty-first century, and the best kind of relationship they can have, if liberated from the shackles of historic issues. The first hurdle to overcome would be to find out how that liberation from history might be achieved. During the first decade of the twenty-first century, a group of Japanese and Chinese scholars tried to work together on establishing an historic record of the Sino–Japanese War, using archive materials from both countries. One of the problems they skirted around was more on the Chinese side than the Japanese: the role of the Communist Party in the final great victory over the imperial aggressors. Most of the propaganda and historiography that is presented in modern China would lead observers to believe that it had been the Communist armies that had brought this success home. But as work by Oxford University's Rana Mitter and others has shown, it was the Nationalist armies under Chiang Kai-shek and his generals who had been the real victors; the Communists had only fought in a number of minor battles. The brunt of the Japanese attack was taken, and ultimately rebuffed, by the reviled Nationalists, whose successor regime is now resident in Taiwan.[5] Its revelations would shatter the fundamental beliefs held by both Japan and China.

This contentiousness doesn't just seep into attempts to establish the facts around the war, but also Chinese politicians' later manipulation of the memory of the war. Mao Zedong actually thanked Kakuei Tanaka in 1972 when he became the first Japanese prime minister to visit the People's Republic. When they met in Nanjing – the site of the 1937 Rape of Nanjing, the most extensive and tragic massacre perpetrated by the Japanese armies on Chinese citizens during the war – Mao stated to Kakuei that

[Japan] doesn't have to say sorry, you contributed towards China, why? Because had Imperial Japan not started the war of invasion, how could we Communists become powerful? How could we stage the coup d'état? How could we defeat Chiang Kai-shek? How are we going to pay back you guys? No, we do not want your war reparations![6]

If this quote is true (and some dispute its veracity), then it proves that Mao was as wily and amoral an historian as he was a guerrilla tactician. The Japanese may have radicalized the Chinese in ways that the Nationalists never did. And this may have led to the vast cohort of victimized, suffering peasants becoming the foot soldiers for Mao's armies. But the idea of claiming that Chinese people paid a fair price in the war in order to bring the Communist Party to power is morally repugnant, especially coming from someone in Mao's position.

In the 1980s, Deng and his fellow leaders looked to Japan in far less controversial ways for inspiration in how to modernize their country. They were impressed in particular by the reforms implemented by Shigeru Yoshida, one of the most prominent of postwar Japanese leaders, who had promoted rapid industrialization and heavy export-led growth. On the basis of this, throughout the 1960s and into the 1970s Japan experienced an era of huge expansion and reconstruction, becoming the world's second-largest economy by the 1980s, and so successful that some suspected it would overtake the United States. These hopes, we now know, proved a little overblown. But the Deng leadership looked hard at the ways in which the Japanese had created modern, effective corporations and built up innovative technologies. It was an appealing model.[7]

Japan was a dynamic partner throughout this era, contributing hugely in terms of aid and investment. In the 1980s it was a far greater investor in China than the United States or Taiwan (whose involvement only really took off in the 1990s). Japanese corporations like car manufacturers Toyota and appliance and technology giants Sony produced vast amounts in the People's Republic for export elsewhere in the world. During this period, the phrase 'Made in Japan' started to really mean 'Made by Japanese corporations in China'. This strong trade and investment relationship prevailed up to the 2000s, when a more strident nationalist tone in the politics of both countries corroded it. Much of the bad feeling between the two was generated by clashes over symbolic issues that related to underlying historic resentments. Junichiro Koizumi, one of postwar Japan's longest-serving prime ministers, exemplified this in his period in office from 2000–5. At a time when China's entry to the WTO had provoked breakneck economic growth, Japan was still stuck in a period of low inflation, low growth and a seemingly perpetual depression, and the two countries should have been creating a new kind of relationship in which they used each other's strengths to mutual benefit. Instead, they remained bogged down in political– historical issues. One of the most provocative acts proved to be Koizumi's insistence on visiting the infamous Yasukuni Shrine in Tokyo, where Class A war criminals are buried. The Chinese were appalled.

For several years, all high-level contact between the two countries was frozen. A brief rapprochement after Koizumi's retirement in 2006 led to Premier Wen Jiabao visiting their maritime neighbour in April 2007 and President Hu Jintao following with a visit the year after that. The two countries talked of 'a warm spring' when Hu was there in 2008.[8] Almost immediately, however, clashes began to occur in the East China Sea, following on from the sale of the Senkaku/Diaoyu Islands by their private owner to the Japanese government, a move taken as provocative in Beijing. (The issue had been blurred before by the fact that the islands had been in private hands, albeit those of a Japanese citizen.)

For Xi Jinping, the relationship with Japan is perhaps the tough- est of his international priorities to deal with. With the United States, the situation is complex – but at least the United States is more remote. Japan sits in the region that China aims to economically dominate. Any moves China makes, therefore, must reckon with how to handle what still remains a hugely important economy, and a very considerable potential diplomatic opponent. Public sentiment towards Japan in China can prove explosive, too, with rallies and protests in the 2000s and most recently in 2014, when even people choosing to eat in Japanese restaurants in China were castigated and some of them physically attacked and humiliated. Despite Xi's frequent-flying style of presidency, Tokyo has conspic- uously not been on the list of destinations for his visits. And when, at the APEC meeting in 2014, Xi and the Japanese prime minister Abe finally managed to meet, the photos of their encounter were almost comical because of the frosty expressions on both leaders' faces and their cool handshake with each other. Chinese netizens started circulating photos of a grumpy cartoon Winnie-the-Pooh standing next to a down-at-heel Eeyore, an image that bore an uncanny similarity to the Xi–Abe encounter.

There have been costs to this fractiousness. Japanese investment in China has fallen since 2010, with more of it going to the United States and other destinations. The Japanese have so far refused to be members of the AIIB, though the AIIB's first two major projects in 2016 were done in partnership with the Asia Development Bank, an entity in which Japan is a major stakeholder. On the other hand, people-to-people links remain strong, with 2015 proving to be a bumper year for tourism as more than four million Chinese people visited Japan.[9] At the elite level, therefore, Japan might be problematic; but among the Chinese urban young, it is still an appealing place. And for them, without the nearly constant government reminders, the history of World War II would probably be growing fainter by the day.

A FRIEND IN NEED: NORTH KOREA

Alongside Japan, there is another close neighbour of China's which Xi Jinping has not visited: the Democratic People's Republic of Korea (DPRK), otherwise known as North Korea. Separate from the south part of the peninsula since World War II and the Korean War from 1950 to 1953, a formal peace treaty has yet to be signed (there is only an armistice in place at the moment). North Korea's early history after 1953 saw relative economic success. With the Soviet Union and some Chinese help it was able to industrialize and build new cities. Indeed, it had a larger economy than the south up until the

1970s. But with the reformation of South Korean industry, and that country's political transformation to a democracy, the two countries' fortunes were reversed. By 2013, the North Korean economy was equivalent to a paltry 2.5 per cent of its southern neighbour.

Beyond the People's Republic, Pyongyang has no other significant diplomatic friends. And even with Beijing, there are huge question marks over what sort of relationship these two actually have. On the level of diplomatic sound bites, they appear deeply committed to each other. In the 2000s, Hu Jintao grew surprisingly poetic when he congratulated the DPRK on the 60th anniversary of its founding by stating that its achievements were 'delightful'. His reward for this was to see a nuclear test the next year, the first of four before 2016. Pyongyang's leader, Kim Jong-il, was taken to China's Special Economic Zones in 2000 and then again a few years later, and granted a tour of Shanghai in 2010 where he was subjected to an advertisement about the wisdom of Chinese-style development under the socialist rubric. But tepid experiments with marketization in North Korea led to a major collapse of its currency, loss of face and the execution of one of its chief finance officials in 2010. With the arrival in power in 2011 of the new leader, Kim Jong-il's son Kim Yong-un, after the former's demise, things have grown even more volatile.

In the Standing Committee of the Politburo, out of the seven members appointed in 2012 the only one with experience with North Korea of any depth was Zhang Dejiang, who had spent two years studying economics at the Kim Il-sung University in Pyongyang in the late 1970s. The idea, however, that this would make the DPRK–China relationship a little easier proved fallacious. Nuclear tests in the first days of 2016 only highlighted just how much the impoverished neighbour of the mighty China wanted its own autonomy. The fundamental characteristic of the bond between these two countries is that while it is true they are 'as close as lips and teeth' (in Mao Zedong's words), like the relationship between lips and teeth, this is not a matter of willing choice but enforced inevitability. The two countries are tied not by bonds of affection and mutual respect, but ones of necessity. They cannot separate and divorce; their geography, economy, history and politics are so wrapped up in each other's that they are almost tied to a single destiny. For North Korea, the strategy for the last seven decades has been to ensure that it balances dependency on its neighbour with defence of its own clear needs and avoidance of complete domination by China. In the recent years of its impoverishment, that has meant facing down its utter reliance on Chinese economic power with a single-track hard-power route, the endpoint of which is to become a nuclear power. Nuclear weapons figure not just to protect the DPRK from the United States; they are also there to save it from complete annexation by China.

In 2017, at least at the elite level, there is an eerie (and for China, unflattering) parallelism. Kim Yong-un, like Xi, is a member of the ruling aristocracy. Both have an almost imperial mandate and imperious personal style. Both are regarded as ambitious and impetuous, and both – in very different ways and in different environments – have been prosecuting purges and attacks against those they see as inimical to their vision, clearing political space around them. The one leader most closely linked to the Chinese in the DPRK system, and regarded as knowledgeable about their economic reforms (and to some extent sympathetic to these) was Kim's uncle, Jang Song-thaek, regarded as the real authority behind the throne when the young regent was elevated to supreme power in 2011. But he was brutally removed from power in late 2013 and summarily executed. Of course, parallels between cleaning up the ranks in the Korean Workers Party and those of the CCP in recent years must be qualified: the CCP is a far vaster, more complex organization. Its days of liquidating opponents in such a transparently old-fashioned, vicious fashion are over. Now it tends to use the outward trappings of due process and quasi-legality.

But just as Jang's execution in the DPRK caused a sharp intake of breath and a realization that the world was not dealing with a benign joke in the country's new ruler, Xi's sanctioning of the prosecution, expulsion from the Party and imprisonment of former Standing Committee colleague Zhou Yongkang in 2014 sent the same message.

The DPRK's nuclear aspirations are the key area of conflict here. Its hopes to become a nuclear state are opposed internationally, violate non-proliferation rules and go against the interests of almost every country in the region, from Japan, to South Korea, to China itself. Why China, even under Xi, has been so passive while Pyongyang has ratcheted up its programme is puzzling. From time to time there have been indications of irritation from Beijing – reports of gas or energy supply being stopped (90 per cent of this comes to North Korea from China), or a postponement of aid – but such periods are brief. Most surmise that China genuinely feels it must endure the status quo because a collapse of the DPRK would mean an unwanted refugee crisis on its north-eastern border or a unification with South Korea and, in effect, a US ally coming right up to China's border, enclosing its space even more.

On North Korea's 2016 nuclear weapons tests, Foreign Minister Wang Yi, when meeting with US Secretary of State John Kerry, came out with bland, formulaic platitudes. According to the *New York Times*, he stated that China 'will not be swayed by specific events or the temporary mood of the moment', going on to say, 'Sanctions are not an end in themselves,' and that the best idea was for the DPRK to return to the negotiating table with the United States and others.[10] This meeting at least made clear that China was willing to tolerate a North Korea with nuclear technology and the ballistics capacity to get it to the West Coast of the United States. The static quality of Chinese policy making on such an important issue is particularly striking because with North Korea, China does have a leadership role, and is the most influential player. The fact that even under Xi it continues to show impotence about this matter and unwillingness to act raises questions about just how much real commitment and resolve China has. If it cannot show mettle over an issue of such immense importance to it so close to home, why expect it to be able to be forceful on issues further from its shores?

There are plenty of analysts in China who argue that North Korea is just part of a larger geopolitical game, and one that is useful as a spoiler against the United States, constraining and limiting its strategic space, preoccupying it and distracting its allies Japan and South Korea. While appealing on a Machiavellian level, this line is flattering to China's overall ability to control circumstances and underestimates the real power of North Korea to spoil its neighbour's backyard, create headaches and generally be an irritant. Life would be much easier for China if the DPRK did not have any nuclear capacity. The fact that China has not done more to stop the DPRK's ambitions is possibly more down to the complex emotional bonds between the two entities and dexterous manipulation of them by all three Kims: Kim Il-sung had been masterful at playing the Soviet Union off against the PRC, and Kim Jong-il had proved as adept at movements of sporadic bad behaviour to extract concessions as he was at demonstrating compliance and apparent outward cooperation. Capriciousness has been the best strategic posture for Pyongyang. It has been predictable solely in its unpredictability. As Andrei Lankov, expert on North Korea, has shown, however, all this indicates is that for the Pyongyang regime there is no plan B.[11] Modest reforms could quickly lead to an endgame for them. Making sure the DPRK's 100,000-strong elite are looked after is the best bet, no matter what vile costs this passes on to the masses of the Korean people. Blackmail and bad behaviour are the only strategic means for it to ensure it survives. This is not sustainable, and one day will need to change. But at the moment, no one in Beijing has the appetite, or the vision, to think about the DPRK in a different way. Historic links are too deep and strong, and challenging them means, in a strange way, challenging the Communist Party's narrative of its own history and identity, because for so much of the time it has said it is engaged in a common socialist cause with its neighbour, and it fought so hard in the war from 1950 to 1953 that cemented the Pyongyang regime. For that reason, North Korea shows more powerfully than any other country the real limits of Chinese foreign policy, even as it (China) rises to become a regional and global power. As the great ancient legalist philosopher Han Fei said, while harm comes from your enemies, calamity will come from those you love. For China, its 'indissoluble' bond with its little brother may, in the very end, prove the source of its undoing – just as the historic prize of becoming a global power is finally within reach.

INDIA AND PAKISTAN

An ancient civilizational state, with huge ethnic diversity and a proud sense of its cultural assets: such a description applies to both China and its western neighbour India. On the surface, they have a lot in common: over one billion inhabitants, economies that have grown over the last three decades, and shared issues such as entrenched poverty, severe pollution and a history complicated by colonialism. However, anyone looking at the relationship today is struck by their clear differences and, in foreign policy and diplomacy, an almost wilful mutual misunderstanding.

China's sole remaining land border disputes are with India, and they look unlikely to be resolved any time soon. India hosts the exiled Dalai Lama, an issue which has been a bone of contention since 1959 when he fled Tibet. It also operates as the world's largest democracy, disproving the assertions of Communist Party officials in China that a country needs to be wealthy and developed in order to allow its citizens the freedom to have a say in who governs them.

Indians look at China with puzzlement. China's rapid growth and the fact that its economy is now three times the size of that of India lies at the heart of this. So too does a certain guarded admiration for Chinese developmental success on the part of many Indians, including some in government. On measures from health, to literacy, to urbanization, China outperforms India.[12] And even though in 2016 India was predicted to have stronger annual GDP growth than China, rising to more than 7 per cent, those who foresee a time when India will overtake China as the world's most dynamic economy, at least in the coming one or two decades, are few and far between.

India and China are not easy bedfellows. They clashed in a war in 1962 which left profound scars on the defeated India and laid the basis for the wary nature of their partnership, which continues to this day. India remains a net importer from its neighbour, with a technology, infrastructure and investment deficit. And even as Xi Jinping and the newly elected prime minister of India, Modi, visited each other's countries over 2014 and into 2015, this wariness did not disappear, despite the evident mutual admiration and personal chemistry between the two. Part of this is down to their respective global position. In the mid-2000s, under US president George W. Bush, there had been hope that India would figure in a new version of trilateralism, counterbalancing China's role in the region and building a closer alliance with the United States.[13] But a combination at that time of India's diffidence and the sheer disparity with China meant this arrangement never gained much traction. Very soon, the United States was distracted by the economic crisis, and the moment of closeness passed.

Under Xi and Modi, however, it is clear that somehow the two have to work out a way of gaining more from each other's respective economies and the potential they offer each other. China is seeing the emergence of perhaps three quarters of a billion higher-consuming, urban-living, service-sector working middle class. That market is of interest to everyone, particularly Indian manufacturers. The rising costs of wages and daily living in China mean that India stands well placed to become a new manufacturing hub. It has the advantage of rule of law and greater transparency, even if its parlous road and rail networks and its often corrupt and byzantine decision-making processes can be intimidating. Modi has attempted to create a better business environment in India, but it has proved challenging. Having partnerships with Chinese companies, with their knowledge of development and wealth creation, would, in theory, prove beneficial. Better access for the Chinese to the emerging India market would also be good. After all, they are so close to each other, both physically and in terms of common ground.

However, is the region big enough for these two? They do not have an easy mutual narrative, and are prone to the same kind of conceit. Both like to be looked up to', and both are seeking regional dominance and status commensurate with their geographical and population size, and strong sense of cultural pride. There is one clear area where India does have a significant advantage, and that is in its cultural reach and appeal. Ironically, Buddhism, which was founded within India, is now overwhelmingly practised more in Communist China. Historically, India's influence on the Asian region has been profound, in its art, literature and music. This is true even into the twenty-first century, where Indian regional cuisines, Indian mysticism and Indian cultural appeal and soft power still outperform China. India, for instance, does not suffer from the image problems that Beijing often complains about, despite the country suffering from huge issues of gender imbalance, sporadic violence against members of low castes, and poor social mobility.

It is striking that while Chinese universities and think tanks are full of specialists on the United States, the EU and the rest of the world (there are 150 study centres focusing on Australia alone), finding experts on India can be extremely difficult. Chinese students seem to have little interest in looking at Indian culture and history, and not many (though the numbers are increasing) travel the relatively short distance to their vast neighbour for holidays. The dominant mindset towards India within China is indifference bordering on sheer ignorance. And while India does put more effort into the understanding of Chinese language, politics and society, it is again underwhelming for two such huge regional partners.

It is highly symbolic, therefore, that when Xi Jinping did eventually visit India in 2014, almost the same moment as his flight was touching down there were violent border clashes between the two countries, which were blamed on the PLA. Speculation continues that these were deliberate, and intended to underline a message that China has the upper hand in military assets. Certainly, it seemed an extraordinary coincidence that this happened when it did. But it was also telling that the rest of the visit, and Modi's return visit to China, proceeded smoothly.

Where China can needle India effectively is in its relationship with Pakistan, one of the most curious of its neighbours. Pakistan's alliance with China is predictable and steadfast. Like the DPRK, Pakistan also declares itself 'as close as lips and teeth'. And for the Belt Road Initiative, Pakistan occupies a key strategic position. Pakistan, as British analyst Andrew Small made clear in a highly readable recent study of the bilateral relationship with Beijing, was a constant ally of the PRC from the earliest days, and the most crucial intermediary during the period of rapprochement with the United States. It is telling that Henry Kissinger made his secret detour to see Mao and Zhou Enlai when pretending to be holed up with an illness in Karachi in 1971.

Pakistan has been a recipient of Chinese largesse as it has grown richer. But its importance to the United States, especially since the 11 September terrorist attacks, has only complicated things. Pakistan's internal instability, and its political and diplomatic complexity, means those declarations that it is a reliable friend to Beijing have been met, in recent years, with what looks a little like weary resignation by elite leaders there. The years of Pakistani prime ministers expecting to extract investments, loans and aid as a matter of course when they visited Beijing were ended under Hu, who refused to commit funds. Gwadar Port, a significant logistics centre in Pakistan, has been talked of as a subject of Chinese interest, creating a strategic Western focus and freeing China up from reliance on its eastern ports and naval supply lines. But the immense amounts of Chinese capital and involvement promised did not live up to expectations. A large part of this was the poor performance on the Pakistani side, with important parts of the project either delayed or not delivered.[14]

CHINA AND ITS FRACTIOUS SOUTH-EAST ASIAN NEIGHBOURS: ASEAN

It is one of the great paradoxes of the modern world that in Westphalia in Europe, the very place where the concept of nation and sovereignty was first codified in 1648, notions of sovereignty are being contested, questioned and eroded. The European Union, with its free trade, employment and free movement of people, has been called a 'post-modernist' entity. The migration crisis from 2015 onwards may well be about to change some of that pooling of sovereignty. Even so, as a multilateral experiment, the EU has been the boldest, and in many areas the most successful. The Association of Southeast Asian Nations might aspire to this level of connectivity and cooperation in the legal, social and commercial sphere, but it operates in many ways as a very much more restricted and circumscribed experiment in cooperation.

Part of this is simply due to the ASEAN member states' attitudes towards the very concept of pooling sovereignty. For all ten members of ASEAN, sovereignty has been hard won, and attempts to even remotely subvert or seem to weaken it end up being short-lived.

The mantra of China – 'non-interference in the affairs of others' –
has particular resonance in countries like Myanmar, Singapore,
Vietnam and Cambodia, all with sharp memories of the experience
of colonization and each of which had, to some degree, to engage
in fights for their eventual autonomy and nation-state identity.
Established in 1967, with membership increasing up to the late
1990s, ASEAN matters to China because it includes some of the
disputants in the South China Sea arguments, and also because these
nations cover a hugely important strategic area, stretching from the
country's south-western border deep into the southern hemisphere.
Throughout this region, there is an important ethnically Chinese
diaspora, a group that contributed hugely to the great call to invest,
trade and work with the motherland when reform and opening up
started in 1978.

ASEAN has great diversity, embracing Communist governments
(Vietnam), democracies (Indonesia), profoundly Buddhist countries
(Thailand) and one containing the world's largest population of
Muslims (Indonesia). Through the subgroups ASEAN + 1 and then
ASEAN + 3, China engages with this group, having signed a free
trade agreement in 2002 which came into effect three years later. This
tangible point of contact between the two illustrates how ASEAN
figures most simply to Chinese leaders as a market, and as a trading
block. On that level, at least, the story is straightforward enough.

In the 2000s, journalists and writers like the American Joshua
Kurlantzick noticed that Chinese investment was increasing in the
ASEAN region, particularly in places like Cambodia, Myanmar
and the Philippines.[15] This was attached to attempts to improve
China's profile in countries which had experienced complex historic
links with imperial and modern China. Vietnam typified these – a
country which had figured in interlinked histories in the region
going back more than 1,000 years and which, for some historians
in modern China at least, had enjoyed something approaching a
vassal–state relationship with imperial courts, either in Beijing or

elsewhere. But Vietnam has also been prosecuting an energetic attempt to maintain its own identity, eschewing the use of Chinese written characters and ensuring that any attempts to influence its politics and domestic society are carefully rebutted, even despite it sharing a similar political system to China post-World War II and the Vietnam War.

Vietnam has what can only be described as a carefully policed, cautious relationship with the PRC in the twenty-first century. Plenty of Vietnamese leaders and business people look to China for interesting ideas about how they can develop their own economy while maintaining a socialist system. But as was proved by the riots in 2015 in Saigon and Hanoi targeting what were thought to be Chinese investments and interests (caused by the Chinese government shifting vast oil prospecting equipment into an area claimed as Vietnamese), such courtesy runs skin-deep. Vietnam, Myanmar, Laos and others have to pursue the ultimate divided strategy, on the one hand embracing economic opportunities with China, and on the other maintaining firm diplomatic and political 'red lines'. As China has grown more prominent, this has become harder.

State Councillor Yang Jiechi, in effect the most senior foreign policy representative in the Chinese government system, stated directly to ASEAN members in 2010 that 'China is a big country and other countries are small countries, and that's just a fact.'[16] Such a declaration, before such a forum, betrayed for many a contemporary Chinese elitist mindset that they were powerful, important and dominant, and that all other parties in the region had to queue up behind them. That ASEAN within itself has often been divided has not helped in articulating an ASEAN consistent policy stance on issues that might counterbalance China. In its annual meeting in 2012, for the first time ever its membership proved unable to publish a press release, because of the desire by four attending nations who had disputes over the South China Sea to express language slightly critical of China in the formal statement.[17] It also downgraded some of its language criticizing Beijing on territorial matters in its communiqué in 2016, reportedly on Cambodia's insistence.

China certainly looms large in the politics of this region, with its influence clearly visible in places like Phnom Penh, where one of the main thoroughfares is named Mao Zedong Boulevard. Large amounts of Chinese investment have been going into Cambodia, and into Myanmar, in recent years. But it is unclear whether the equation that Chinese investment equals immediate political influence is ever as neat as commentators like Kurlantzick make out. As the account of China's activities in Africa and the Middle East will show, rather than money buying love, it often buys scepticism and antagonism. Myanmar is the classic example, a country which for years had a close relationship with China and which was protected by its huge neighbour throughout the years of isolation when its governing military junta had made it an international pariah. China's almost amoral stance meant that it continued to be a conduit for trade and goods when almost no one else was active in the country. This was not due to any profound allegiance in Beijing to their south-western partner, but because of interest in its plentiful energy resources. With reforms from 2012, however, the political opening up of Myanmar to the outside world transformed it, introducing the EU, then the United States, as new actors there, seeing a visit by President Obama and in effect integrating the country into a much more diverse group of relations. It was clear that reliance on China was regarded as a huge strategic vulnerability. The years of superficial declarations of allegiance and closeness from the Myanmar state therefore, proved just that – rhetoric with no real depth.

That cautiousness among smaller nations in Asia – a desire for diversity and to reduce reliance on China – is testified to in the investment flows across the region as a whole. Apart from Singapore, in 2014 China only accounted for 2.4 per cent of overall investment stock in the ten countries, at least according to one report. And while China is important as a manufacturing, exporting country, the relationship is less overwhelming than might be imagined: 'It is fair to say,' the report stated, that 'Chinese outbound investment in ASEAN is still early-stage.'[18] The conclusion has to be that even in the region closest to China, where the gains of trading and investing in each other are most tangible, and the motivations strongest, there is an ambiguity to China's relationships and its role.

In the realm of security, this ambiguity grows even stronger. Paradoxically, the greater China's wealth, the more willing it is to spend this on its neighbouring ASEAN countries, and the more reservations and doubts these countries have towards their newly generous partner. This seems to be a modern Chinese trap, a devil's gambit where China is damned if it shows its hand, and damned if it doesn't.

RUSSIA AND CENTRAL ASIA

The Soviet Union served as the most influential international patron and partner to the Chinese Communist Party during its rise to power. And after 1949, the USSR still exercised great control, despite Mao Zedong's clear attempts in the realms of ideology and practice to differentiate the movement in China from that in Russia. Russian troops, for instance, did not leave the north-eastern region of the country until the mid-1950s,[19] and Russian experts helped the PRC to eventually construct its own hydrogen bomb. Even so, the political relationship was always prickly, and as Chapter 3 made clear, part of China's motivation in the late 1960s for rapprochement with the United States came from real fears on the Chinese side of Russian intervention and bullying.

With the resolution of the border disputes in the 2000s between Russia and China, one major area of uncertainty and contention was removed. Under Putin, China has also been able to deal with a more secure and stable leader in Moscow. Rumours in 2012 that

Xi Jinping felt Putin's style of leadership was something he wanted to mimic were perhaps overblown; even so, the highly centralizing style of these two leaders is striking, as is their annexation of political space in their respective countries. More practically, Russian isolation over the annexation of Crimea in 2014 pushed Putin neatly towards closer relations with the PRC. He visited China in May that year and signed a major deal for gas supply from Siberia on terms which were regarded as generous. As of early 2017, however, nothing much has materialized from this deal.

Russia's contemporary relationship with China has been described as an axis of convenience.[20] The question has increasingly become who is more convenient to whom, however. Russian antagonism towards the United States and Europe is useful up to a point for Beijing in distracting the two major powers, although speculation about Chinese support for Putin's aggression towards Ukraine was just that – speculation. This is simply because a more assertive Russia in the long term would clearly be a bad thing for China, creating rivalries both in the Asia region and throughout Central Asia, where China is now becoming an increasingly important player. The relationship is currently a profoundly distrustful one, however, despite Xi Jinping according the country the honour of his first visit abroad as president in early 2013. (Hu Jintao had done the same a decade earlier on his elevation, indicating the kind of continuities in Chinese strategy that persist despite all the editorials and arguments about radical change.)

In what ways are China and Russia (in the terminology favoured by the foreign-policy establishment in Beijing) 'comprehensive strategic partners'? For Russia, Chinese designs on Siberia and the Far East are regarded with unease. The 150,000 Chinese business people now working in this region are viewed as potential agents for a Beijing grab on territory which is vulnerable and contains plenty of resources China would like to get its hands on. These fears of Chinese creeping control of the region are long-standing, and go back to before the founding of the PRC. Even so, they still figure in Russian thinking – though they are important more as a perception than a reality. Even so, they still figure in Russian thinking – though they are important more as a perception than a reality. As one Russian academic stated at a London conference about Russia–China relations in the mid-2000s, 'There is one good reason why Chinese are unlikely to want to take over Siberia: It is not a very nice place, and a hard one to live and work in. Why take responsibility for that?'

When visiting Moscow in 2013, Xi Jinping went out of the way to burnish his Russian literary credentials, mentioning in one speech a phenomenal list of writers and intellectuals, from Dostoyevsky to Tolstoy and Gogol.[21] One of his predecessors, Jiang Zemin, was even able to speak good Russian, gained from a two-year stint studying there in the 1950s, when the relationship between the two countries was good. This was not unusual for people of his generation. However, despite this appearance of mutual warmth towards each other, do Russian and Chinese elites really share reciprocal complementary visions for their nations, ones that they each can buy into and work towards? Russian resentment at its loss of status after the collapse of the USSR resembles Chinese anger over what it views as its humiliation at the hands of the West in an earlier era. The only difference is that the memories for Russia are more recent, and therefore stronger.

There are ways in which this suits Chinese aims. It means they are never considered to be (at least at the moment) a target for Russian frustrations. They are factored in as more supportive and useful. But that sort of strategic 'marriage of convenience' could easily dissipate. Russia's more imperial, nationalist dreams are not ones the Chinese would share because they carry clear territorial aims that China would disagree with and find threatening.

In that sense, a weak but stable Russia is a Russia that China under Xi would support. That means a country that does not cause it problems within its region, has a benign economic relationship with China, largely figures as a resource supplier, and continues to distract the attention of countries like the United States. In that framework, Putin's Russia is almost ideal, except for its worrying upward trend of nationalism and its own inherent economic woes. There too, it reflects China – compensating for internal challenges and weaknesses by presenting a pushy, assertive face to the outside world. Does the Asian region have space for two such huge, assertive actors? History strongly suggests not.

One of the dynamics playing into China's extension of diplomatic and political reach in the Central Asian period after 2010 is an attempt to diversify its space, to seek other arenas and means of influence beyond the coastal areas, beyond the current realm of security, where it feels boxed in by the United States. Turning attention to the western region of China works on many levels. It is an area where China's own domestic configuration is vulnerable, with the Tibet and Xinjiang autonomous regions in particular figuring as places of instability and sensitivity. From 1999, the central government promoted a grand new initiative, called 'Opening Up the West', in many ways something that prefigured the Belt Road Initiative ideas of over a decade later but mapped out in the domestic rather than international space.

This kind of paradigm shift has meant China now works in areas it has never properly been exposed in. Through the Central Asian states, it has sent out diplomatic and economic feelers, with Xi Jinping himself undertaking an extensive tour there in 2013 and visiting Turkmenistan, Kazakhstan, Uzbekistan and Kyrgyzstan. Resources were of course uppermost in his mind, along with securing allies in a region which figures as a potential supply route.

From 2000, the Opening Up the West initiative had aimed to develop 11 of China's western provinces, places which had been left behind by the extraordinary pace of reform on the coast. While Fujian, Guangdong, Zhejiang and other eastern suburbs had created manufacturing clusters, raised GDP, built large amounts of infrastructure and become integrated into global supply chains, and middle provinces like Henan, Hunan, Hebei and Hubei had seen some trickle-down effects of this process, further west the state-owned enterprises still dominated, GDP levels were low, poverty was common and the infrastructure poor. Even asking wealthier provinces to pair up with these western ones proved challenging. They were, in the end, very remote, even from other places in China.

In terms of ethnicity, culture, history and other links, however, a natural place to look for partnerships was in the closer Central Asian area. Trying to build bridges here gave the Opening Up the West story greater vibrancy, so what initially looked like a domestic issue came eventually to have profoundly international dimensions. The Belt Road Initiative story can be seen as a continuation of this, even to the extent of sharing some of its haziness and epic quality. And like Opening Up the West, BRI operates more as an attempt to create a framework, a normative environment, rather than something which has detailed, prescriptive policies. It is an endeavour by China to carve out meaningful, sympathetic space for itself in areas that matter to it.

When touring Central Asia, Xi did refer to the 'win–win' rubric, a phrase that had appeared about all sorts of foreign-affairs issues until then. The SCO, which had been created in the late 1990s, was resurrected by Xi's foreign-policy activism and as a result of the new, more intense interest in this region. It figured as part of an attempt to create a world of valid and viable Chinese activity away from the constant intervention and interference of others, particularly the United States. It meant that China was able to demonstrate leadership in areas where it wanted to do so, but in ways and about issues that did not make others too suspicious and at least protected its interests. And it also meant it could link important domestic and external issues with each other. With rising restiveness in the Islamic areas of Xinjiang, and with major riots there in 2009, it was important to have at least some conduit for dialogue with partners in the region who could help it in controlling its own security issues.

THE BELT ROAD INITIATIVE: THE HUNT FOR A COMMON CHINESE LANGUAGE

Locating the genealogy of the Belt Road Initiative in the Opening Up the West policy of over a decade before at least helps to understand a bit better what sort of thing it is: an initiative rather than a policy, one involving a raft of different proposals and funding streams and where there are multiple angles of engagement, combined by all working within one 'master story'.

BRI also operates as part of a grand Chinese external narrative, one which has been presented at events like the huge Boao gathering in the southern island of Hainan each April. In this context, BRI is a contribution to Asia's hunt for a common destiny. Boao was also a good place to confront some of the problems of this grand idea, however – an unconvincing attempt to influence international foreign-policy thinking and debates by stuffing various musty halls in a somewhat remote, purpose-built function centre with individuals who, mostly, could be trusted to say the right thing. Squadrons of largely Chinese media were unleashed onto speakers once they had finished their sessions, with the great event being a declaration by a major leader – usually Xi himself, or, some years, Li Keqiang.

Anyone wandering around the halls of Boao would be struck by the idea that they were witnessing China's confusion over and fleshing out of its message to the world. Friendly Japanese, Taiwanese and some other representatives of neighbouring countries were granted access, but on the whole the absence of major figures from the United States, Japan or Europe has shown that there are some misgivings about exactly what Boao is trying to achieve both on the part of the organizers, who clearly want a massive PR project, and the audience, who often come away feeling like they have been unwittingly recruited as walk-on parts in a promotional event rather than taken part in any meaningful discussions. In any case, the notions of common destiny in Asia have grown more vapid since 2013: 'environment', 'stability' and 'sustainability' are all good buzzwords and attract no dissent; the region certainly needs to focus on all of these. But once it gets down to detail, things tend to rapidly disintegrate. China is seen by some living in the same area as a power simply manipulating its new-found wealth in order to shape a region convenient and malleable to its political aims. And for all the talk about 'win–win', in the end China's military imprint is increasing, and its attempts to influence space right out to the edges of Malaysia are regarded as being nothing more than the behaviour of a revisionist superpower-in-waiting (ready to dominate, settle some historic scores and impose a new imperium where the US one had left off). Some have caustically commented that 'win–win' has a simple definition: China wins twice!

The point made here is not so much about what China has been saying and how it has been behaving, but about the clear lack of consensus among those outside its borders – from ASEAN to India to others – about what relative weight to give to each side of the economics and security equation. There were clearly many who felt that China as an economic actor was a good thing, and something to be supported and worked with. But there were others who also saw its economic ascendancy clearly linked to a major political agenda, with the two marching side by side with each other. In 2014, a year marking the centenary of the start of World War I, the Japanese prime minister explicitly referred to the situation in Asia mirroring that which had prevailed in Europe so many years before. 'The comparison,' a journalist writing for the *Financial Times* commented on hearing this, 'lies in the fact that Britain and Germany – like China and Japan – had a strong trading relationship. But in 1914, this had not prevented strategic tensions leading to the outbreak of conflict.'[22]

Such parallels were seen at the time as far-fetched. But the suspicion about Chinese intentions in the long term in the region have not shifted, even when something like the Belt Road Initiative tries to concentrate on pure economic space. In terms of reputation, image and trust, China seems unable to remove deep-seated opposition and suspicion. This is also a characteristic of its relations with the third zone: the European Union.

5

ZONE THREE
THE EU AND CHINA –
CIVILIZED PARTNERS TALKING PAST EACH OTHER

Speaking at the first ever visit by a Chinese head of state to the headquarters of the European Union (EU) in Brussels in 2014, Xi Jinping made a declaration during a speech at the College of Europe in the beautiful city of Bruges that China and the EU were 'civilizational' partners. Outlining the cultural, historical, intellectual and material assets of China over what he called its 'time-honoured civilization', he reverted to the trope favoured by Communist leaders since the era of Jiang Zemin of 5,000 years of 'uninterrupted' history and civilization. In this context, Xi drew a flattering parallel with Europe:

> China represents in an important way the Eastern civilization, while Europe is the birthplace of the Western civilization. The Chinese people are fond of tea and the Belgians love beer. To me, the moderate tea drinker and the passionate beer lover represent two ways of understanding life and knowing the world, and I find them equally rewarding. When good friends get together, they may want to drink to their heart's content to show their friendship. They may also choose to sit down quietly and drink tea while chatting about their life.

In China, we value the idea of preserving 'harmony without
uniformity', and here in the EU people stress the need to be
'united in diversity'. Let us work together for all flowers of
human civilizations to blossom together.[1]

In many ways, Xi's words were at least an attempt to solve a conundrum for Chinese leaders, officials and people. For them, making
sense of this expanding group of EU members – whose numbers
had risen to 28 from a mere nine in a little under two decades –
with all its internal linguistic, cultural and social diversity, proved
tough. What precisely was the EU? It was not a country, nor a
continent (several European countries are not in the EU). And for
all its tantalizing unity, it manages as a trading block to throw up
endless challenges to China, and as will be seen later in this chapter,
Chinese tourists love coming to Europe, and Chinese students certainly appreciate the United Kingdom and (increasingly) Germany,
Holland and France. But there has been something about the EU
since the very early days that has grated with the Chinese – its
proclivity to place values at the heart of political discussion, on the
assumption that it represents something ideal and more futuristic
which China should emulate. But the real effrontery is that it does
this with no substantial hard power to back up its outward facade of
influence, and, in addition, does so despite its cumbersome history
of massive violence through colonialism and both world wars. What
right had the EU to lecture China with this sort of historical baggage
attached to it? Conferring on the EU the abstract label of 'civilizational partner' seemed at least to solve some of these problems. It
stressed parity between the two (getting rid of any sense that China
needed to be culturally and philosophically beholden to the EU),
recognized the genuine Chinese admiration for Europe's immense
contribution to modernity through the scientific revolution, and
somehow created a discursive link between a country on the one
hand, and a consortium of nations on the other. The only problem

with the 'civilization partners' rubric was that no two people seemed to be able to agree what, in practice, it actually meant.

Not that the Chinese were alone in this bafflement. US academic Perry Anderson stated that even most citizens of the EU have a weak understanding of what precisely this Union is. A pragmatic collection of states focused on optimizing internal free trade arrangements (something the Chinese really bought into)? Or something more substantive, a pooling of sovereignty which is on its way to becoming the sort of superstate alluded to by some of the founding fathers of the whole project – Jean Monnet, for instance?[2] British journalist David Goodhart, writing on British identity and immigration policy in 2012, referred to the ways in which the EU has evolved so that it seeks to present itself as a post-modern polity, the sort of place we are heading to when the states that grew up as a result of the Westphalian model wither away. But for him, this outcome is highly problematic:

> Although the EU mimics the nation state in some trivial ways, it is not a nation state and to the extent that it commands loyalty it is at a far lower level than national loyalty. Very few people would die for the EU and very few would make big economic sacrifices for another EU state. We have seen this clearly in the case of Germany, one of the least overtly nationalistic of the big European states, which was happy to spend about one trillion dollars on unification with East Germany but is very reluctant to spend far smaller sums helping to support the Greek economy and what they call a European 'transfer union'.[3]

Despite this, there is the powerful moral vision of the EU, something articulated and defended by thinkers as diverse as German philosopher Jürgen Habermas, British commentator Mark Leonard and former European Union official Robert Cooper.[4] These opinions

stand against daily experiences of the Union along the lines that
Anderson noted – of something remote, which people in Europe feel
little emotional or political attachment to, an entity that in many
places is starting to repel people and which, because of the ongoing
financial crisis that began in 2008, is failing to deliver the very thing
it is regarded as being strongest at: economic efficiency. The latest
blow to this immense unifying project has been the decision taken
during the referendum held in the United Kingdom on 23 June
2016 to leave the Union, the first time a fully signed-up member
has decided to quit the grouping.

In view of all this, placing the EU as a contested, evolving,
dynamic entity beside China (in the context in which they share
such a huge trade partnership with each other and are also hugely
integrated in terms of imports, exports, research, investment, education and cultural links) has proven a vastly complex endeavour. It is
a task on which many officials, academics and other actors in both
areas (the EU and China) have spent a lot of time and effort. The
fact that there are up to 80 policy- or technological-level dialogues
across economic, political and cultural areas alone testifies to the
complexity of the relationship. It deserves to be taken seriously,
and is one of the key relationships of the modern world. And yet it
is also one beset by frustration and lack of mutual understanding.

On top of all of this, the EU and China have both changed so
profoundly since they since they developed formal linkages for the
first time in 1975 that they simply lack the right architecture to
deal with each other – they desperately need a flexible, more fit-for-
purpose framework to aid mutual understanding. There is no lack
of nice aspirational language, but in terms of the daily machinery of
engagement, there needs to be a radical rethink – and this applies to
both sides. The second point here is that in a strange way, each has
a moral and cultural vision of itself that jars with how it views the
other partner; this vision in fact creates problems with how the two
engage and interact. Until these issues of internal self-identity are

dealt with, external relations are unlikely to get any easier. The simple fact is that, in different ways, the EU and the PRC as they currently stand are recent inventions, born from horrific suffering and conflict, both on a vast journey of self-articulation and self-discovery. And then there is the nitty-gritty, specific issues where the two prove that they really do come from different worlds: the controversial meeting between British prime minister David Cameron and the Dalai Lama in 2012, the solar panel arguments in 2013, and policy over foreign direct investment issues. Finally, there is 'the vision thing': the way they both talk about their ideas of the future strategic directions in which they aspire to travel. In a strange way, the two have more in common than they think, but do less than they could simply because of their lack of an internalized and integrated vision of who they are and how they can best relate to each other. The series of crises which have been besetting the EU recently, from migration to the Brexit referendum decision of June 2016, illustrate this: unlike Russia, China wants the EU to remain unified and sees value in this. In that sense, it is in the strange position of being an ally of EU integration – even if this could make it a threat.

THE STARTING POINT

The EU and the PRC trace their first diplomatic recognition of each other back to 1975. But at that time the EU was simply called, somewhat technocratically, the European Economic Community (EEC), with nine member states. It had nothing approaching the scope and form it assumed after the Maastricht Treaty of 1992, which created the single currency and structured the resultant Union itself under three pillars – the European Community, the Common Foreign and Security Policy, and Justice and Home Affairs. In 1975 too, the PRC was radically different to that which was to gradually come into existence after the Third Plenum of the Eleventh Party

Congress in 1978. It did not embrace the market, did not allow
foreign capital inside the country, and adhered to class struggle as
the key objective of Party policy. In 1975 China was still under
the leadership of Mao Zedong, and the radical leftists that became
known as the Gang of Four were still immensely influential. Indeed,
in that year one of their members, Zhang Chunqiao, produced
a diatribe against marketization and possible liberalization, 'On
exercising all-round dictatorship over the bourgeoisie in China'.[5]
This set the political tone for this period in China.

The legal basis of the relations between the EU and China to
this day remains the EEC–China Trade and Economic Cooperation
Agreement, signed on 16 September 1985. While both the EEC
and the PRC had changed over the decade since their recognition,
there were still radical differences between the situation in 1985
and that which prevails now. The overwhelming dominance of
trade issues in this agreement therefore is unsurprising. It was and
remains a soft-trade concord. Its main provisions relate to customs
duties, tariffs, regulations of trade and taxes, and internal charges. It
states in its preamble that it grants both sides 'most favoured nation
status', and sets out a number of key sectors where each will grant
more liberal access to the other.[6] There have been revisions to this
agreement over the last three decades, with a strategic partnership
agreed in 2003 and the issuing of 'guidelines' in a document issued
by the European Commission to the Council and the European
Parliament in October 2006 entitled 'EU–China: closer partners,
growing responsibilities'. A further communication, updating this,
was issued a decade later, ironically on the same day as the UK referendum to leave the EU. But these update the document signed
in 1985, rather than replacing it.

While the trade-focused basis of the EEC (from 1992 the EU) and
China relations has some sort of legal basis and is well established, as
the EU has evolved in more ambitious directions over the last two
decades, both sides have started to use more aspirational language in

documents spelling out the nature of their relationship. The October 2006 document referred to in the paragraph above spelled out an ambitious menu of common concerns. These embraced:

- supporting China's transition towards a more open and plural society;
- sustainable development (in terms of energy, climate change, international development and sustainable economic growth);
- trade and economic relations;
- strengthening bilateral cooperation (between the EU and China); and
- supporting and promoting international and regional cooperation.[7]

The journey from setting out the sort of objectives tabulated in 1985 with those in 2006 is also the journey of the EEC's transformation into the EU, and of its expansion of membership up to 28 nation states, with a greater sense of its economic attractions and of its need to build common values and coherence within itself. For some, like British analyst Mark Leonard, it is the way in which Europe, through the EU, can articulate and put into practice a radical new polity that is significant, aside from its economic weight. In its founding charters it can now speak of ethical and cultural issues on which it leads the world, and indeed offers a counterbalance to the sole remaining superpower, the United States. This at least was the case before the economic trauma that started in 2007. For this reason, Leonard states grandly that Europe is a transformative power:

> By creating the largest single internal market in the world, Europe has become an economic giant that, according to some calculations, is already the biggest in the world. But it is the quality of Europe's economy that makes it a model:

its low levels of inequality allow countries to save on crime and prisons, its energy-efficient economies will protect them from the hike in oil prices. Europe represents a synthesis of the energy and freedom that come from liberalism with the stability and welfare that come from social democracy. As the world becomes richer and moves beyond satisfying basic needs such as hunger and health, the European way of life will become irresistible.[8]

It is interesting that this statement was written almost at the time the new guidelines between the EU and China were being discussed in 2006. They share an idealism and confidence in the nature of the whole EU project, something that would be fundamentally questioned when the economic crisis set in two years later. The 2016 update only served as a statement of greater intensification and specificity of the parameters set out in 2006. It was twice the length of the earlier document, and more specific on investment, technical cooperation and the mechanics of engagement, perhaps as an admission that on this level the two did have more fruitful ways of engaging with each other.

Idealism was not just on the side of the EU, with its notion of being able to somehow transform by example and act as a moral exemplar to China; the Chinese government itself produced a brief official white paper at the same time as the strategic partnership between the two was announced in 2003. In this, it states that:

The EU is now a strong and the most integrated community in the world, taking up 25 and 35 percent of the world's economy and trade respectively and ranking high on the world's list of per capita income and foreign investment.

Recognizing that China attaches great importance to the relationship, it goes on to say, 'There is no fundamental conflict of interest between China and the EU and neither side poses a threat to the other,' and that despite differences in cultural outlook, politics and world views,

> The common ground between China and the EU far out-weighs their disagreements. Both China and the EU stand for democracy in international relations and an enhanced role of the UN. Both are committed to combating international terrorism and promoting sustainable development through poverty elimination and environmental protection endeavors. China and the EU are highly complementary economically thanks to their respective advantages. The EU has a developed economy, advanced technologies and strong financial resources while China boasts steady economic growth, a huge market and abundant labor force. There is a broad prospect for bilateral trade and economic and technological cooperation. Both China and the EU member states have a long history and splendid culture each and stand for more cultural exchanges and mutual emulation. The political, economic and cultural common understanding and interaction between China and the EU offer a solid foundation for the continued growth of China–EU relations.[9]

Even with strongly aspirational language on both sides, the decade of 2003–13 was to throw up challenges that have caused the two sides to fundamentally reappraise their views of each other. The simple fact is that the current framework (initially established in 1975 and then placed on a more legal basis in 1985, with subsequent guidelines issued) and other key official constitutive documents between the two are no longer capable of capturing the complexities of the relationship. Since 2003, the idealistic language has been toned down somewhat, firstly due to arguments over the EU's failure to lift its arms embargo towards China, imposed because of US pressure after the student uprising in 1989, followed by arguments over the EU's refusal to grant China 'market status', despite doing so with Russia and other economies, and finally due to a number of complex and protracted trade disputes.

This is best exemplified by a second White Paper issued almost simultaneously with Xi's visit to Brussels in 2014. There the language is much harsher, and the red lines more categorical. While acknowledging that 'China and the EU stand as two major civilizations advancing human progress,' the paper goes on to state that, 'With no fundamental conflict of interests, China and the EU have far more agreement than differences. Both sides are at a crucial stage of reform and development and China–EU relations face new historic opportunities.'[10] While listing the various economic, environmental and other areas where the two have achieved unity and cooperation in the last decade, once the paper hits the question of Taiwan, Tibet and human rights, the tone is markedly sharper than in 2003. On Taiwan, China 'asks the EU and its member states not to support Taiwan's accession to any international organization whose membership requires statehood'. On Tibet, China asks the EU to

> not allow leaders of the Dalai group to visit the EU or its member states under any capacity or pretext to engage in separatist activities, not arrange any form of contact with officials of the EU or its member states, and not provide any facilitation or support for anti-China separatist activities for 'Tibet independence'.

And on human rights in general, 'the EU side should attach equal importance to all forms of human rights, including civil, political, economic, social and cultural rights and the right to development, view China's human rights situation in an objective and fair manner, stop using individual cases to interfere in China's judicial sovereignty and internal affairs.'

CHANGING PLACES

Back in 2003, when the then Chinese premier and head of the State Council Wen Jiabao heralded the establishment of the strategic partnership, he talked in terms of a relationship which was able to deal with challenges but where people stuck at it and did not give up. Over the following decade, however, there were two radically transformative moments. These have pushed the strategic relationship to the extreme and made deep changes to its internal dynamic and composition, something testified to by the shift in language in the two White Papers referred to above. The first of these is the impact since 2007 of the financial crisis. The EU's previous language describing itself as an exemplar, an economic and political model (often used to emphasize differences between itself and China), has become much harder to use since the crisis, certainly since the Eurozone travails really set in from 2009 and the brutal fracture following on from the Brexit vote. From this period onwards, we can see clear changes in the tone of Chinese leaders towards the EU. While this could not quite be described as condescending, the ways in which Chinese officials and politicians started expressing concern about the EU after the onset of this crisis is symbolically and politically meaningful. Such solicitous language is exemplified by Gao Hucheng, China's then international trade representative, who stated on 6 October 2009 that 'China is confident that Europe has what it takes to weather the current crisis.'[11] Quoted in an editorial in Xinhua issued on the day that the European leaders had finally managed to hammer out their stability deal two years later in 2011, and while Klaus Regler, chief executive of the European Financial Stability Fund (ESFS), was already on his way to China, Premier Wen Jiabao reinforced this by declaring that 'China stands up ready to improve co-ordinating and co-operation with the EU and contribute to the global economic recovery,' but, 'Emerging economies should not be seen as the EU's Good Samaritans – in the end the EU has to pull itself out of the crisis.'[12]

The sudden appearance of the Chinese lecturing the EU about its lauded economy is politically fascinating. But this is also within a context in which the EU itself has undergone further deep internal changes, with the signing into law of the Lisbon Treaty in 2009. This treaty was carried after lengthy and often fractious internal arguments, and was only fully voted on in some of the member states – Ireland, the Netherlands and France, for instance. This gave the treaty an immediate problem with legitimacy. The document set out the creation of a unified and enhanced link between the EU parliament and the Commission, granting the parliament more powers and creating a presidency of the Commission, and it also set out aspirations towards a more unified foreign policy with the creation of an external action service and a high-level representative for foreign affairs.

Under Lisbon, the EU has become a different kind of diplomatic actor, one that superficially looks more joined-up and should act in a more coordinated way. Practically, however, the Lisbon outcome has created even more complexity for China in its engagement. As head of the State Council, Wen Jiabao (and Li Keqiang, his successor after 2013) has had to engage with both presidents of the Union, one from the Council (the first initially being Herman Van Rompuy, replaced by Donald Tusk in 2015) and one from the European Commission (José Manuel Barroso, replaced by Jean-Claude Juncker in 2015). The question of who to speak to about what has therefore become more complex. Once one factors in the natural importance of the heads of the nation states that are part of the EU – from the chancellor of Germany to the president of France, or (until the Brexit vote) the prime minister of Great Britain – it is understandable that Chinese leaders experience confusion when they are trying to work out who is supposed to deal with what within this complex architecture.

While the tectonic plates of the world's geopolitics have shifted since 2008 because of the impact of the financial crisis, the Brexit vote and the election of Donald Trump, injecting a harder realism into the ways in which the EU and China relate to each other, it is also helpful to look at the issues of disagreement to see how the relationship between the two is evolving. China and the EU enjoy great economic links, for example. This at least everyone knows. By 2014 EU and Chinese bilateral trade had risen to 466 billion euros, with the EU being the largest destination for Chinese exports and the second largest supplier of goods to China.[13] Even in the harsh years of trade from 2007 to 2011, trade rose 9 per cent per annum, almost double the rest of the world. China accounted for 17 per cent of EU imports, and nearly 9 per cent of exports.[14] If there was one reason why the two profoundly mattered to each other it was here, in the trade and (increasingly) investment flows between the two. But the key strategic documents that have been issued jointly between both parties over the period following 2003 have striven to look to a world beyond simple trade links, and therein lies the problem. They speak of ways they can influence each other's behaviour, speak to each other as development and cultural partners and have a deeper impact on the ways the other is growing. It is in this realm where the biggest challenges are occurring, where the notion of 'civilizational partnership' is just the most recent staging post.

THE BATTLE OVER VALUES, MARKETS AND KNOWLEDGE

When looking at the internal configurations of power within each of the two entities and how each regards its own political identity, the three hardest areas for the EU and China to cooperate in are those pertaining to values and rights, questions of how each understands the principles of fair access to its own domestic market, and uncertainties surrounding intellectual property rights and trust. On each of these, the EU experiences the same clashes as the United States does with China, but fares somewhat differently in terms of how its opinions are heard and what outcomes it obtains.

The first issue is best demonstrated by Tibet, and in particular the meetings by EU leaders with the Dalai Lama. Tibet is one of the biggest problems for internal Chinese politics. This has worsened since the uprising in Lhasa in March 2008. The handling of this autonomous region involves profound issues of national legitimacy. The EU and China have a human rights dialogue and a number of modes of interaction, and these provide the framework within which problems like Tibet should be raised. But far from allowing positive outcomes, these dialogues have created mechanisms in which, according to one critical assessment, they have allowed politicians on both sides to say they have engaged in tough issues when in fact this has been fielded out to experts who have then engaged in technical but largely abstract discussions.[15] This has created a certain amount of cynicism in the EU about the effectiveness of continuing this sort of debate in this way.

Things are not helped by the fact that the new Europe, represented in large part by the EU, comes with an immense amount of colonial history issues like Tibet. Great Britain in particular was involved in Tibet from the early part of the twentieth century onwards, and it participated in moves to discuss the issue of the region's status at the United Nations in 1949 when the People's Republic was founded. This sort of history poses a particular source of irritation for the current Chinese government, which was only partially ameliorated by the revision of the British official policy in 2008 to recognize only Chinese suzerainty in Tibet, rather than full sovereignty.[16] Even in the so-called 'golden age' of United Kingdom–China relations, ushered in since Xi Jinping's visit to the United Kingdom in 2015, Tibet is an issue that still has the power to disrupt and complicate the relationship.

Detailed discussions between the two countries on abstract issues of rights and obligations have taken place in the last decade, with an attempt to set out a framework to explicitly discuss highly sensitive issues for the Chinese like Tibet. Often issues between member states and China then escalate to EU level. When both German chancellor Angela Merkel (in 2007) and French then president Sarkozy (in 2008) met with the Dalai Lama, this led to deep anger by the Chinese government, the boycott of the 2008 annual EU–China Summit and a large campaign in China against French brands like Carrefour. All of this was made worse by demonstrations and the manhandling of a disabled Chinese athlete by French spectators during the Olympic torch ceremony in the summer of 2008 in Paris.

By 2012, it was clear that there were few heads of state across the EU who would meet with the exiled Tibetan religious leader because of the strength of feeling from the Chinese government and the ways in which they had responded from 2008 onwards. The award of the Nobel Peace Prize to Chinese dissident Liu Xiaobo in 2010 only exacerbated matters, with Chinese attempts to block EU leaders and others from attending the award ceremony in Oslo that year, which led to China strongly condemning and isolating the Norwegian government despite its non-involvement in the award. Nor is Norway a member of the EU. Even so, it is clearly a major country in Europe and one that some in the EU wanted to show solidarity with. The simple fact was that the Chinese government showed in its assertive behaviour that it was unwilling to endure European 'moral haughtiness' and lecturing on an issue it was sensitive about. Nor was it willing to tolerate external intervention over issues it regarded as domestic. And unlike in the past, its economic importance now gave it the leverage to do this. By the time of writing this book in early 2017, remarkably, this diplomatic freeze has still not thawed, with Norwegian ministers still not able to get full access within China.

The meeting between British prime minister David Cameron and the Dalai Lama while the latter was in London in May 2012 to receive the Templeton Peace Price was conducted in the usual low-profile way, with the justification that had been used for most of the last two decades: the Dalai Lama was being met as a religious leader, not a political one, by the serving prime minister. Even so, the response by the Chinese government was immediate and severe. A high-level visit to the United Kingdom by the then second-ranking member of the Communist Party's Politburo Standing Committee Wu Bangguo was cancelled. A BBC report stated that the Chinese government, through its Ministry of Foreign Affairs, had issued a statement complaining that Cameron's actions had 'seriously interfered with China's internal affairs, undermined China's core interests, and hurt the feelings of the Chinese people'.[17] Britain, needless to say, had a long and illustrious history of hurting Chinese feelings, but this time suffered a pushback that took even its most hardened officials by surprise.

Over the ensuing year, according to the *Financial Times* in April 2013, only one formal vice-ministerial meeting had occurred between two British and Chinese counterparts, with one other having taken place informally. The successful visit by French president François Hollande to Beijing in April that year, soon after his election, only highlighted just how differently the two EU member states were faring. As the paper reported, while Hollande received red-carpet treatment and access to President Xi Jinping, Premier Li Keqiang and a number of other leaders in China, Cameron's attempt to visit was snubbed.[18] Things only started to improve in July 2013.

The 28 members of the European Union have joint commitments to issues of rights and values which are enshrined in their constitutional documents, the most recent of which is the Lisbon Treaty. In order to become a member of the EU, candidate states have to show that they adhere to shared democratic values and are committed to freedom of speech, assembly and religious belief, as well as a range of other social, political and legal issues. But on a more detailed level, things are more complex. On the issue of balancing how to deal with senior political leaders meeting with the Dalai Lama, and how to promote stronger support for human rights in China, there are evidently deep differences of opinion within the Union. Little solidarity was shown with the United Kingdom over this issue, as Hollande's visit illustrates. His own discussions with China on rights issues seemed suitably abstract to not cause problems for his hosts.[19]

Because of the complex history outlined above – and the issues arising from questions of self-determinacy, freedom of religion, freedom of association and a host of other contentious subjects that this raises – finding a common language in which to talk about Tibet with the Chinese, in order to build and maintain policy consensus, will remain among the toughest tasks for the EU in issues regarding China. So far, the case of British prime minister Cameron meeting the Dalai Lama in 2012 and the fallout from this shows that the EU member states within themselves have not been able to achieve that meaningful unity. They operate therefore within a framework which promises agreement on rights issues but then is undermined by evidence that they seem to have separate understanding of what this means, with some more broadly liberal and some more pragmatic. It is therefore not surprising that China is both confused by this position and also willing, when it is useful diplomatically, to exploit it. Cameron was finally allowed back into China in late 2013, and somewhat surprised journalists by brushing off their questions about any planned future meetings with the Tibetan religious leader by saying none were planned. In 2014 and 2015, the United Kingdom pursued a ruthlessly economic relationship with China, with the British Chancellor of the Exchequer George Osborne even briefly visiting Xinjiang in what many interpreted as a colossal act of appeasement and penance in September 2015. On top of this, the United Kingdom, as already stated, was one of the earliest to join the AIIB, against US wishes.

TRADING BLOWS

With the vast flow of trade referred to above, it is clear that as markets, the EU and China matter immensely to each other. And yet the issue of how mutually fair they are in granting equal access has been a long-standing one. China and the EU experienced complex negotiations in the run-up to the former's eventual joining of the WTO in 2001. Sectors which proved particularly problematic over this period were telecommunications, agriculture and financial services. To both sides, they were key areas of economic importance, and ones they needed to know they were not exposing to unfair competition.

In 2005, the EU imposed tariffs on Chinese textiles and entered into a lengthy dispute on anti-dumping. This was among the first (and the most difficult) trade disputes. From 2012, one of the most contentious issues arose from EU claims that the country's government was subsidising the manufacture of solar panels by Chinese companies. On 8 May 2013, after a lengthy investigation and numerous rounds of discussions with Chinese trade officials, the then trade commissioner at the European Commission, Karel De Gucht, announced that 47 per cent tariffs would be imposed on solar panels imported from China into the EU. This had largely been provoked by Chinese imports climbing from almost zero in the late 2000s to more than US$ 27 billion worth of goods, 80 per cent of the market, by 2012. This rapid market dominance had been helped by the fact that Chinese goods were almost half the price of those of competing manufacturers in Europe.[20] The Chinese response was to target luxury goods like wine, on which it slapped a retaliatory high tariff in late May.

This dispute has brought to the surface the different dynamics of trade between separate EU member states and China. German chancellor Angela Merkel stated during her visit to China in September 2012 that she did not wish to see any kind of trade warfare and wanted to pursue a political route.[21] She was to repeat these sentiments in late May 2013, directly to the new Chinese Premier Li Keqiang. Germany alone of the then 27 members of the EU has often enjoyed an export surplus with China, largely due to its strengths in the car and machinery sectors. It has the most to lose from any kind of tit-for-tat levying of tariffs if these impact on sectors that matter to it. The Chinese choice of retaliatory tariffs on luxury wines was likely to hit Germany the least.

Bottom-line trade disputes like this confront the rhetoric produced by both sides about harmoniously seeking win–win outcomes with a harsher reality. In many ways they are not only the world's largest trade partners, but also the world's biggest competitors. Frustration became clear in an editorial in the official *People's Daily* issued on 8 June the same year:

> There are at least two negative messages out of the EU's decision to impose punitive duties on solar panels from China: first of all, the EU lacks courage to face the fact and the ability of solving dispute through dialogue. In terms of decision-making, the EU's mechanism has flaws; otherwise, Karel De Gucht, EU trade chief, could not have dominated such sensitive issue [*sic*] alone.

The article said that while trade war is the last thing China wants, 'China did nothing wrong to make its solar industry competitive in price, which is the result of declined price [*sic*] of the raw materials and industrial progress. It has nothing to do with dumping and subsidies.' However, it concluded:

> Reviewing China–EU ties in recent years, the conclusion is that if China and the EU move forward into [*sic*] same direction and focus on cooperation, there is no difficulty that both sides will fail to overcome. But if the [*sic*] both sides don't

take each other's interests and concerns into consideration,
or lack the sincerity of solving disputes through talks, China
and the EU will hardly realize a sound development of the
bilateral ties and economic cooperation.[22]

This follows the traditional patter of Chinese diplomatic attack
on the EU, deployed several times in the past. The personaliza-
tion of the role of De Gucht, painting him as somehow isolated and acting against the interests of EU members, means
that China can carve out space to be friends with those in the
EU who don't agree with this stance. There is a stress on China's
reasonableness and collaborative nature, and its being a victim
rather than a protagonist. There is also the familiar deployment
of veiled threats, and the interesting use of the 'win–win' phrase
elsewhere in the article, with a statement that in this case that
option is simply not going to be achieved unless the EU backs
down. Beyond a categorical general rebuttal, however, the article
is silent on the accusation that subsidies are granted by the state
in China, and on how this might create an unfair advantage for
Chinese manufacturers. Underlying this is a long-standing ideological difference, which is that the EU does not accept that the
state plays the same role in the Chinese economy as European
states do in Europe's. Despite highly detailed and comprehensive
trade agreements and protocols, and many years of experience of
working with each other in the trade area, the EU and China are
still, on this fundamental issue, evidently split in their interpretations and understanding of what a valid free market is. This
is something that the solar panels dispute brings to light. It also
shows that there are no easy means for the two to address this
sort of fundamental difference in outlook.

This issue has not gone away. In 2016, according to some interpretations, the EU was due to accord China 'market economic status'
under the WTO. But with fears of Chinese steel being dumped,

flooding the markets of Europe, and huge lobbying by manufacturers in that and other sectors across the 28 member states, EU
lawyers were still grappling with what latitude they had to oppose
full recognition of China as a market economy, and the concomi-
tant free access it gave to the EU. In this area, at least, trade issues
become deeply political, with arguments raging on both sides about
hypocrisy and double standards. The European Commission's final
proposal for resolving this issue was the logical move of talking not
about countries wholesale as market economies, but about specific
sectors. In this way, China's overcapacity and its claimed dumping
of steel and other goods on the global markets, depressing the
economies there, could be discussed in a framework which was less
politically charged.

MUTUAL INVESTMENT

As already noted, Chinese elite leaders and their spokespeople often
talk of 'win–win' situations. And direct outward investment should
fall happily into this category where the EU is involved. China has
accrued a massive amount of foreign exchange through its exports
in the last three decades, and particularly since joining the WTO. It
needs to find ways of utilizing this capital, and foreign investment
should be an easy one. Since 2008, there have been a number of
attractive assets available in Europe, from financial entities to infrastructure and companies going cheap. China invested in a Greek port
in 2010, and a Chinese company bought Volvo in 2009. Huawei, the
Chinese telecoms company, also has significant interests in Europe,
from the United Kingdom to Germany. Among the key drivers that
have so far been seen of Chinese outward investment, the EU at
least satisfies those that support sales markets and those which are
technology-driven. Even so, the overall amounts of investment from
China in Europe are low. More surprising, European investments

into China, while ranking sixth overall, were less in 2012 than they were in Kazakhstan.[23]

Why this hesitancy on both sides? Jeremy Clegg and Hinrich Voss, in a paper for the EU-funded Europe China Research and Advice Network project, showed the very real differences between member states in their stance on attracting Chinese investment. Some, like the United Kingdom and Germany, have proactive inward investment policies, with an infrastructure to support this. Others have been relatively passive. Despite the competency for inward investment being passed to the European Commission's Directorate-General for Trade from 2012, national members of the Union are least likely to find common cause in this area. They compete between themselves, sometimes undercutting each other. And to Chinese potential investors the barriers to entry that the EU throws up are formidable, with different regulations, tax regimes and employment rules across the member states.[24] The statement by Goodhart at the start of this chapter about few being willing to die for the EU can perhaps be formulated in a new way: few in the member states would even be willing to see growth-generating investment from China go to their neighbours if they do not perceive themselves as directly benefiting from this.

The EU evidently needs more investment, and yet an ambiguity remains about what kind of Chinese investments are welcome, and how they are directed. Huawei has already been noted. It raised particular issues because of the sensitivity of the telecoms sector, and has posed problems in the United States, Australia and other areas. But in the EU, this complex response is reflected across the terrain of the 28 member states, with the United Kingdom allowing large amounts of Huawei involvement, and France and Germany being more wary. The irony therefore of the United Kingdom – a country which has had the most contentious relationship with China since 2012 over issues like Tibet – also being the most open to investment by Chinese companies in sensitive sectors only shows that there is little uniformity across the three issues discussed here. Good investment from China does not follow necessarily from good political links; and poor links do not exclude good economic relations. In this sense, Wen Jiabao's statement about a strategic relationship seeing off the good and the bad issues and giving some stability might make some sense. Where there is pragmatic understanding of material, tangible benefits coming that suit both sides, then no matter how shrill political or trade disagreements might be, these links continue.

This has only been sharpened by the United Kingdom's zealous attitude towards gaining Chinese investment over 2015 and into 2016. The Chinese started to invest in Heathrow Airport, in Anglia Water, bought old brands like Weetabix and Pizza Express, and even Wentworth Golf Course, where they experienced a spectacular fallout over raising membership fees, an act which had antagonized the local community and alienated most of their members. With the proposed idea of Chinese partial investment in the planned nuclear reactor, the first to be built in a generation, at Hinckley Point, a new line seemed to have been crossed. China certainly was building more nuclear power stations than any other nation on earth. But concerns about safety, security and viability lapped against the proposal, with some elsewhere in the EU seeing it as a sign of remarkable nonchalance verging almost on recklessness.

GOING FOR THE BIG PRIZE

Investment matters because the EU and China are interested in each other most where they offer vast and relatively unified markets. This crucial fact is often forgotten. Despite the immense internal differences and wealth levels across the EU and China, therefore, when they are seen as marketplaces, and unified at least around this attribute, then relations between the two make immense sense – and the wisdom of the 1985 agreement and why it still stands today, despite the huge changes that have occurred elsewhere, becomes clear. For Chinese actors, whether government or non-state, and in whatever sector, the EU remains a source of almost half a billion consumers, with per capita levels that, even in the poorest EU member state, at present rank seven times more than those which are the average in China. This per capita wealth difference is often forgotten. The EU includes countries which at the time of writing (2017) rank in the top global economies, from Germany (fourth), France (fifth), the United Kingdom (sixth), Italy (ninth). This is a collection of highly desirable markets to sell into. Seen this way, the Union makes huge sense as a place for China to be interested in, and one where it wants to do much better.

For an EU where growth has been stagnant across the Eurozone and beyond since 2009, access to China's market of emerging consumers is also of immense interest. China's growth rates may fall below the double-digit levels posted during the 2000s, but their current level at around 6.5 per cent means that the country will double its GDP by 2020. There is nowhere else that will see this amount of raw growth and where more middle-class consumers will come online, ready to buy both goods and services. Getting access to this market, and being able to sell into it, offers the single strongest prospect of future growth for European manufacturers and financial service providers. For them, the attractions of being able to sell into the unified, albeit complex market that China offers, with single tariff rates and customs demands, reflects Chinese interest in the unified market of the EU. As market entities, therefore, the EU and China are entirely compatible, and as markets want, and have the incentive, to keep each other as close as possible.

Indeed, the differences between provincial wealth levels in China are far steeper than those between EU states, and in that sense show that it is a more divided and complex internal market than the EU.

Per capita levels of wealth in Shanghai were close to middle-income country levels in 2015, whereas Gansu and other western provinces still rank as poor. These dramatic differences are a much greater challenge to creating a level regulatory, tax and developmental field in China than they might be in the EU. As a market, therefore, the EU still has many advantages and strengths over China. In many ways, its chief economic objective in the next five to ten years is to be able to enjoy a period of strategic advantage over its trading partner to ensure it leverages access to this market.

Making China a potential customer of EU services in the financial and invisibles sectors will be critical here. The EU economies produce more than 80 per cent of their GDP in the service sector. In China, this has yet to reach 50 per cent. The EU has to compete in a global marketplace where China is increasingly regarded as a target, and where fighting for access there is important. As a consortium of nations, the EU has created a natural advantage. It now needs to engage in opening up China to become a consumer of its services, to be a place where its financial sector can operate, and where it can start to see a source of growth.

ONTOLOGICAL DISSONANCE

In their internal configuration, in the very nature of their separate polities, China and the EU have very evident differences, something that the idea of 'civilizational' partnership is evidently geared at trying to come to terms with. This can be called ontological dissonance. In their core identity, in their very nature, they are existentially different. One is a unified sovereign state, and one a coalition of separate nation states. This seems straightforward enough.

Beyond this, however, there are also surprising parallels. China's internal economic diversity is also mapped in the political sphere, where it almost operates like a modern empire rather than a single state, unified by language and certain administrative functions, but also often bewilderingly disparate. This disparity is sharpest in the autonomous regions of Tibet, Xinjiang and to some extent Inner Mongolia, where development levels, language, ethnicity and other markers show difference. Even so, the centralized government in place since 1949 has prevailed, creating a unified fiscal and administrative system which holds everything together. This unity was hard won, and is something the ruling Communist party is keen to boast of in moments of national celebration like the 60th anniversary of the founding of the PRC, in October 2009.

Despite this, it can be challenging to be precise about what sort of state China is. While British journalist Martin Jacques and others have described it as a civilization state, others have more accurately questioned the coherence and continuity of the many entities claimed to have been historic precursors of the modern Chinese state. Questions of state identity, and the ways in which people feel engaged and related to the nation and the state across China, are sometimes as vexed as they are among EU citizens in relation to the EU. At this level, the two share some surprising similarities. Their complexity and vastness alienate people at the grass roots, who wish to relate to something more local and identifiable.

Despite ontological dissonance, the EU and China also share some surprising common frameworks. For example, they are constructs largely of a small elite. In the case of the CCP, this is made up of the 3,000 or so vice minister-level cadres and above who shape it. For the EU, the elite is a centralized bureaucracy of only 18,000. In these two administrations, the deployment of vocabularies has overlaps. The term 'China Dream' used from late 2012 by Xi Jinping occupies the same space as the EU's view, as articulated by people like Mark Leonard, of its mission to raise the living standards of members of each of its states. Hu Jintao, when Party secretary and president in China, talked of the 'historic mission', of China restoring its dignity after what is articulated as the century of humiliation at the hands of foreign and colonial oppressors. Oddly, the EU also has an historic mission, led by its desire to avoid more conflicts like its horrific experiences during World Wars I and II in the first half of the twentieth century, which lay at the heart of the birth of the EU vision and has often been used to justify its increase in scope.

The EU and China refer to their experiences of history, and to being modern entities in charge of ancient historic polities. They also share similarities in their belief in a renaissance, a return to their justified historic space. In this sense, the contentiousness of their relationship is as much due to these ideational similarities as it is to clear market differences.

The impact of the Brexit vote and the ongoing internal challenges of the EU from 2016 onwards matter to China because the stability of the EU matters. The Chinese leaders, inasmuch as they ever take any public position on a matter which is internal, felt that the United Kingdom should remain within the network that EU membership offers. From a country that sets such store in defence of its own sovereignty, this was a telling piece of advice. The decision to leave on 23 June 2016 was greeted initially by bewilderment in Beijing, and then an acknowledgement that a country which had for so long been one of its historic foes and interferers was now in a greatly weakened position and more in need of China's help. Chinese business people began to contemplate the ways in which a developed, highly regulated economy like Britain's would now need to liberalize even more towards foreign investment, and that China would figure high on the list of initial targets. Despite this, China's main interests in the United Kingdom – finance, investment and intellectual partnerships – will all be threatened by a badly handled Brexit. For the EU, too, existential doubt about its fundamental cohesion took the intensity out of its ability, and appetite, to lobby China about human rights and other issues.

It is clear that the EU and China are stuck in a relationship in which they have to work with each other and yet find many areas of dissatisfaction. Perhaps if they were clearer about how they conceptualize each other and were able to locate each other in better frameworks this might help. They need a more sophisticated conceptual language by which to understand each other.

This is a top-down process, and one that can only be done at the level of the most senior leadership – and it is here that there is the largest problem. Wen Jiabao famously committed huge efforts to making sure the EU–China relationship was on the right track. This was despite the challenges that the failed attempt to lift the arms embargo in the early 2000s referred to above had brought, and despite multiple arguments over trade, diplomatic and other matters. With Li Keqiang, from 2013 the EU had to deal with a new and largely untested interlocutor, and within the new Chinese leadership Li initially had to find the Chinese conceptual language for how to engage better with the EU, in a context in which this is clearly not an easy relationship, but one that can't afford to fail. The early hopes of the EU being some kind of benign counterweight to US dominance in a multipolar world are long over. But at the very least, on specific trade and economic issues, the EU does offer an alternative voice which sometimes helps China. The question is whether the label 'civilization partners' helps at all in clearing up these mutual misunderstandings and conceptual lapses. As of early 2017, the auguries are mixed.

6

ZONE FOUR
THE WIDER WORLD

Beyond the United States, the Asia region and the EU, there is a group of other relationships that China has. As an intrinsically global power, it is active in particular as an investor and resource procurer in Africa, Latin America and the Middle East. Each of these regions has developed specific relations with China, but the story is not a straightforward one. Across the 54 countries of the African continent, Chinese influence promised to intensify in the decade after 2005. But this proved a mixed story, with issues looming from 2008 onwards over poor governance of Chinese projects, involvement in arms dealing and evidence of Chinese complicity with local human rights abuses. For the Middle East, China engaged in a delicate balancing act, dependent for much of its imported oil on the region and yet desperate to evade its endless, complicated politics. For Latin America, China's main interests were in securing resources, with huge deals signed during a visit by Li Keqiang in 2015 and by Xi in a follow-up visit in late 2016. This was also a place where Huawei and other Chinese companies were allowed less fettered access than in North America, Australia or Europe. Finally, right on the periphery, there was the question of Chinese emerging interests and activities in the South and North Poles. If nothing else, its figuring in the geopolitics of these remote regions was truly a sign that the era of Global China had well and truly arrived.

Speaking about China's emerging role in the developing world, many commentators regarded this as a new phenomenon. But it was something that had been present, with varying levels of intensity, for many decades. In 1974, when Deng Xiaoping was rehabilitated for the second time, he attended a UN conference where he outlined one of Mao Zedong's pet theories, that of the Third World. Using language that would have sounded very strange coming from his mouth a few years later after the reforms he first sponsored in 1978, he declared that:

> At present, the international situation is most favourable to the developing countries and the peoples of the world. More and more, the old order based on colonialism, imperialism and hegemonism is being undermined and shaken to its foundations. International relations are changing drastically. The whole world is in turbulence and unrest. The situation is one of 'great disorder under heaven', as we Chinese put it. This 'disorder' is a manifestation of the sharpening of all the basic contradictions in the contemporary world. It is accelerating the disintegration and decline of the decadent reactionary forces and stimulating the awakening and growth of the new emerging forces of the people.[1]

In the following paragraph, he went on:

> Judging from the changes in international relations, the world today actually consists of three parts, or three worlds, that are both interconnected and in contradiction to one another. The United States and the Soviet Union make up the First World. The developing countries in Asia, Africa, Latin America and other regions make up the Third World. The developed countries between the two make up the Second World.

Although it was not explicitly stated, China promoted itself as taking the leadership role for the Third World. Delegations of left-wing groups from Africa and Latin America trooped through Beijing, granted aid and largesse, and often were received by the Chairman himself (see later in this chapter). For a country that had, at least on the level of rhetoric, resolutely set itself against all forms of hegemony, there was a clear need to avoid acting like it aimed to be dominant in any way. But critics did find echoes of a new Chinese colonial mentality, with smaller, poorer countries almost figuring as vassal states.

Through the 1990s and into the 2000s, Chinese approaches to what was once called the Third World became more variegated and complex. The 1980s were an anomalous decade, one in which the spotlight was shone on developed countries like Japan, the United States, European nations or Singapore. A look at the top-level leadership delegations over this period testifies to this. Xi Jinping himself first visited the United States in 1985. He was in good company. Deng and almost every other top-level Communist leader took the opportunity to go and take a good look at a country once branded as a die-hard enemy. There was little interest at that time in wandering around Africa or South America. The key objective in these years, instead, was to secure capital – but, more importantly, know-how and technology. The developed world was the clear repository for that.

During the 1990s, however, with its wealth increasing, China figured increasingly as an exemplar, a potential model of development. As one official at the World Bank in Beijing reported to me in 2009, since 1978 China had accrued a huge amount of knowledge about how to develop an economy, and what sort of tactics might work, and it therefore had ways of sharing this with others. The question was, though, whether there was any associated political agenda. The clearest answer to this was in the battle to get diplomatic recognition shifted from the Republic of China on

Taiwan to the PRC. In the 1990s, the situation developed into a multi-nation game of table tennis, where countries vying for support from either Taiwan or China would play one off against the other, shifting allegiance almost overnight. Liberia in 1993, Lesotho and Burkina Faso in 1994, Niger, Senegal and Chad in 1996 and 1997, all ceased recognizing Taiwan. In 2004, Vanuatu managed to maintain diplomatic links with Taiwan for all of seven days before reverting to the PRC, and Dominica shifted allegiance away from the disputed island the same year, with its South American cousin Grenada following in 2005. The net result of this was that by 2009 only 23 countries still recognized Taiwan, although they were mostly tiny. Only Paraguay figured as a significant country in terms of geographical size and population. A diplomatic thaw across the Strait under Hu Jintao and Ma Ying-jeou meant that the jockeying for links ceased, at least until 2013, when Gambia also decided to recognize the PRC instead.

The idea that a cashed-up China was able to buy allegiance from smaller developing countries was one seized on by critics in the United States and elsewhere. Was this a new, more subtle way of the PRC exercising influence and power and bending the world to its own aims during its era of renaissance and re-emergence onto the global stage? Was this a place where evidence could be found of China shaping external relationships in ways which accorded with its own self-centred objectives and preoccupations?

CHINA IN AFRICA: A STORY IN SEARCH OF A PLOT

When European countries and the United States express consternation about Chinese strategies in Africa, they have to confront a sharp problem: their own lamentable history of colonization, enslavement, brutal exploitation and violence across the continent.

This meant that when China established the Forum on China–
Africa Cooperation (FOCAC) in 2000, with meetings held every
three years thereafter, the primary approach was to create a set of
relationships between China and the attending heads of state or
government from approximately 40 countries which were freed of
colonial history and the heavy sense of obligation, with all its associated political issues, that existed when Europe or North America
had attempted to convene large meetings in this way.

China's resurrection in Africa is a fascinating story. Academic
Donovan C. Chau's study of the Maoist era and its strategy towards
the continent covers ambitious aid projects to gain political interference, the importation of as many as 70,000 Chinese to work
on the Tanzanian railways in the late 1960s, the visits by senior
Chinese leaders to court African ones and vice versa, all of which was
occurring from the late 1950s onwards and all of it foreshadowing
behaviour that China was then accused of using 40 years later, in
the twenty-first century.

Things were very different in the mid-twentieth century, though.
Much of its engagement in the past was driven by the PRC's desire
to get enough votes at the UN to acquire the seat occupied by the
Republic of China on Taiwan, which was occupying it at that time. It
achieved this in 1971. China was also far more heavily and explicitly
engaged with internal politics in some of the countries in which
it was present, being linked to support for internal revolutions in
Algeria, where it funded and provided logistics and training to support the anti-French colonial struggle, and less happily in Ghana and
Tanzania, where it got dragged into clashes between post-colonial
competitors in the 1960s. Perhaps the unhappy memory of these
involvements explains China's current wise distancing from most
overt contemporary political engagement in Africa. In the twenty-first century, it is insistent that it is all about material help and
commercial partnership rather than supplying ideological support.
As Li Keqiang said during his 2014 tour of several African countries,

China is a partner that does not lecture. This prior era of closeness
in African–Chinese relations, with all the headaches it led to, must
be the basis behind that principle.[2]

China's engagement post-2000 could be described as amoral and
largely driven by self-interest. Whatever the appetite elsewhere, the
promotion of some kind of illusive China model was not something officials from the Chinese government tended to mention.
To them, the continent was a source of resources, a potentially
important market, and an ally in the UN when their backs were
against the wall. Howard French, a journalist with experience in
both China and several African countries, referred to an extended
visit to the northern and central part of the continent in 2013–14
where he came across many Chinese communities who had come
to live, work and do business. The sense conveyed by his book
was more often than not about individuals pursuing commercial
opportunities, though some of them were linked to the state companies, particularly in the energy sector. Perhaps as many as 750,000
Chinese were resident. The majority of them were unknown to the
Chinese government back home.[3]

The state enterprises – in particular, ones like Sinopec, PetroChina
and the CNOOC – had appeared on analysts' radars from quite
early on. Around 2008, there was talk of a Chinese takeover of
Africa. This was reinforced by the language used by some leaders.
The then president of Senegal, Abdoulaye Wade, in an article
in the *Financial Times*, referred glowingly to his meetings with
Chinese leaders:

> China's approach to our needs is simply better adapted
> than the slow and sometimes patronising post-colonial
> approach of European investors, donor organisations and
> non-governmental organisations. In fact, the Chinese model
> for stimulating rapid economic development has much to
> teach Africa.[4]

This did not stop fierce criticism of Chinese involvement in Sudan, where a vicious civil war was going on and the local leadership were accused of genocide. Nor did it help when a Chinese ship reportedly bearing arms for the pariah state of Zimbabwe was stopped at the dock in South Africa and prevented from making its onward delivery. And the claim that China had tried to influence the 2006 elections in Zambia added fuel to the criticism. By 2007, the situation had become such a reputational problem for China that Liu Guijin was appointed as Special Representative of the Chinese Government on African Affairs. Someone deeply experienced in African diplomacy, Liu had served in the continent and back in Beijing on Africa-related affairs for many decades. But his position was an unenviable one, with the 2008 Olympics and claims that it was a 'genocide games' because of China's African ventures proving particularly taxing.

Human Rights Watch, in a hard-hitting report from 2011, looked at the behaviour of Chinese state mining companies in Zambia. The picture was not good. Long shifts and poor to non-existent safety regimes painted a picture of the Chinese as neo-colonial in their mindsets and acting little different to imperialists from another era. Those that did protest were dismissed by their bosses, or had intolerable pressure placed on them. 'While Zambians working in the country's Chinese-run copper mines welcome the substantial investment and job creation,' the report stated, 'they suffer from abusive employment conditions that fail to meet domestic and international standards and fall short of practices among the copper mining industry elsewhere in Zambia.'[5] British-based academic Stephen Chan, who had himself lived in Africa for a number of years, refers to a Chinese approach to the continent that is often inward-looking and culturally insensitive. Chinese investments in Botswana, with its stable legal system and good levels of governance, or those in South Africa, are a different matter to those in the Democratic Republic of the Congo or Liberia. In that sense,

Chinese economic interaction and behaviour are opportunistic, rather than being led by some grand strategic vision from Beijing.[6]

Chinese leaders have certainly spent quality time in Africa. Hu Jintao and Wen Jiabao went there often enough to earn the label 'frequent flyers'. In 2014, Wen's successor Li Keqiang made one of his most ambitious tours, with an eight-day, four-country trip covering Ethiopia, Angola, Nigeria and Kenya. Showering the usual trade and aid favours liberally as he went, Chinese aid was lifted to US$ 12 billion and a US$ 3.6 billion deal was signed to construct a railway line from Nairobi to Mombasa. Xi Jinping himself visited a year later, attending the FOCAC meeting in Johannesburg, where he grandly announced US$ 60 billion of aid, and the supply of 200,000 technicians. He also embraced a visit to Zimbabwe, source of so much criticism for China only a few years before. 'China supports the resolution of African issues by Africans in the African way,' he stated, promoting the notion of a non-judgemental, sympathetic alternative partner to the West with its moralizing, conditions and demands, even over small amounts of aid.[7]

Some years ago, however, during a conference on EU–China–Africa relations held in Oporto, Portugal in 2006, a European analyst had warned Chinese partners attending that they should beware: 'Africans will use you for Africa's purpose. So don't get too taken in by the warm words and talk of deep partnership.' Xi's approach to the continent can be typified in 2016–17 as more cautious, the harsh lessons of the mid-2000s taken on board and a more pragmatic tone dominating. The ageing leader of Zimbabwe, Robert Mugabe, made a visit to Beijing in August 2014, seeking investment and support at a time when the domestic economy was still ailing badly. For all the talk of friendship and close alliances, the message that Zimbabwe was sent home with was a harder-edged one: to make friends with the West and develop his economy; China could not sign blank cheques. Expectations of up to US$ 27 billion of trade and deals signed while he was courting Chinese leaders did not come through. In the words of one analyst, 'In the end, Mugabe and his team coaxed a less-than-expected deal out of the Chinese authorities, apparently on terms largely set by China.'[8] Soon after, Zimbabwe adopted the US dollar as their national currency, a further sign of trying to look a little less to the East and a bit more to the West, despite the years of antipathy and ill feeling.

Nor was it all roses within Africa itself. China had to contend with suspicion and ill feeling among Africans, who felt that cheap Chinese goods were flooding the local market and that their workers were coming and taking local jobs. Chinese aid projects often stipulated that Chinese workers had to come in and do the labour. There was little visible benefit for ordinary Africans, nor much sign that the two communities intermixed much. And as with so many other areas of the world, the excited talk from 2005 onwards of an imminent Chinese takeover and burgeoning Chinese investments ran alongside a more prosaic story. It was true that in the decade up to 2014, the net annual flows of Chinese money across the continent had skyrocketed to US$ 3.2 billion per annum. And by 2014, it was also true that the stock of Chinese investment had shot up to US$ 32 billion, a 20-fold increase.[9] But despite all this sound and fury, by 2015 Chinese investment only accounted for 3 per cent of total foreign capital being deployed in the continent. It was still overwhelmingly American, French and British actors that were active there.

Perhaps the most significant long-term move over this period has been the appearance of a stronger security dimension in the Africa–China dialogue. Bearing in mind all the previous comments about China historically not being a naval actor, and not wanting a prominent role outside its own region, the announcement that it was proceeding with establishing a naval logistics facility on the east coast of Africa in the impoverished state of Djibouti, mentioned in the Introduction, aroused huge interest: 'by establishing an outpost in the Horn of Africa – more than 4,800 miles away from Beijing and near some of the world's most volatile regions,' the *New York*

Times commented, 'President Xi Jinping is leading the military beyond its historical focus on protecting the nation's borders.'[10] Here was something that could prove truly groundbreaking and significant, especially as this facility was close to a much larger and more comprehensive US one.

The Chinese government themselves were keen to stress, however, that the core driver behind Djibouti was to service its civilian ships taking oil from the Middle East, the largest external source of supply, down towards the Straits of Malacca and into the Indian Ocean and South China Sea. Ships here were vulnerable to attack by pirates, and China had worked with the UN and EU in supplying forces to anti-piracy patrols. Its explanation for a presence in the region therefore was a viable one: solely looking after its own interests, not as some meaningful marker of greater regional dominance. This example demonstrates how tough it was proving for the Chinese to avoid being viewed with suspicion when doing anything outside their region.

To the proposition 'China is promoting a new colonial strategy', a balanced assessment of the country's decade of renaissance and renewed activity across Africa up to 2017 would have to deliver a 'case not proven' verdict. Its trade and investment links, while expanding, have proved modest. Its political role has become more cautious since 2007. Involvement in poorly managed projects was soon recognized as bringing it big reputational losses and was largely addressed. No Chinese state company went into Africa with a cast-iron ambition to exploit and ride roughshod over the local populations. They shared the same hunger for driving hard bargains and getting the best for themselves as anyone else, but the main difference is that they were unrestrained in going full-out for this by opinions back home, which meant they acted impulsively and sometimes without due caution, making mistakes that way. Some Chinese may well have had a sense of superiority and arrogance towards local cultures and populations – but once again this reprehensible behaviour was not without precedent, with North Americans and Europeans having done far worse things in the last century and a half. Interestingly, for Xi Jinping there were no grand new narratives and stories about the continent. It seemed like it intrigued and interested him far less than his own region, the United States or Europe. African countries did not figure in the Belt Road Initiative, nor in the AIIB (except for the membership of South Africa), and only really once again through South Africa in the BRICS bank that China had set up jointly with others in this 'imagined community' and then located in Shanghai. By early 2017, however, BRICS has become less prominent than during its hot phase only a few years before, and currently China's role in Africa still seems to be a story in search of a plot. The earlier excited talk of China being guilty of bullying and hegemony has been replaced by a more nuanced one, where it is often more about mutual confusion.

THE MIDDLE EAST: HIDE AND SEEK[11]

If confusion is the order of the day for China in Africa, in the Middle East it is far more about Beijing seeking desperately to avoid being sucked into commitments and the quagmire of politics in the region. Unlike the United States or the EU, China does not have a specific Middle East policy as such at the moment. It relies on the standard parameters for its foreign policy elsewhere: respect for sovereignty of others, non-interference in the domestic affairs of foreign countries, and support for a multipolar world order opposing great-power hegemony. Unlike the situation in Africa, while China has been diversifying its links across the Middle East region, the political complexity of the area and the ongoing conflicts there have made a risk-averse Chinese leadership even more wary of taking any initiatives.

All this was clear to see when Xi Jinping made his first ever visit to the region in January 2016. As has become the habit under his leadership, a White Paper was issued while he was setting foot in the first country of his three destinations – Egypt. This contained the usual rhetoric about going for 'win–win' outcomes. 'China firmly supports Arab national liberation movement,' the paper's preamble stated, 'firmly supports Arab countries' struggle to uphold sovereignty and territorial integrity, pursue and safeguard national interests, and combat external interference and aggression, and firmly supports Arab countries' cause of developing the national economy and building up the countries.' But the rest of the document is light on specifics, despite this bold start, stating that

> China will continue to carry forward China–Arab traditional friendship, enrich and deepen our all-round, multilayer, wide-ranging cooperation, promote sustainable and sound development of our strategic cooperative relations featuring all-round cooperation and common development, and safeguard peace, stability and development of the region and the world at large.

This simply piles up largely meaningless stock phrases. On the most important and vexed issue of all, security in the region, the paper simply states that

> China calls for a concept of common, comprehensive, cooperative and sustainable security in the Middle East, and supports Arab and regional countries in their efforts to build an inclusive and shared regional collective cooperation security mechanism, so as to realize long-term peace, prosperity and development.[12]

The Middle East in itself is a complex and disunited region, and this complexity is mapped in the modes of engagement between China and its partners there. There is a China–Arab States Cooperation

Forum, founded in 2004, and China has relations with the League of Arab States and the Gulf Cooperation Council. But these are currently low profile and probably not geared up for more ambitious engagement. No Middle East powers sit in the BRICS grouping. In the G20, only Saudi Arabia and Turkey are members. China has not talked, as it does with the EU, of anything approaching a 'strategic partnership' in the existing region, although it has recently started to initiate the desire for this. Its dominant discourse has been almost wholly in terms of economic cooperation, as the 2016 White Paper evidences. And while it has expended time and effort on some of the major countries, it has not, as Russia did over Syria at the UN in 2012, stuck its neck out and defined a policy position which might isolate it. It has followed the lead of others, as it did with the veto at the UN over action in Syria, where it followed Russia's lead.

Where the Chinese–Middle Eastern relationship is unique is in both partners' dependence on China's domestic energy policies and its energy needs. This means that Chinese policy in the region is almost solely driven by the imperative to preserve its access to resources there by maintaining close relationships with its core suppliers in the Middle East. It is likely that unless China finds alternative sources of energy, it will need to deepen its political and security role in the region for this reason alone, and that the management of this will require considerable diplomatic skill. However reluctant, therefore, China is likely to become an increasingly important player for the Middle East, with a potential knock-on effect in its relations with other key players there – particularly the United States and Russia. As Xi Jinping moved through the region in January 2016, his tour captured this, going from the firmest and most long-standing of Beijing's allies, Egypt, the earliest Arab state to confer recognition on the PRC, to Saudi Arabia and Iran, which were embroiled in a furious argument over the execution by Riyadh of a Shia cleric the month before. China's Middle East relations are best described as a resolute attempt to keep things simple, focus on one specific area and avoid the temptation to make things more complex by getting involved in other problems which Beijing is unwilling, and unequipped, to cope with, focused on one specific area, and avoiding the intrusion of other problems which Beijing does not feel it should get involved with, nor believe it has any specific measures or ideas to cope with.

For all the sporadic frustration that the outside world might express towards China on this position, there are sound reasons for holding to it. For it, the Middle East is high-risk territory. It is largely as a zone under the influence of either the United States or in some cases Russia, a place which had highly problematic internal politics, and where there is the lack of a grand overarching narrative for relationship with China. The main forum for discussions between the two is the Gulf Cooperation Council and the China–Arab States Cooperation Forum (CASCF), low-profile multilateral gatherings. This is despite all the grand talk in the 2016 White Paper of relations having a history going back two millennia. Foreign Minister Wang Yi, for instance, at the sixth ministerial meeting of CASCF held in Switzerland in January 2014, simply stated that both sides needed to 'enhance communication and cooperation'. With the Gulf Cooperation Council, China has largely been discussing a free-trade agreement. But this is a long way from the coherence and ambition of the bold narrative frameworks mentioned previously in this book, of 'great power relations' with the United States and 'civilizational partnership' with the EU. Whatever solidarity China gains from its status as a post-colonial survivor now on the trajectory to being a major power again, the Middle Eastern post-colonial legacy has been marred by continuing disunity and state breakdown, from the Iran–Iraq War of the 1980s to the first and second attacks on Iraq by the United States in the 1990s and 2000s, to the wave of protests from 2010 which created the Jasmine Revolution. For the Chinese, the Middle East post-colonial response is one of failure and instability.

Were the Middle East to have no oil reserves, China would almost certainly steer clear of any significant commitment at all. But it is in this one area at least that the region is of great strategic importance, and it has to be given higher priority. So while Chinese policy makers in many ways operate according to the historic template discussed above in terms of traditional diplomacy, relegating the Middle East to the outer zone of their interest, it is prioritized as a partner when it comes to oil supply. This perhaps explains some of the slightly schizophrenic behaviour of Chinese policy in the region – sometimes close and enthusiastic, but sometimes tepid and risk-averse. The region belongs to two places in the Chinese conception of its world, and there is no fresh consensus on where precisely it should be located.

Bluntly stating that the region is important as an energy supplier is, understandably, not that satisfying. But the provision of something deeper and more 'shared' between both regions is hardly assisted by the great cultural distance between the two, and the disparity among China's specific bilateral bonds in the region. Up until now China has guided its actions in the Middle East on the principle of not wanting to expend precious geopolitical capital there, particularly against the United States, when it has other areas to prioritize such as its own regional neighbourhood. Avoiding getting sucked into obligations that tie its hands, and engaging in a mission to limit itself to rhetorical commitments without being recruited to support any of the opposing parties in the area, is hardly an exciting and dynamic framework within which to operate.

China's energy links have become increasingly important, however, due to rising domestic demand and a need to diversify its supply partners, and this now gives it a new imperative to revitalize and refresh this framework. Its preferred position of neutrality is being challenged, and it will in the future need to make larger and bolder commitments to partners in the region, even if only to preserve its self-interest. This is not just about oil, however. China also looks upon the terrorist ideology and mission of more extreme actors in the Middle East with real concern, as this reflects the increasingly unsettled situation in China's western regions, particularly in Xinjiang. Ominously, late in 2015 a Chinese national, Fan Jinghui, was taken hostage by Daesh, the insurgent force controlling large swathes of Syria, and brutally executed in November. So far, the links between extremists in China and those in the Middle East are low priority for Daesh and others, but Beijing has figured in their language as a legitimate target for anger and recriminations because of its control over Xinjiang. It would be a nightmare for Xi Jinping's China to suddenly face an increasingly internationalized extremist terrorist group, adding to the pain and panic that has already been caused by events such as the suicide bombs in Beijing and mass knife attacks in Kunming over 2014.

In the area of economic cooperation, at least, things should be straightforward, and statistics bear that out. Up to 2016, the most that Chinese leaders were willing to say was that they were 'eyeing the establishment of a strategic partnership, using the FTA as a driving force to boost pragmatic cooperation in all fields' (the words of Foreign Minister Wang Yi, in January 2014). During Xi Jinping's visit, trade and economic links figured high in the agenda as usual. US$ 55 billion was offered in aid, with bilateral trade with Iran scheduled to reach US$ 600 billion before 2015. In view of the fact that this only stood at US$ 54 billion in 2014, this was an ambitious target. The difference was that after 2016, China could enjoy the lack of US-imposed sanctions on a denuclearizing Iran. The region also figures in the Belt Road Initiative universe, at its edges.

In the last three decades, China's greatest feat has been political: its maintenance of good relations with almost all Middle Eastern countries, who on the whole have sought to reciprocate this. It has experienced none of the conflicts over human rights, Tibet or Taiwan that tend to complicate its relations with the EU, the United States and other partners. In Latin America and Africa, for example, a number of countries still recognize Taiwan, whereas none do in the Middle East. The Middle East countries, in addition, are not likely to discover a deep interest in the issue of Tibet or to put pressure on China over human rights, as many of them have been repeatedly castigated by international agencies for having even worse records.

With the Israel–Palestine conflict, China has maintained a position where it enjoys good links to both parties – and indeed was a strong ally of the Palestinian Liberation Front under Arafat in the 1980s – yet avoids being sucked into taking sides. It has friendly relations with Israel, even to the extent that Israel was accused in the 1990s of supplying it with sensitive radar equipment, offending its key ally, the US. Some have even speculated about whether China can fulfil a peace-brokering role because of its unique position, but so far it has resisted this, simply standing by its rhetoric of preserving peace and stability.

The Jasmine Revolution period, which began in 2010, posed a difficult moment of uncertainty and offered the strongest test to its pragmatic, largely non-committal stance. Beijing banned discussion of the revolutions on the internet domestically, and clamped down on any activists after 2010 who attempted to draw parallels with the situation in Egypt and Libya and what was happening in China. Some Chinese officials simply stated that the Jasmine protests were against inefficient governance, and in China's case no such charges could be laid against it. Despite this, the removal of Mubarak in Egypt, the collapse of Gaddafi's regime in Libya and the uprisings in Syria deeply unsettled China. In Libya, it simply abstained from the 2011 UN vote supporting military involvement, feeling when the full NATO actions occurred that it had been short-changed into something far greater than it had originally expected. It had to ship out more than 36,000 citizens from the area in its largest ever repatriation, revealing just how extensive its energy and economic interests had grown in the region.

The Libya experience framed its subsequent response to Syria, where it stood with Russia despite immense pressure from the United States and the United Kingdom, and voted against any military involvement. In view of the ongoing instability in Egypt and Libya, it now probably feels vindicated in its belief that the United States and its allies were naive in thinking that political reform along the lines originally envisaged was really going to offer quick and sustainable solutions. As a pragmatic actor, China seems to understand the highly tribal and disunited nature of politics in the Middle East area.

Since 2011, the horrendous conflict in Syria, and the subsequent emergence of ISIS, has shown the strengths and weaknesses of the Chinese position. While it has been proved right in its scepticism about the effectiveness of sweeping away former regimes and replacing them with new, weaker ones, the moral bankruptcy of simply standing back and watching Syria self-destruct has shown that the world's second biggest economy has little geopolitical imagination when it comes to trying to solve the problems of a region to which it has increasing material links. Despite sporadically promising to take a more active stance, the most that China has offered is humanitarian assistance. The ISIS challenge does link to radical Muslim action in its own country, and a spate of terrorist attacks in China has only heightened this awareness. China, therefore, whether it likes it or not, has gradually been forced to take a position because of domestic challenges arising from international issues in the Middle East. Dependence on oil imports is only likely to accelerate that trend.

Focus on oil gives coherence to the Chinese story in the region. While China's prime source of energy is coal, 20 per cent now comes from oil. This is unlikely to change. Since 1993, China has imported more oil than it can source domestically, and now more than 50 per cent of oil imports come from the Middle East. This, more than anything else, gives China a direct interest in the Middle Eastern region. It has signed major deals with Iran, Saudi Arabia and others. Within the Belt Road Initiative rubric, revivifying logistics and trade routes between China and Europe through Central Asia and into the Middle East supplies much-needed diversification.

In terms of tangible economic links, China's figures have grown despite the unrest since 2010, with Saudi Arabia, Iran, Egypt, the UAE and Iraq figuring among its top commitments pre-2014. Middle Eastern investments into China are negligible by comparison, with only Turkey, Israel and Kuwait making any meaningful commitments, and none of these more than US$ 189 million worth of stock (Israel). The vast majority of Chinese involvement is in energy projects, with some diversification recently into tourist infrastructure. China's most important economic actors in the region are the state energy companies – Sinopec, PetroChina and the Chinese Offshore Overseas Oil Corporation.

With Iran, China has intimated at something more substantial, flowing from the political into the economic and highlighting an area where it is able to work with partners like the United States and the EU over contentious issues. China was a significant investor in the country even during the period when it was in effect a pariah state after being named one of the three members of the 'Axis of Evil' by George W. Bush in his State of the Union address in 2002 (the others were Iraq and North Korea). China continued to enjoy positive relations with Iranian leaders through their attendance as observers at the SCO, a Central China and Inner Asia grouping of powers. When visiting Tehran in May 2014, Chinese minister of defence Chang Wanquan alluded to something deeper when he stated that he wanted to 'deepen defence relations'. According to the Xinhua news agency, Chang told Iranian defence minister Hossein Dehqan that the development of bilateral relations has 'remained positive and steady, featuring frequent high-level exchanges and deepened political mutual trust'. This was in the context of US accusations that a Chinese businessman had imported arms to Iran, something which China expressed anger over and where some aspects

of relations between Iran and the United States and EU showed the
first signs of thawing.

In 2015, as the United States and its partners edged closer to a
freeze on Iran's nuclear production, China took a supportive role,
using its leverage in Tehran. Chinese foreign minister Wang Yi,
when visiting the country in February 2015, said, 'Talks on the
Iran nuclear issue face an historic opportunity, and striking a comprehensive deal on schedule is the trend of the times and the desire
of the people,' urging his Iranian hosts on by stating:

> Reaching comprehensive agreement is beneficial to Iran
> upholding its own legal rights, including the right to the
> peaceful use of nuclear power, and for the people of Iran to
> throw off the difficulties of sanctions as early as possible and
> focus on energetically developing the economy.

This was the sort of statement that Beijing was making as a matter
of course to its so-called ally in Pyongyang.[13] With the successful
completion of the deal in July of the same year, and the benediction
of China as a permanent member of the UN Security Council, China
stood to gain from the lifting of sanctions and the possibility of
further investment into Iran unfettered by legal constraints. It was
also an example of where China could say it was supporting prin-
cipled behaviour – stopping proliferation of nuclear weapons – in
concert with other partners, and acting in a properly multilateralist
way. The only downside was the way in which its support for Iran's
denuclearization laid it open to pressure to be more bullish towards
North Korea, which, in principle, offered a very similar case.

Despite this example of proactivity, in their mission to find more
diverse diplomatic partners the current leadership in China will
regard Africa, Latin America and others as far more straightforward
than ones in the Middle East. Saudi Arabia remains the most stable
and substantial. Historic links to Egypt are good, but marred by

the present instability in the country. It is therefore unlikely that Xi Jinping or his colleagues will want to take the risk of a new approach to the Middle East, unless they are forced to. The latter is made more likely by the increasingly worrying disunity in the region, and by the threat of the United States through isolationism pushing China into having to take a more proactive stand simply to protect its own interests. Sitting on the fence – China's preferred option – has worked fine up to now. But the fence is looking increasingly wobbly, and China will, whether it likes it or not, have to think very hard of feasible actions to take once its comfortable neutral position is blown away.

CHINA IN LATIN AMERICA: THE WEAKEST LINK?

South America offers a specific set of challenges to Chinese foreign policy. Rich in resources that China currently needs, it also poses sharp political issues; a number of Latin American countries still recognize Taiwan over Beijing, and it remains firmly, almost jealously, within the US zone of closest military and political influence. The last thing China would wish for would be to be accused of meddling in the region. It does not have specific forum as with Asia, Europe, Africa or the Middle East to collectively engage with Latin American countries except through the tepid, and somewhat tendentious BRICS framework. Nor does Latin America figure in the imagined Belt Road Initiative community, or take any role beyond Brazil's membership in the AIIB. And yet under Xi, it is seeking what has been described as 'an upgraded relationship', something new and meaningful, backed up by an increase in high-level visits and promises of trade and investment increases since 2013. What designs does China have on an area in which it has only weak historic links, and very faint cultural and geopolitical ones?

Some analysts try to make sense of this by applying the 'south–south' concept. In this theory, Chinese approaches and ideas about development are taken as inspirational by countries seeking to develop their economies, manufacturing industries and infrastructure. This idea is partially behind the 'Beijing Consensus' model which had been discussed earlier in the 2000s. If a 'south–south' mentality did exist in the minds of Beijing officials, then it was an important change, signalling a clearer connection with the Latin American world. In the Maoist period, the only real link had been through support of the revolutionary struggle in Cuba, and of other workers' movements. Che Guevara had even met with Mao Zedong as part of a delegation to Beijing in 1960. While the approach, showing solidarity and sometimes giving financial support to left-wing protest groups, was similar to that deployed in Africa, what was different was the lack of any significant aid projects.

Such paucity of clear content was evident almost three decades later when a White Paper was issued on the region and the Caribbean by the State Council in 2008. That had dealt with the relative lack of shared history by blandly stating that the region mattered to China because 'Latin America and the Caribbean have a long history, vast territory and abundant resources, and the region enjoys a good foundation for economic and social growth and huge development potential.' To fulfil this, the paper proposed four pillars of engagement: promote dialogue, deepen cooperation, draw on each other's strengths to boost common progress and adhere to the 'one China' principle.[14]

This stark combination of the search for some kind of mutual cultural recognition alongside the promotion of raw-blooded economic cooperation based on self-interest has been well illustrated by high-level visits since 2013. After having no top leaders descend on their neighbourhood for over a decade, Xi Jinping came not once but thrice between 2013 and 2016, with his second visit, in

July 2014, lasting an epic ten days. Quite why a Chinese premier wished to lavish such attention on the area does need an explanation, with his first trip – embracing Trinidad and Tobago, Costa Rica and Mexico – fitted in just before his visit to Sunnylands in the United States to see President Obama, and his second taking in Brazil, Argentina, Venezuela and Cuba. The third was largely to attend the Asia–Pacific Economic Conference in Peru. As US analyst Michael Swaine pointed out, beyond the geopolitical fun of messing around in the United States' backyard, returning it some of the favours it has been handing out in China's area of strategic interest in Asia, there was something very striking. Between 2000 and 2013, Chinese trade across the whole Latin American area had skyrocketed from US$ 12 billion to US$ 261 billion, with US$ 65 billion in direct investment. These figures had made China the second largest trading partner, after the United States, and the third largest investor.[15]

But the focus on pursuing economic opportunity has also been cloaked in a more ameliorating language of cultural appeal and the creation of people-to-people links. In this context, the lack of any heavy history of colonial mutual involvement or victimhood serves as a liberating factor, and an opportunity. When Premier Li Keqiang made his visit to four countries in the region in May 2015 – Brazil, Peru, Colombia and Chile – the descriptions emanating from the tour had an almost dreamlike quality, a world away from the hard and fast statistics usually showered down when top Chinese leaders visited. For Colombia, the idea was 'literature as the bridge'. 'Li has proposed that China and Latin America strengthen not just material but also spiritual cooperation,' the Xinhua report recorded, after his attendance at a literature summit in which Nobel Prize laureate Mo Yan had been in attendance, 'and rely on the power of literature to achieve heart-to-heart communication.'[16] For Peru, the idea was 'ancient civilizations, modern connections'. For the region as a whole, it was 'mutual understanding'.

Is there much mutual understanding at present? If it is strengthened, then it has to take into account a number of factors impacting
on it. Criticisms of China in the region focus on two main areas.
The first was in claims that Chinese investment in commodities was
having a deleterious impact on the environment. A report issued
in 2015 by Boston University's Global Economic Governance
Initiative stated that

> The Latin American commodity boom was largely driven by
> new trade and investment with China, and concentrated in
> the petroleum, mineral extraction, and agricultural sectors –
> sectors endemic to environmental degradation and often the
> source of social conflict over rights and working conditions.[17]

The report made clear that China should not take sole responsibility for this. As in Africa, there were plenty of issues with poor
governance and corruption in the host countries. But through the
1990s and into the 2000s, it was predominantly Chinese state
companies that were accused of involvement in serious environmental issues with their South American investments. These figured
in the previously cited Joshua Kurlantzick study of soft-power
issues, with Peruvian mines and their particularly poor safety and
environmental record under a Chinese state owner coming in for
particular criticism. A particularly hysterical account of the negative
sides of Chinese investment into the region appeared in a further
study published by two investigative reporters a few years later. For
Heriberto Araújo and Juan Pablo Cardenal, the issue almost figured
as a global 'yellow peril' phenomenon, in which masses of Chinese
workers were fanning out over the planet, taking up jobs, investing
in order to control and manipulate, and generally exemplifying the
emergence of a new imperium.[18]

The second was the uncomfortable fact that, for all the talk of
grand amounts of investment and new project financing going into

the region from Beijing, what was promised and what was delivered rarely matched up. This issue had been pointed out earlier, and in a more general context, by economist Joe Studwell in a book on the disparity between the huge figures promised when Chinese leaders travelled abroad, and what actually happened after they had returned home.[19] Even when China had been a far smaller economy, these trade deals had reached eye-watering amounts. By the 2010s, the usual figure was in the billions. Li's trip to the region in 2015 saw US$ 53 billion signed up. A Brazil–China Business Council report sobered up excited observers by showing that in the period from 2007 to 2012, only a third of the announced figures of inward investment were actually realized.[20] Those listening to Li's announcements in 2015 who had been present during previous high-level outward visits from China might have been forgiven for having reservations.

Added to these two issues is the simple fact that, as of early 2017, of the 22 countries in the world remaining who still confer diplomatic recognition on the Republic of China on Taiwan, 12 of them are in Latin America, with countries such as El Salvador, Guatemala, Nicaragua, Honduras, Panama and Paraguay all still recognizing Taipei. Throughout the early 2000s, a diplomatic tussle took place with some Latin American countries and their diplomatic allegiances. Costa Rica was infamously 'bought' (according to its critics) by hefty aid and investment inducements to shift recognition to Beijing in 2007. Taiwan was able to persuade St Lucia to swap from recognition of the People's Republic back to Taiwan the same year. A truce in seeking diplomatic recognition and swaps has largely been in place since the return of the nationalists under Ma Ying-jeou in 2008. However, the election of Tsai Ing-wen as president of Taiwan at the head of the more pro-independence Democratic Progressive Party in 2016 might prefigure another era of diplomatic tussles. China will base this on the immense economic leverage that it is starting to have in the region.

BEYOND ALL OF THIS: THE POLAR CAPS

One of the unique features of Xi Jinping's CV was the fact that, by 2014, he had visited every single state and territory in Australia in the previous three decades except the remote southern island of Tasmania. That was rectified in November 2014, when, after the G20 was convened for that year in Brisbane in the north-east of Queensland, Xi took a flight first to Canberra, and then from there on to Hobart, the small city facing out to the Antarctic Ocean on the southern point of the island.

There was a good strategic reason for this brief visit. The Antarctic is the ultimate form of diplomacy in the style of Chinese 'Go'. A 1956 treaty ratified in 1983 by China and involving 52 countries prohibits military activity and resource exploitation on the vast polar caps in the Southern hemisphere. But as a report made clear in 2013, there might be as much as 200 million barrels of oil in the region. It was for this reason that Xi Jinping was quoted as stating at a Politburo meeting that China needed to 'take advantage of ocean and polar resources'.[21] The most remarkable issue around the Antarctica region is that sovereignty over parts of it seems to be a matter of planting a flag next to an installation and laying a claim to it. As of 2017, the United States has five such structures, with the Australians operating three. China is making up for lost time, with four already functional, including the Great Wall Station on the periphery of the ice mass, another on King George Island, opened in 1985, and three other 'research stations' dotted across the vast territory.

The Antarctic clearly has value for everyone in terms of its untapped water, resources and fish. It is also a beautifully remote part of the earth, one which receives next to no attention while everyone's eyes are diverted to places like the Middle East, Europe or North America. The fact therefore that in such a supremely isolated and harsh place China has upped its investments in the last few years to US$ 55 million is striking.[22] The 1956 treaty is due for review in 2048, and at that stage there might be options to develop more resource exploitation with technology which is better and more suited to the unique attributes of the region than that which exists today. Meanwhile, China is staking out spaces of interest and control, in ways that almost map its general geopolitical strategy.

What is most remarkable about the Chinese strategy in the South Pole (and it clearly is a strategy, linked to Xi Jinping's benediction from 2013 at the Politburo meeting mentioned earlier in this chapter and his subsequent physical visit so close to the area) is how Chinese thinking can now embrace a region and area which is so far from its traditional zones of focus and concern. If there was proof of China's graduation to a truly global power, then this is it. It is supplemented by China's interests in the North Pole, through its admission in 2013 as an observer to the Arctic Council, a forum set up by states with territory in the Arctic, founded in 1996. As with Antarctica, China's interests are a mixture of strategic and practical. But the Arctic is a busier space, with major players like the United States, Canada and Russia all claiming large parts of the marine territory through the extent of their Economic Exclusion Zones (EEZ). While investing more in the North Pole (where it has more latitude), the South Pole has importance as a potential source of resources (though very hard to access and exploit at the moment), shipping lines (the ship *Xuelong* was able to make the first ever Arctic crossing by a Chinese vessel in 2012, cutting a possible 6,000 kilometres off the alternative route via the Suez Canal and through the Indian Ocean, though through waters unnavigable for much of the year) and science. The last of these should not be underestimated. Both in the North and South Poles, China has the opportunity to demonstrate that it can be on the cutting edge of research, looking to extract, for instance, buried ice which contains molecules from over a million years before, giving evidence of the earth's climatic situation then.

For all the tepid talk about China simply being an observer, and being present through an interest in generic issues like climate change, research and environmental protection, the activities of its state and non-state companies, in, for instance, trying to buy tracts of land in Greenland for iron ore, or Iceland for tourism, arouse complaints that there is a larger strategy behind all of this. One of the anomalies of the Arctic region is that it is a place with no sovereignty, which has prompted Chinese thinkers to argue that China has as much right to be there as anyone else. Interestingly, this desire overrode its fury at Norway for giving the 2010 Nobel Peace Prize to imprisoned Chinese dissident Liu Xiaobo. For all the splenetic rage it expressed back then, China maintained dialogue over Arctic issues – around which, of course, Norway is an important player – and also established a research base in 2014 on the Norwegian peninsula. China has travelled in the space of half a century from having one ambassador based abroad in 1966, to drawing close to having Arctic and Antarctic strategies. This is a remarkable testament to its reach and global status.[23]

CONCLUSION
TELLING THE CHINA STORY

Of all its major contradictions, one of the most evident is that China is old and new at the same time. Its leaders never cease to enjoy deploying the line that China is an ancient civilization, with Jiang Zemin even inflating the period of antiquity from four to five thousand years. His successors have been more than happy to echo this line, with Xi Jinping stating proudly in his address to the EU in 2014 that China's continuous civilization is the oldest on the planet, marking the country out for special treatment. Trying to work out the tangible source of this claim to continuity has proved hard work. It is certainly true that in terms of continuous use of a specific 'script', a recorded imperial history and its associated culture, then China does have (using what the late anthropologist Benedict Anderson called in a different context) an imagined community – albeit one which is complex and diffuse.

This diversity in China's many pasts, and the many places where that past has taken place, stands alongside the stark and irrefutable fact that the People's Republic of China has only existed since 1949. This is a very new history, and the PRC is a very young country. It stands beside the United States, with territorial integrity and political structures largely in place for a century and a half, or European countries like Great Britain, with state traditions and habits that reach back over 1,000 years. China is a new member of this community, made all the newer by being a country that has only figured as a member of the United Nations since 1971, and one which has only appeared on any economic radars since the late 1970s. This has given the PRC a layered identity which is fresher, and more recent, than any other power of a similar size and reach.

The sheer scale of the PRC's emergence and rise is something that has woven its way through this book, and gives a leader like Xi Jinping an enormous political asset. China's status on the world stage is hugely important domestically, and is something that recent leaders have gained from. That their country is now included in almost all top decision-making bodies, and is an important player in all key global debates, from the economic to the political to the environmental, goes without saying. The story behind Xi Jinping's remarkably high number of foreign trips from 2013 onwards is simply to make crystal clear how truly global his country is now. And its global era really only began after the reforms of 1978. Before that, China had only the faintest interest in playing anything like a global role, and regarded the outside world mostly as a place of threat, potential interference and hostility. It was a country that had taught itself enclosure and self-protection.

This newness means that the high expectations we sometimes have of Chinese diplomacy are misplaced. In many ways it is remarkable how few arguments China has had with the world since 1979. The choice of pursuing a relentlessly economic priority has meant that it has been able to create a parallel order, a power demonstrated not through guns, weapons and naval assets, but through trade links, investment and reciprocal demonstration of material interests. Looked at this way, the 120 plus countries in which the United States has military installations pale in comparison with the 130 plus countries with whom China enjoys the status of largest trading partner.

This prominence is far harder to interpret as predatory and controlling. It is, as China's frequent language about 'win–win' and mutuality makes clear, all about both sides seeing clear benefit. That approach is appealing. It sits next to the declarations of non-inter-ference, non-judgemental postures and good old-fashioned respect. China is a new kind of opportunity, a new kind of actor in the tale, embracing the world through its outward-looking leader, contrib-uting simply by being able to feed, clothe and look after the fifth of humanity living within its borders. This China offers a fresh take, replacing the weary tropes of US dominance.

The development of this story, however, is now at a very sig-nificant and potentially very treacherous moment. We return to the Djibouti installation with which this book started, and the immediate suspicion this aroused in 2015. We also address the complaints among its neighbours that China is assertive, building permanent structures in the South and East China Sea, staking out territorial claims like some wily player of the ancient 'Go' chess game (a metaphor returned to several times in this book), studying Kissinger tactics and carefully delineating, then annexing, space. For the key tacticians in China, at least since the 2000s, the effort has been how to avoid the sort of Mearsheimer nightmare of great-power conflict. The premise here is that China will achieve its aim and become a great power. The issue is how the United States will respond, and what sort of space it will grant to a new, non-hegemonist, but aspiring great power. Xi Jinping's words in the United States in 2013 about the Pacific being big enough for both countries sounded bold at the time, and they may simply prove wrong. China's attempts to convey a message in which it is regarded as benign, positive and good sit beside the amorality of some of its state companies' behaviour, the clear distrust surrounding its cyber-security tactics, the real issues with its resistance to responsibility to protect ideas, and, finally, the greatest elephant in the room – its unique domestic politics and the way these sit antagonistically beside the grand narratives of democratic development being pursued and supported by the United States and its allies. All of this has only been exacerbated by the election of Donald Trump, who puts China in a rather bewildering position: on the one hand, his election offers the PRC a great opportunity, and on the other the new president's unpredictable nature and contradictory statements on China make the United States potentially a very serious threat.

A democratic China, with multiparty elections and a nice, civil four- or five-year cycle of presidential plebiscites, would be a fine thing, the delivery of a dream to many in the Washington establishment. Commentators there felt the whole point in engaging with the Communist-led country from the 1970s onwards was to see it finally change and become like them. But as my chapter on the United States–China relationship made clear, when the moment of great opportunity came in 1989, the United States lost its nerve, and the Communist Party was given breathing space. It reasserted authority and control, poured even more resources into the track it was following – of economic development as the key to everything – and, on this immense gamble, was proved resoundingly right. The USSR fell in 1991, along with half of the one-party regimes in Eastern Europe. In the 2000s, the colour revolutions upended the politics of Central Asia in the zone of the former Soviet empire. Mongolia held elections from the early 1990s, right next to China's northern border, and in 1996 Taiwan held its historic first democratic presidential campaigns.

But through all this change, while China's economy and society were convulsed by an almost feverish transformative energy, the Communist Party maintained control. In early 2017, under Xi Jinping, it looks further from falling from power than it has done at any time in the previous two decades. He has proved, so far, a popular leader on the street, with his anti-corruption struggle and the fulfilment of the promise that constituted the very first words he spoke when emerging as the key leader in November 2012: to 'close the gap between the people and the Party'.

For Xi's China, the outside world is infected by this ambiguity that presides over almost everything the PRC gets involved with.

The outside world is a theatre of opportunity, but China must resolutely resist some aspects of it. It is fine for the PRC to comply with other countries' norms when dealing with the outside world, but within the country itself, its companies, organizations and people must operate on China's terms. He and his colleagues, in word and deed, know the importance of the world around them. But laden down with the resentment which originates in the long history of humiliation, they are also married to a domestic political strategy of demonstrating whenever they can that the outside world must increasingly deal with China on its own terms. And that includes accepting its political model and the idea that far from being an alien construct, the Chinese Communist Party in the twenty-first century is an expression of the country's unique cultural identity, and inextricably linked to its aspirations to be a great, modern power restored to its rightful moral and geopolitical place.

For Xi Jinping, the current era of China's development is a treacherous one. The 'middle-income trap' – where rising manufacturing costs lead to relocation of factories outside of the country but new industries don't grow quickly enough to replace them in the economy – is one of a whole range of headaches. Trying to maintain growth and momentum during the transition from export-orientated, primarily industry-led manufacturing models to a high-consuming service-sector model is another. So is keeping up with people's vast expectations, their desire for a decent health service, good social welfare, pensions and the other good things that more and more of them see with their own eyes as they travel around Europe, Australia or America and directly experience lifestyles there. In this era of hard change, many things can go wrong. And the old mantra in the Hu years of simply referring to spectacular growth, and allowing that to silence critics, no longer pays off. The simple fact is that the whole message of the ruling Party under Xi must change – and it *is* changing.

Throughout 2013 and on into the following years, during his 'frequent flying' era, Xi showed that not only was he the face of China, but its flatterer-in-chief. The world had asked for more of an indication of what role China wanted to take, and how it saw its new status, and Xi fulfilled that with the grand narrative frameworks discussed throughout this book, mapping out a world of zones of importance around China, from the United States outwards. But in addition to this, he married remarkably harsh and authoritarian actions back home (230 plus rights lawyers apprehended during 2015 alone, with many handed sentences or sent to trial) with words of soothing reassurance while he travelled throughout Russia, America and Europe. Speaking in Seattle in 2015, Xi declared that there was no 'house of cards', a reference to the popular TV drama series about the brutal politics involved in the anti-corruption struggle at the top of the US system. China was simply cleaning up its governance, making itself more efficient, showing greater stability. Surely that was good for the world? In ways that his predecessor Hu Jintao never had, Xi gave interviews to the media, no matter how tightly managed these interactions were. He referenced Russian authors in Russia, German ones in Germany, and made the obligatory reference to Shakespeare while lauding the emergence of the United Kingdom–China 'golden age' in London in 2015.

One often overlooked angle of these overseas trips is related to who the audience is. As the world's second most powerful leader after the US president, it would be fair to think Xi might be a household name. However, his 2015 visits to the United Kingdom and the United States proved this would be a bold claim to make. In the United Kingdom, beyond media coverage about protestors and controversy over proposed Chinese investment in a potential nuclear plant, the only images of the PRC leader that gained much traction were ones of him sipping a pint of IPA beer in a country pub, and a selfie with a Manchester City soccer player and British prime minister David Cameron. The recognition of Xi's name in the

United Kingdom remained remarkably low. In the United States, this was even more striking. In a visit taking place at the same time, ironically it was Pope Francis, the leader of the only European country to still recognize Taiwan, who featured most in the press; Xi barely registered on news media. This was not down to his personality – he is not an introvert like his predecessor Hu Jintao – but largely because the US newspaper-buying and news-watching public were not that interested in knowing about him.

Nor did Chinese media handlers allow Xi much public access in the countries he went to – the danger of mishap was too high. High levels of control and media planning mean that he exists behind a phalanx of bodyguards and minders. The key audience for his travels was the people back in China, who were exposed to their globetrotting leader conquering the world through his speeches, investment figures and soothing messages about the rise of a new, proud country. Observing these foreign visits by Chinese leaders, particularly those of Xi himself, gives rise to an impression of a parallel universe, where on the one hand there is jubilant, all-conquering diplomatic success, and on the other extraordinarily retentive indifference or ignorance about China within the countries he travels to. For the domestic constituency, the danger is overstating China's role in the world from the manipulation of the media information they are fed. For those outside of China, it is underestimating it.

Within China, foreign interests have taken a battering. The travails of GlaxoSmithKline (GSK) in 2014 are a case in point, with the detention of some of its staff and their incarceration for alleged corruption and mis-selling of pharmaceutical products to Chinese doctors. Pharmaceuticals have been a growth area in China, with a population increasingly suffering from the same ailments as the West – obesity, lung and heart disease, cancers – the grim downside of the new Western lifestyles the Chinese are experiencing. Increasingly, Western-style medicine and medicine practices are the treatment of choice. And with low trust in local products, carrying a brand from Europe or the United States goes a long way. Doctors overprescribe medicine because of the kickbacks they get. Revenues are high. No foreign company can truly afford to be out of this market with its seemingly limitless long-term potential for growth.

In the boom years under Hu, corruption was regarded as a simple by-product of fast growth. Analysts like Andrew Wedeman looked closely at Party tactics – trying to keep its head above water by going for a few cases, but on the whole letting 99 per cent of the rest happen while everyone tried to make more money.[1] With falling growth under Xi, and the start of what looks like austerity with Chinese characteristics, such indulgence no longer makes political or economic sense. By 2013, not just domestic companies but also multinationals active in China started to get swept up in the invasive work of the greatly feared Central Discipline and Inspection Commission. The corruption clampdown was already starting to accelerate. The managing director of one of these multinationals was caught in an explicit film with a Chinese colleague. Another consultant to the company, a long-term British resident in China, was taken in and paraded on Chinese TV making what looked like a forced confession.

The Chinese government seemed to be making a point. In the old days, the received wisdom was that foreign companies were given special status in China, and allowed to operate with a freedom and autonomy their local equivalents envied. There were sporadic exceptions to the rule – the issues hitting Rio Tinto in 2008, when some of their company representatives in Shanghai were accused of involvement with corruption, landing them in jail, was perhaps the highest-profile case during that decade. But overall, the technology, know-how and the international branding of foreign companies gave them a high status. Under Xi, that atmosphere has changed. As part of strengthening the country's image abroad, the idea is now to clearly show that China does not allow foreign companies to regard the country as just a limitless opportunity for profits.

Working locally on Chinese terms to aid Chinese interests is fine. Making a mint out of China and walking away scot-free is not.

This is just one dimension of the story running through much of this book: under Xi, the imperative has been to get the message right. This message is not about fawning to foreign interests, or bowing down before superior Western technology, systems and governances. It is about relentlessly asserting China's uniqueness, its hybridity, its exceptionalism. Almost every idea is localized by having 'with Chinese characteristics' added to it, from capitalism, to socialism, to democracy, to development. Understanding China's national conditions (what it calls its *guoqing*) is critical. Those that prove oblivious to this only testify to their ignorance, their words dismissed. Those that have traction in China demonstrate sympathy with and understanding of the unique attributes of the Chinese experiment in modernity. For all foreigners, therefore, from companies, to people, to thinkers, to whole countries, the new framework is a nuanced one. Yes, Xi's China continues to say, you matter deeply to us, we need you, we want you to understand us, we want you to respect us and help us and work with us, and we can help you – but never on asymmetrical terms, always on the basis of parity, and always when we feel it is in our national interest to do so.

That invitation to work in parity with China is an enticing and persuasive one. Global environmental deals without China are meaningless. When China is onside, as it was during the Paris negotiations in late 2015, things happen. China's involvement in the Iran nuclear deal made a difference. Attempts to balance the global financial and economic order have to involve China. Richard Nixon was right in 1968 – it is both wrong, and impossible, to even try to exclude China from a major place in all of these debates. On some issues, China is growing closer to taking the leading role. Surely that is a good thing? But there is a clear trust deficit, suspicion about each other's intentions, which is most intense when it relates to China's regional interests but still lingers, even in the remote haunts of the Arctic or Antarctic. Chinese investments are regularly used to demonstrate some major move to dominate and control global agendas. Its diplomacy is accused of being sly and underhand; accusers argue that on the surface it adheres to principles, but then subtly undermines them. In some ways, the Communist Party and its opaque decision-making system take the blame for this. Even with a more visible, expressive and seemingly in-command leader like Xi, this distrust of China by outsiders derives from its system of governance.

That makes the central paradox that many countries are wrestling with in the era of Xi's charismatic and activist leadership even more complex to handle. For many countries in Asia, but now increasingly further afield, in Africa, the Middle East, Central Asia and Latin America, they have to balance a set of security concerns – in which the United States and its vast system of alliances are central – with considerations of where China offers the greatest economic benefit. How do they manage this sustainably?

One of the countries that offers the sharpest example is Australia. The world's sixth largest country by landmass, it sits at the heart of key strategic territory. Embraced by the United States in the Australia, New Zealand and United States Security Treaty (ANZUS), under the Mandarin-speaking prime ministership of Kevin Rudd from 2007 to 2010 the country grew almost frenetically conflicted. Rudd himself went to Beijing just after the Tibetan uprising of 2008 and grandly stated at Peking University that the two countries were 'true friends', meaning they could speak openly and frankly to each other. His frankness evidently irritated his hosts, who curtly reminded him Tibet was an internal affair he would be best to keep out of. Rudd's real crime, however, was to agree the rotation of US marine troops from the Pacific fleet in Darwin, right up in the northern tip of the country, and, in a defence paper in 2009, to announce language reminiscent of 'Chinese threat' thinking and make it clear that while China was welcome to invest in mines and trade in resources with Australia, it was not in a security alliance with the PRC.

Rudd's successors have not done much better with the balancing act. Telecoms provider Huawei was in effect blocked from bidding for a national broadband system in 2012, and attempts to develop a more positive relationship with China often collapsed due to pro-United States Australian politicians accusing the country of being pushy and threatening in the South China Sea. During the short-lived premiership of Tony Abbott, Japan was named as the country's key regional ally, much to the anger of figures in Beijing. Abbott went further in describing the attitudes towards China as ones dominated by fear and greed. As far as enjoying the benefits of Chinese investment, trade and economic growth, Australia was fine. But public views on Chinese citizens coming to buy residential housing in cities like Sydney or Melbourne sometimes gave rise to ugly racist sentiment. Perhaps the most remarkable moment in recent years in this particular bilateral relationship was when Xi Jinping visited Canberra and, in the same place where President Obama only a few years before had declared the rebalancing back to Asia, demanded more 'imagination and vision' by Australians in the relationship towards China. This had followed an event reported some months before where Australia had desisted from becoming a member of the AIIB due to US pressure, only to change its mind and join when the United Kingdom, Germany and many others went ahead.

Australia was in good company. Throughout the region, from Indonesia, to the Philippines, to Malaysia, to Pakistan, Central Asia and spanning out from there, countries have to constantly calculate the risks of 'offending the feelings of the Chinese people'. They also have to factor in the downsides of having Chinese investment in critical infrastructure, broadband and other strategic areas. As the discussion of the One Belt, One Road initiative in Chapter 4 made clear, while it is easy to spell out a common economic destiny, the brutal truth in the security realm remains that most countries do not share China's dominant concerns. They do not, for instance, agree with its maritime border disputes. They do not feel they need to support at any cost the continuation in power of the Chinese Communist Party. They do not appreciate Chinese politicization of issues from environment to energy security, and nor do they buy into some of the guiding Chinese historic narratives which are based on resentment and feelings of injustice. In these areas, there is anything but consensus. And around the handling of Taiwan or Hong Kong the problems grow even more contentious.

Taiwan is the central issue in far more profound ways than is often appreciated. The island's successful and largely peaceful transition to a democracy in 1996 had immense symbolic importance, not least in proving that an ethnically Chinese community could successfully run as a multiparty, largely harmonious entity. Mainland Chinese tactics for dealing with Taiwan over the years have varied from shrill criticism to patient negotiation. Under Hu, the PRC and the Republic of China shifted to working together mostly in the economic realm, and the two entities are now interlinked by air, postal services and people-to-people links in ways that were unthinkable a decade before. But the strategic attitude of Xi Jinping could not be clearer. Taiwan remains a renegade province, and despite the meeting with President Ma Ying-jeou in Singapore in November 2015, the ultimate aim of the Communist Party is to see reunification. Nor has Beijing relinquished the threat to use force to achieve this in the event of a unilateral declaration of independence by Taipei.

For Xi, it is clear that the opportunity for China to be a truly regional, dominant power is within the country's grasp. This gives the underlying energy to its assertiveness in the South and East China Sea, with complex claims being made over disparate parts of maritime territory. The unifying feature is that they are all mapping out strategic space for China, zones where it can truly be free of

US influence, or that of its allies, and have regional autonomy in ways appropriate to such a large economy. Xi's narrative of national regeneration and renaissance needs to be exemplified in this space. Hong Kong has been used in particular by Xi as an example of how Beijing, and Beijing alone, calls the shots now, and will take no heed of foreign declarations and protestations. There was always very little the United Kingdom could do to maintain much relevance and influence in the city after its handover in 1997. In fact, it is questionable if it had much clout before this time. In the end, under Xi, Hong Kong is firmly part of China's domestic space, and the outside world has next to no influence on the politics there. It is a lost cause.

The success of this Beijing-centric approach to Hong Kong might embolden Xi and his advisors to move even further towards their regional aspirations and make a bid for Taiwan. Foreign policy, as argued earlier in this book, is often not so much about logic but instead about countervailing emotions. For Xi, the prize of being the leader to see complete reunification and a return to the mythical great, single China of the past, would mean he truly would rank alongside Deng and Mao in a great troika of leaders and claim a major place in history. Much of the testing of commitments and resolve that China is clearly involved with around the region – building installations on islands, using proxy agents to clash with others and demanding observation of borders right down to the coast of Malaysia – shows how much latitude China has. It is able to spot weaknesses, chinks in people's armour, and raise questions of whether, in a crisis, people would really stand by their alliances.

These questions are most sharp and difficult around Taiwan. Would the United States really stand by the Taiwan Relations Act and its security commitments to the island if China were to one day make a hostile move? Would a deal be possible where China could aim for a 'one country, two systems' outcome, the model originally devised for Taiwan but then used for Hong Kong, allowing it a high degree of autonomy but reclaiming it as sovereign territory? For Beijing leaders, the logic of these ideas is compelling, even though it is clear that the vast majority of Taiwanese see their identity as being independent in all but name from the mainland, and who view the outcome of the one country, two systems idea with dismay in Hong Kong, where the emphasis since 2014 has clearly been increasingly on the 'one country' part of the phrase.

No one knows whether the world would stand by Taiwan if a hostile Beijing move was made on it, if push came to shove. Xi himself, speaking in 2014, complained that the two sides could not always put off talking about politics and just engage economically. The trajectory of almost everything China does in the area, from building up its navy to mapping out areas of control in the maritime region, does seem to move towards some ultimate showdown of reclamation over the island. This is supported by strong public sentiment supporting the PRC's governmental policy. Would the United States, and the region, be willing to face China off on this issue? Or would the time come when the calculation would be that Taiwan is expendable, and has to be left to its own fate (much as Hong Kong has been)?

Taiwan matters because it is an ideological and visionary divide, not just a territorial one. It is in this space that the Xi vision of Chinese regional and global order becomes real. If it is here that the US-led notion of a rule-based global order clashes with the reality of a Chinese alternative, valid perhaps only for China but embracing Taiwan, it would be a clash between the island's democratic vision and that of an autocratic, single-party state. That is why Taiwan is truly the ultimate interface between the People's Republic and the outside world. What matters here in the coming decade or so will truly reveal the face of Chinese power in its reality – is it something that is offering 'win–win outcomes' or simply a throwback to an older vision of power based on physical might, coercion, suppression of criticism and civil freedom? – and, in effect, whether China is the enemy of the whole modernist and post-modernist experiment to make state behaviour and governance humane. We shall have to wait and see. We are still living in an era of ambiguity, and at the moment, while it is undecided about what it wants for its future, that probably suits China just fine.

This book listed the main actors in Chinese foreign policy in Chapter 2, but there was an important partner and influence missing: the outside world. Like it or not, the outside world does have an immense influence on how China develops. This is probably not in the way the country wants, and not perhaps what it might expect. But decisions made by the average Chinese person about which luxury brands to purchase and where to send their children to be educated prove that the outside world impresses and appeals to them. The idea since 1989 of working with China in order to help it solve its internal problems so it becomes more like 'us', where 'us' is the liberal West, has so far failed. But there are many other areas where the world's impact on China has been huge – from supplying competition to improve China's domestic economy, to being the core economic and technology partner. Chinese people's lives have improved immeasurably since 1978, and that is in no small part due to the country's opening up to the world; this is even acknowledged in the official Chinese government term for this period – 'reform and opening up' (*gaige Kaifeng*). Without opening up, reform would never have achieved what it has, and the links with the outside world have been crucial in this process. China, as stated above, is probably, in its heart, undecided about where it is heading. 'Great strong nation' is, after all, a highly abstract term. What will this look like when China arrives there? Will it even know when it has arrived? The outside world, therefore, as Xi Jinping's multiple travels around the world from 2013 onwards make clear, is probably in the strongest position to influence China's formulation of foreign policy. The question is how it does this, and how it allows China to influence its trajectory. A good outcome could see an extraordinary moment when a nation which was almost crushed and annihilated by invasion and slaughter in the middle of the twentieth century becomes the key shaper of the twenty-first. If it achieves this, in ways which are harmonious, consensual and supported by the rest of the world, it will be a true victory for humanity. That, and that above all, is why Chinese views of its global role matter, and will continue to matter long into the future.

NOTES

INTRODUCTION

1   Jane Perlez and Chris Buckley, 'China retools its military with a first overseas outpost in Djibouti', *New York Times* (26 November 2015). Available at https://www.nytimes.com/2015/11/27/world/asia/china-military-presence-djibouti-africa.html.

2   Con Coughlin, 'China is moving into the Middle East – why is no one worried?' (17 December 2015). Available at http://www.telegraph.co.uk/news/worldnews/middleeast/syria/12055805/China-is-moving-intyo-Syria-why-is-no-one-worried.html.

3   Bruce Cumings, *Dominion from Sea to Sea: Pacific Ascendancy and American Power* (New Haven, CT: Yale University Press, 2009).

4   Han Fei Zi, *Basic Writings*, trans. Burton Watson (New York: Basic Books, 2003), p. 80.

5   For the next decade, initially under Chen Yi, poet and diplomat, the Ministry of Foreign Affairs was convulsed by internal battles and attacks from radical Red Guard groups outside. See Ma Jisen, *The Cultural Revolution in the Foreign Ministry of China* (Hong Kong: Chinese University, 2004).

1   THE PRINCIPLES OF CHINESE FOREIGN POLICY

1   See William T. Rowe, *China's Last Empire: The Great Qing* (Cambridge, MA: The Belknap Press of Harvard University Press, 2010), John Keay, *China: A History* (New York: Basic Books, 2009), along with Immanuel Hsü, *The Rise of Modern China*, 2nd ed. (Oxford: Oxford University Press, 2000).

2   William Callahan, *China: The Pessoptimist Nation* (Oxford: Oxford University Press, 2009).

3   Constitution of the People's Republic of China [English version] (amended 14 March 2004). Available at http://www.npc.gov.cn/englishnpc/Constitution/2007-11/15/content_1372962.htm.

4   Xi Jinping, 'Full text of speech at commemoration of 70th anniversary of war victory', *China Daily* [website] (3 September 2015). Available at http://www.chinadaily.com.cn/world/2015victoryanniv/2015-09/03/content_21783362.htm.

5   See 'China's initiation of the Five Principles of Peaceful Co-Existence', Ministry of Foreign Affairs of the People's Republic of China [website] (n.d.). Available at http://www.fmprc.gov.cn/mfa_eng/ziliao_665539/3602_665543/3604_665547/t18053.shtml.

6   The issue of principle versus practice is discussed at length by Sophie Richardson in *China, Cambodia, and the Five Principles of Peaceful Coexistence* (New York: Columbia University Press, 2009).

7   M. Taylor Fravel, *Strong Country, Secure Nation: Cooperation and Conflict in China's Territorial Disputes* (Princeton, NJ: Princeton University Press, 2008).

8   The modern form of this argument is put most persuasively by Martin Jacques in *When China Rules the World: The End of the Western World and the Birth of a New Global Order* (London and New York: Penguin, 2008).

9   Christopher Coker, *The Improbable War: China, the United States and the Logic of Great Power Conflict* (Oxford: Oxford University Press, 2015).

10   'Deng Xiaoping Tao guang yang hui waijiao zhenlue de laili' [The origin of Deng Xiaoping's diplomacy strategy], china.com [website] (1 March 2012). Available at http://news.china.com/history/all/11025807/20120301/17065999.html.

11   Sun Tzu, *The Art of War*, in *The Seven Military Classics of Ancient China*, trans. Ralph D. Sawyer (New York: Basic Books, 1993).

12   Han Fei Si, *Basic Writings: Translations from the Asian Classics*, trans. Burton Watson (New York: Basic Books, 2003), p. 35.

13   Henry A. Kissinger, *On China* (New York: Allen Lane, 2011).

14   Alastair Iain Johnston, 'Cultural realism and strategy in Maoist China', in Peter Katzenstein (ed.), *The Culture of National Security: Norms and Identity in World Politics* (New York: Columbia University Press, 1996), pp. 216–68.

15   Lawrence Freedman, *Strategy: A History* (Oxford: Oxford University Press, 2013), p. 193.

16 For Xi Jinping's views of the party he heads, see Kerry Brown, *CEO, China: The Rise of Xi Jinping* (London: I.B.Tauris, 2016).

17 Zheng Bijian, 'China's "peaceful rise" to great-power status', *Foreign Affairs* (September/October 2005). Available at https://www.foreignaffairs.com/articles/asia/2005-09-01/chinas-peaceful-rise-great-power-status.

18 Bates Gill, *Rising Star: China's New Security Diplomacy* (Washington DC: Brookings Institute Press, 2007).

19 Susan Shirk, *China: Fragile Superpower* (Oxford: Oxford University Press, 2008).

20 Yan Xuetong, *Ancient Chinese Thought, Modern Chinese Power* (Princeton, NJ: Princeton University Press, 2011), p. 16.

21 Joshua Cooper Ramo, 'The Beijing consensus: notes on the new physics of Chinese power' (London: Foreign Policy Centre, 2004), p. 4. Available at http://fpc.org.uk/fsblob/244.pdf.

22 Daniel A. Bell, *The China Model: Political Meritocracy and the Limits of Democracy* (Princeton, NJ: Princeton University Press, 2015).

23 See in particular Stein Ringen, 'Is Chinese autocracy outperforming Western democracy?', openDemocracy [website] (12 June 2015). Available at https://www.opendemocracy.net/stein-ringen/is-chinese-autocracy-outperforming-western-democracy.

24 See 'Security Council – veto list, Dag Hammarskjöld Library [website]. Available at http://research.un.org/en/docs/sc/quick.

25 Robert Zoellick, 'Whither China: from membership to responsibility?', remarks to National Committee on US–China relations, US Department of State [website] (21 September 2005). Available at http://2001-2009.state.gov/s/d/former/zoellick/rem/53682.htm. Emphasis in original.

26 Dai Bingguo, 'The core interests of the People's Republic of China', *China Digital Times* [website] (7 August 2009). Available at http://chinadigitaltimes.net/2009/08/dai-bingguo-%E6%88%B4%E7%A7%89%E5%9B%BD-the-core-interests-of-the-prc/.

27 Robert Cooper, *The Breaking of Nations* (New York: Atlantic Books, 2004).

2 THE WORLD ACCORDING TO XI JINPING

1 Fei Xiaotong, *From the Soil: The Foundations of Chinese Society*, trans. Gary Hamilton and Zheng Wang (Oakland: University of California Press, 1992).

2   This is dealt with in greater detail in Chapter 3, on US–China relations.

3   Kerry Brown, *CEO, China: The Rise of Xi Jinping* (London: I.B.Tauris, 2016).

4   For an overview of the role of Leading Small Groups throughout the history of the People's Republic of China, see Alice L. Miller, 'The CCP Central Committee's Leading Small Groups', *China Leadership Monitor*, Hoover Institute, No. 26 (Autumn 2008). Available at http://www. hoover.org/sites/default/files/uploads/documents/CLM26AM.pdf.

5   For a provocative overview of Taiwanese settlement, see J. Bruce Jacobs, 'Taiwan's colonial experiences and the development of ethnic identities: some hypotheses', *Taiwan in Comparative Perspective*, vol. 5 (July 2014), pp. 47–59.

6   John Garnaut, 'China's great wall of sand is theatrical bluster', *The Age*, (29 October 2015). Available at http://www.theage.com.au/comment/ chinas-great-wall-of-sand-is-theatrical-bluster-20151028-gkksbt.html.

7   See David Bray, *Social Space and Governance in Urban China: The Danwei System from Origins to Reform* (Chicago, IL: Stanford University Press, 2005) and Michael Schoenhals, *Spying for the People: Mao's Secret Agents, 1949–1967* (Cambridge: Cambridge University Press, 2013).

8   OECD, *Economic Survey of China 2005*, (Paris: OECD 2005), available at http://www.oecd.org/china/economicsurveyofchina2005.htm

9   See James Kynge, *China Shakes the World: The Rise of a Hungry Nation* (London: Weidenfeld & Nicolson, 2006).

10   Michael Smith, 'Spy chiefs fear Chinese cyber attack', *Sunday Times* (29 March 2009). Available at http://www.thesundaytimes.co.uk/sto/ news/uk_news/article158319.ece.

11   Maggie Lu-YueYang, 'Australia blocks China's Huawei from broadband tender', Reuters [news agency] (26 March 2012). Available at http:// www.reuters.com/article/2012/03/26/us-australia-huawei-nbn- idUSBRE82P0GA20120326.

12   Yasheng Huang, *Selling China* (Cambridge: Cambridge University Press, 2003).

13   Roland Barthes, *Travels in China* (Cambridge: Polity Press, 2011).

14   See Kerry Brown, *Ballot Box China: Grassroots Democracy in the Final Major One-Party State* (London: Zed Books, 2011).

15   Bo Yang, *The Ugly Chinaman and the Crisis of Chinese Culture* (Sydney: Allen and Unwin, 1992).

16   See Brown, *CEO, China*, for a description of this inner network.

3 CHINA AND THE UNITED STATES: THE ULTIMATE LOVE–HATE RELATIONSHIP

1 'US charges five Chinese military hackers with cyber espionage against US corporations and a labor organization for commercial advantage', FBI (19 May 2014). Available at https://www.fbi.gov/pittsburgh/ press-releases/2014/u.s.-charges-five-chinese-military-hackers-with-cyber-espionage-against-u.s.-corporations-and-a-labor-organization-for-commercial-advantage.

2 'Is the story "Dulles refusing handshake with Chou En-lai" true?', *Guanming Online* [website] (20 June 2013). Available at http://en.gmw. cn/2013-06/20/content_8019674.htm.

3 For an account of Maoist influence in France in the era of student protests in the 1960s, see Richard Wolin, *The Wind from the East: French Intellectuals, the Cultural Revolution and the Legacy of the 1960s* (Princeton, NJ: Princeton University Press, 2010).

4 For a full account of this era, see Margaret Macmillan, *Seize the Hour: When Nixon Met Mao* (London: John Murray, 2006).

5 For the full released transcripts, both of Kissinger's preparatory meetings and then of Nixon's encounters with Chinese leaders during this time, see William Burr (ed.), *The Kissinger Transcripts: The Top Secret Talks with Beijing and Moscow* (New York: Diane Publishing Co., 1999).

6 See Robert S. Ross, *Chinese Security Policy: Structure, Power and Politics* (London: Routledge, 2009).

7 Deng Xiaoping, 'We are working to revitalize the Chinese nation' (7 April 1990). Available at https://archive.org/stream/ SelectedWorksOfDengXiaopingVol.3/Deng03_djvu.txt.

8 'US–China Strategic and Economic Dialogue outcomes of the Strategic Track', US Department of State [media note] (24 June 2015). Available at http://www.fmprc.gov.cn/mfa_eng/wjdt_665385/2649_665393/ t1173628.shtml.

9 'Chinese leader Xi Jinping joins Obama for summit', BBC News [website] (8 June 2013). Available at http://www.bbc.co.uk/news/ world-asia-china-22798572.

10 'Remarks by President Obama and President Xi Jinping of the People's Republic of China after bilateral meeting', Office of the White House Press Secretary [media note] (8 June 2013). Available at https://www. whitehouse.gov/the-press-office/2013/06/08/remarks-president-obama-and-president-xi-jinping-peoples-republic-china-.

11   Aaron L. Friedberg, *A Contest for Supremacy: China, America, and the Struggle for Mastery in Asia* (New York: W. W. Norton, 2010).

12   John J. Mearsheimer, *The Tragedy of Great Power Politics* (New York: W. W. Norton, 2001).

13   Wang Hui, *The End of the Revolution: China and the Limits of Modernity* (London: Verso Books, 2010).

14   Wang Xiaodong, Song Shaojun, Huang Jilao and Song Qiang (eds), *Zhongguo bu gaoxing* [Unhappy China] (Nanjing: Phoenix Publishing and Jiangsu People's Publishing Company, 2009).

15   Christopher Coker, *The Improbable War: China, the United States and the Logic of Great Power Conflict* (Oxford: Oxford University Press, 2015).

16   Mandiant, 'APT1: exposing one of China's cyber espionage units' (2013), p. 2. Available at https://www.fireeye.com/content/dam/fireeye-www/services/pdfs/mandiant-apt1-report.pdf.

17   Quoted in Mark Landler, 'Offering to aid talks, US challenges China on disputed islands', *New York Times* (23 July 2010). Available at http://www.nytimes.com/2010/07/24/world/asia/24diplo.html?_r=0.

18   Barack Obama, 'Remarks by President Obama to the Australian parliament' [press release] (17 November 2011). Available at https://www.whitehouse.gov/the-press-office/2011/11/17/remarks-president-obama-australian-parliament/.

19   Robert D. Blackwill and Ashley J. Tellis, 'Revising US grand strategy toward China', Council on Foreign Relations (April 2015), p. 4. Available for download at http://www.cfr.org/china/revising-us-grand-strategy-toward-china/p36371.

20   Ibid., p. 5.

21   Ibid., p. 38.

22   Sun Tzu, *The Art of War*, in *The Seven Military Classics of Ancient China*, trans. Ralph D. Sawyer (New York: Basic Books, 1993).

23   Marcel Mauss, *The Gift* (London: Routledge, 1990).

24   Mearsheimer, *The Tragedy of Great Power Politics*.

25   Ewan MacAskill, 'WikiLeaks: Hillary Clinton's question: how can we stand up to Beijing?', *Observer* (4 December 2010). Available at http://www.theguardian.com/world/2010/dec/04/wikileaks-cables-hillary-clinton-beijing.

4 ZONE TWO: THE ASIA REGION

1   Mark Edward Lewis, *The Early Chinese Empires: Qin and Han* (Cambridge, MA, and London: The Belknap Press of Harvard University Press, 2007), p. 143.

2   Wu Jiao and Zhang Yunbi, 'Xi in call for building new "maritime silk road"', *China Daily USA* [website] (4 October 2013). Available at http://usa.chinadaily.com.cn/china/2013-10/04/content_17008940.htm.

3   Quoted in Nguyen Hong Thao, 'Why the US–China summit failed on the South China Sea', *The Diplomat* (9 October 2015). Available at http://thediplomat.com/2015/10/why-the-us-china-summit-failed-on-the-south-china-sea/.

4   See Bill Hayton, *The South China Sea: The Struggle for Power in Asia* (New Haven, CT, and London: Yale University Press, 2014) for an overview of the history and current status of this issue.

5   See Rana Mitter, *China's War with Japan 1937–1945: The Struggle for Survival* (London: Penguin, 2013) for a masterly overview of this era.

6   This comment appears to derive from the vast unattributed statements of Mao, many of which arose from the Cultural Revolution era. It is referred to on the BBC History website in the article 'China and Japan: seven decades of bitterness' (13 February 2014). Available at http://www.bbc.co.uk/news/magazine-25411700.

7   For an exhaustive account of Deng's visits to other countries, including Japan, during the early phase of the so-called Reform and Opening Up era after 1978 see Ezra Vogel, *Deng Xiaoping and the Transformation of China* (Cambridge, MA: The Belknap Press of Harvard University Press, 2013).

8   See Kerry Brown, *Hu Jintao: China's Silent Ruler* (Singapore: World Scientific, 2012).

9   Alyssa Abkowitz, 'China is now the top source of foreign tourists to Japan', *Wall Street Journal* (2 December 2015). Available at http://blogs.wsj.com/chinarealtime/2015/12/02/china-is-now-the-top-source-of-foreign-tourists-to-japan/.

10 Jane Perlez and David E. Sanger, 'John Kerry urges China to curb North Korea's nuclear pursuits', *New York Times* (27 January 2016). Available at http://www.nytimes.com/2016/01/28/world/asia/us-china-north-korea.html?_r=0.

11 Andrei Lankov, *The Real North Korea* (Oxford: Oxford University Press, 2013).

12 For comparative material on this, see Amartya Sen and Jean Drèze, *An Uncertain Glory: India and Its Contradictions* (London: Penguin, 2013).

13 See Bill Emmott, *Rivals: How the Power Struggle Between China, India, and Japan Will Shape Our Next Decade* (Boston, MA: Houghton Mifflin Harcourt, 2009).

14 See Andrew Small, *The China–Pakistan Axis: Asia's New Geopolitics* (New York and London: Hurst, 2015).

15 Joshua Kurlantzick, *Charm Offensive: How China's Soft Power is Transforming the World* (New Haven, CT, and London: Yale University Press, 2007).

16 John Pomfret, 'US takes a tougher line with China', *Washington Post* (30 July 2010). Available at http://www.washingtonpost.com/wp-dyn/content/article/2010/07/29/AR2010072906416.html.

17 *The Economist*, 'Divided we stagger' (18 August 2012). Available at http://www.economist.com/node/21560585.

18 Nargiza Salidjanova and Iacob Koch-Weser, 'China's economic ties with ASEAN: a country-by-country analysis', US–China Economic and Security Review Commission (March 2015), p. 6. Available at https://www.uscc.gov/sites/default/files/Research/China%27s%20Economic%20Ties%20with%20ASEAN.pdf.

19 See Paul G. Pickowicz and Jeremy Brown (eds), *Dilemmas of Victory: The Early Years of the People's Republic of China* (Cambridge, MA: Harvard University Press, 2007), for an overview of this era.

20 Bobo Lo, *Axis of Convenience: Moscow, Beijing, and the New Geopolitics* (Washington DC: Brookings Institute Press, 2009).

21 See Xi Jinping, *The Governance of China* (Beijing: Foreign Languages Press, 2014).

22 Gideon Rachman, 'Davos leaders: Shinzo Abe on WWI parallels, economics and women at work', *Financial Times* (22 January 2014). Available at http://blogs.ft.com/the-world/2014/01/davos-leaders-shinzo-abe-on-war-economics-and-women-at-work/.

5 ZONE THREE: THE EU AND CHINA – CIVILIZED PARTNERS TALKING PAST EACH OTHER

1 Xi Jinping, 'Speech by H. E. Mr Xi Jinping, President of the People's Republic of China at the College of Europe' (Bruges, 1 April 2014).

Available at https://www.coleurope.eu/events/president-peoples-republic-china-he-mr-xi-jinping-college-europe.

2   Perry Anderson, *The New Old World* (London: Verso Books, 2009), p. 3.

3   David Goodhart, *The British Dream: Successes and Failures of Post-War Immigration* (London: Atlantic Books, 2013), p. 2.

4   Jürgen Habermas, *Europe: The Faltering Project* (Cambridge: Polity Press, 2009); Mark Leonard, *Why Europe Will Run the 21st Century* (London: Fourth Estate, 2005); Robert Cooper, *The Postmodern State and the World Order* (London: Demos, 1996).

5   Available at https://www.marxists.org/reference/archive/zhang/1975/x01/x01.htm.

6   Details of the agreement can be found at the European Union archive: http://europa.eu/legislation_summaries/external_relations/relations_with_third_countries/asia/r14206_en.htm.

7   Summary of paper at http://europa.eu/legislation_summaries/external_relations/relations_with_third_countries/asia/r14208_en.htm. The paper itself in full can be found at http://eur-lex.europa.eu/legal-content/EN/TXT/?uri=celex:52006DC0631.

8   Leonard, *Why Europe will Run the 21st Century*, chapter 1.

9   'China's EU policy paper', State Council Information Office (October 2003). Available at http://www.china.org.cn/e-white/20050817/.

10 Ministry of Foreign Affairs of the People's Republic of China, 'China's policy paper on the EU: deepen the China–EU Comprehensive Strategic Partnership for mutual benefit and win–win cooperation' (2 April 2014). Available at http://www.fmprc.gov.cn/mfa_eng/wjdt_665385/wjzcs/t1143406.shtml.

11 *Straits Times* (7 October 2011). Quoted at https://wikileaks.org/gifiles/docs/13/137615_-os-china-eu-econ-gv-china-expresses-confidence-over-europe.html.

12 Quoted in Kerry Brown, 'Decision time or moment of truth for China and the EU', *China Brief* 11 (12). Available at https://jamestown.org/program/decision-time-or-the-moment-of-truth-for-china-and-the-eu/.

13 European Commission statistics. Available at http://www.consilium.europa.eu/uedocs/cms_data/docs/pressdata/en/ec/132478.pdf.

14 EU–China summit September 2012 [factsheet]. Available at http://eeas.europa.eu/china/summit/summit_docs/20120920_factsheet_en.pdf.

15 For an excellent discussion of this, see Katrin Kinzelbach and Hatla Thelle, 'Talking human rights to China: an assessment of the EU's approach', *China Quarterly* 205 (March 2011), pp. 60–79. Available at http://www.jstor.org/stable/41305194?seq=1#page_scan_tab_contents.

16 The best and most accessible single-volume treatment of this is to be found in Tsering Shakya, *The Dragon in the Land of Snows: A History of Modern Tibet Since 1947* (London: Pimlico, 1999). Despite its title, the first and second chapters of this work give context to colonial involvement, in particular by the British, from the late Qing era before 1911 up to 1947.

17 'David Cameron's Dalai Lama meeting sparks China protest', BBC News [website] (16 May 2012). Available at http://www.bbc.co.uk/news/uk-politics-18084223.

18 Jamil Anderlini, Simon Rabinovitch, George Parker and Hugh Carnegy, 'Chinese roll out red carpet for Hollande', *Financial Times* (24 April 2013). Available at https://www.ft.com/content/03182260-acef-11e2-b27f-00144feabdc0.

19 According to some news reports of the visit, however, in private Hollande did raise the specific issue of the self-immolations in Tibet during his official meetings. See 'French President Hollande talks of human rights during China visit', *Europe News* (26 April 2013). Available at http://www.euronews.com/2013/04/26/french-president-hollande-talks-of-human-rights-during-china-visit/.

20 Robin Emmott and Francesco Guarascio, 'EU agrees China solar panel duties in boldest move yet', Reuters [news agency] (8 May 2013). Available at http://www.reuters.com/article/us-eu-china-solar-idUSBRE9470CO20130508.

21 'Merkel urges dialogue to solve EU–China solar dispute', *China Daily USA* (18 September 2012). Available at http://usa.chinadaily.com.cn/business/2012-09/18/content_15764937.htm.

22 'Solar dispute: China hopes for best but prepares for the worst', *People's Daily* (8 June 2013). Available at http://english.peopledaily.com.cn/90778/8278183.html.

23 For the drivers of Chinese overseas investment and how this relates to the EU, see Kerry Brown, 'Chinese overseas investment in the European Union', *International Spectator*, Vol. 47, No. 2 (June 2012).

24 Jeremy Clegg and Hinrich Voss, 'Chinese direct investment in the European Union' (London: ECRAN, 2012). Available at https://www.chathamhouse.org/publications/papers/view/185555.

6   ZONE FOUR: THE WIDER WORLD

1   Deng Xiaoping, 'Speech by chairman of the delegation of the People's Republic of China, Deng Xiaoping, at the special session of the UN General Assembly' (10 April 1974). Available at https://www.marxists. org/reference/archive/deng-xiaoping/1974/04/10.htm.

2   Donovan Chau, *Exploiting Africa: The Influence of Maoist China in Algeria, Ghana, and Tanzania* (Annapolis, MD: Naval Institute Press, 2014).

3   Howard W. French, *China's Second Continent: How a Million Migrants are Building a New Empire in Africa* (New York: Knopf, 2014).

4   Abdoulaye Wade, 'Time for the west to practise what it preaches', *Financial Times* (23 January 2008). Available to subscribers at http://www.ft.com/cms/s/0/5d347f88-c897-11dc-94a6-0000779fd2ac.html#axzz40KSgVuae.

5   Human Rights Watch, '"You'll be fired if you refuse": labor abuses in Zambia's state-owned copper mines' (4 November 2011). Available at https://www.hrw.org/report/2011/11/04/youll-be-fired-if-you-refuse/labor-abuses-zambias-chinese-state-owned-copper-mines.

6   Stephen Chan (ed.), *The Morality of China in Africa: The Middle Kingdom and the Dark Continent* (London: Zed Books, 2013).

7   Lily Kuo, 'China's Xi Jinping pledges $60 billion to help Africa solve its problems its own way', *Quartz Africa* (4 December 2015). Available at http://qz.com/565819/chinas-xi-jinping-pledges-60-billion-to-help-africa-solve-its-problems-its-own-way/.

8   Bob Wekesa, 'Mugabe visits China: Zimbabwe's "Look East" policy reloaded' (2 September 2014). Available at http://www.ccs.org.za/wp-content/uploads/2014/09/CCS_Commentary_Mugabe_China_Visit_BW_2014.pdf.

9   Chinese Minister of Foreign Commerce figures, quoted in *The Economist*, 'Chinese investment in Africa: not as easy as it looks' (21 November 2015). Available at http://www.economist.com/news/middle-east-and-africa/21678777-western-worries-about-chinas-burgeoning-influence-africa-may-be-overblown-not.

10   Jane Perlez and Chris Buckley, 'China retools its military with a first overseas post in Djibouti', *New York Times* (26 November 2015). Available at http://www.nytimes.com/2015/11/27/world/asia/china-military-presence-djibouti-africa.html?_r=0.

11   Some material in this section appeared in a previous publication (Kerry

Brown, 'Mixed signals: China in the Middle East', FRIDE [policy brief] (December 2014). Available at http://fride.org/download/PB_190_China_in_the_Middle_East.pdf.) It has been extensively revised, updated and rewritten for this book.

12 'China's Arab policy paper' (English version), Xinhua [news agency] (13 January 2016). Available at http://news.xinhuanet.com/english/china/2016-01/13/c_135006619.htm.

13 Ben Blanchard, 'China's foreign minister pushes Iran on nuclear deal', Reuters [news agency] (16 February 2016). Available at http://www.reuters.com/article/us-iran-nuclear-china-idUSKBN0LK05Q20150216.

14 'Full text: China's policy paper on Latin America and the Caribbean', Xinhua [news agency] (5 November 2008). Available at http://news.xinhuanet.com/english/2008-11/05/content_10308117_1.htm.

15 Michael Swaine, 'Xi Jinping's July 2014 trip to Latin America', *China Leadership Monitor* (5 September 2014). Available at http://www.hoover.org/sites/default/files/research/docs/clm45ms-xi_jinpings_trip_to_latin_america.pdf.

16 'Spotlight: Cultural exchange to usher in new era of China-LatAm sustainable cooperation', *Xinhuanet* [website] (31 May 2015). Available at http://news.xinhuanet.com/english/2015-05/31/c_134284655.htm.

17 Rebecca Ray, Kevin P. Gallagher, Andres Lopez and Cynthia Sanborn, 'China in Latin America: lessons for south–south cooperation and sustainable development' [working group report], Global Economic Governance Initiative, Boston University (2015), p. 2.

18 Heriberto Araújo and Juan Pablo Cardenal, *China's Silent Army: The Pioneers, Traders, Fixers and Workers Who Are Remaking the World in Beijing's Image* (London: Penguin, 2013).

19 Joe Studwell, *The China Dream: The Elusive Quest for the Last Great Untapped Market on Earth* (London: Profile Books, 2002).

20 'Chinese investments in Brazil 2007–2012: a review of recent trends', China–Brazil Business Council (2013), p. 33. Available at http://cebc.com.br/sites/default/files/pesquisa_investimentos_chineses_2007-2012_-_ingles_1.pdf.

21 Nicola Davison, 'China eyes Antarctica's resource bounty', *Guardian* (8 November 2013). Available at http://www.theguardian.com/environment/2013/nov/08/china-antarctica-trip-icebreaker-snow-dragon.

22 'They may be some time: putting down roots in Antarctica', *The Economist* (16 November 2013). Available at http://www.economist.

com/news/china/21589908-putting-down-roots-antarctica-they-may-
be-some-time.

23 For a good, contextual overview of China in the Arctic, see Sanna Kopra,
'China's Arctic interests', *Arctic Yearbook* (2013). Available at http://www.
arcticyearbook.com/images/Articles_2013/KOPRA_AY13_FINAL.pdf.

CONCLUSION: TELLING THE CHINA STORY

1 See Andrew Wedeman, *Double Paradox: Rapid Growth and Rising
Corruption in China* (Ithaca, NY: Cornell University Press, 2014).

SUGGESTED READING

INTRODUCTION

In 'The Beijing consensus: notes on the new physics of Chinese power' (London: Foreign Policy Centre, 2004), available at http://fpc.org.uk/fsblob/244.pdf, Joshua Cooper Ramo sets out the core argument for the Beijing vision of state development, or at least his perception of it. In Yan Xuetong's *Ancient Chinese Thought, Modern Chinese Power* (Princeton, NJ: Princeton University Press, 2011) there is an excellent and lucid outline of China's potential to be a moral and cultural superpower, not just an economic one. This is supported by the interesting, sometimes challenging defence of the Chinese political system by Daniel A. Bell, *The China Model: Political Meritocracy and the Limits of Democracy* (Princeton, NJ: Princeton University Press, 2015). Robert S. Ross, *Chinese Security Policy: Structure, Power and Politics* (London: Routledge, 2009), particularly chapter 2, 'The Geography of Peace', is an excellent overview of China's history as a land rather than sea power, up until modern times. In *China Goes Global: The Partial Superpower* (Oxford: Oxford University Press, 2013), David Shambaugh covers Chinese soft power and investment issues. For different treatments of China's global role, see Susan Shirk, *China: Fragile Superpower* (Oxford: Oxford University Press, 2008); Bates Gill, *Rising Star: China's New Security Diplomacy* (Washington DC: Brookings Institute Press, 2007); and Martin Jacques, *When China Rules the World: The End of the Western World and the Birth of a New Global Order* (London: Penguin, 2008). An excellent attempt to see China as an intellectual entity rather than a diplomatic one is in Kent G. Deng's essay, 'A swinging pendulum: the Chinese way in growth and development from 1800 to the present day', in *China's Many Dreams: Comparative Perspectives on China's Search for National Rejuvenation*, ed. David Kerr (Basingstoke: Palgrave Macmillan, 2015).

On the history of Chinese interaction with the outside world, see Odd Arne Westad, *Restless Empire: China and the World since 1750* (New York: Basic Books, 2012) and Julia Lovell, *The Great Wall: China Against the World, 1000 BC–AD 2000* (New York: Atlantic Books, 2006), the latter of which offers a highly readable overview of Chinese imperial and modern views of the outside world. And in *China Under Mao: A Revolution Derailed* (Cambridge, MA: Harvard University Press, 2015) Andrew G. Walder is highly critical of Mao Zedong in his summary of the domestic drivers of policy from 1949 onwards, which shows how some of these drivers related to China internationally.

1   THE PRINCIPLES OF CHINESE FOREIGN POLICY

On the principles of Chinese foreign policy, see Alastair Iain Johnston, 'Cultural realism and strategy in Maoist China', in Peter Katzenstein (ed.), *The Culture of National Security: Norms and Identity in World Politics* (New York: Columbia University Press, 1996), pp. 216–68. For rhetoric about this, see the collection 'China's Peaceful Rise: Speeches of Zheng Bijian, 1997–2004' at https://www.brookings.edu/wp-content/uploads/2012/04/20050616bijianlunch.pdf. On the overall culture of Chinese strategic thinking, see the first and second chapters of Henry Kissinger's *On China* (London: Penguin, 2011). On the division between principles and practice, see Sophie Richardson, *China, Cambodia, and the Five Peaceful Principles of*

Coexistence (New York: Columbia University Press, 2009). Finally, William A. Callahan's *China: The Pessoptimist Nation* (Oxford: Oxford University Press, 2010) addresses the link between Chinese modern history and its current world view.

2   THE WORLD ACCORDING TO XI JINPING

The most concise and best description of core actors of Chinese contemporary foreign policy is in Linda Jakobson and Dean Knox's 'New foreign policy actors in China', SIPRI Policy Paper 26 (September 2010), available at http://books.sipri.org/files/PP/SIPRIPP26.pdf. On the drivers of Chinese overseas investment, see Peter J. Buckley, L. Jeremy Clegg, Adam R. Cross, Xin Liu, Hinrich Voss and Ping Zheng, 'The determinants of Chinese outward foreign direct investment', *Journal of International Business Studies* 38 (4), *International Expansion of Emerging Market Businesses* (July 2007), pp. 499–518. In *The Improbable War: China, the United States and the Logic of Great Power Conflict* (Oxford: Oxford University Press, 2015), Christopher Coker offers an excellent analysis of resentment carried over from history and its continuing role in Chinese foreign policy today. The best treatment of China's interest in borders and their negotiation over the last 65 years is in M. Taylor Fravel's *Strong Borders, Secure Nation: Cooperation and Conflict in China's Territorial Disputes* (Princeton, NJ: Princeton University Press, 2008).

A good discussion of the ways in which China's involvement in international economic and finance entities gives insights into it being either a rule-observer or -breaker is in the contributions to Eric Helleiner and Jonathan Kirshner's *The Great Wall of Money: Power and Politics in China's International Monetary Relations* (Ithaca, NY: Cornell University Press, 2015), particularly chapter 2, which deals with the role of China in the IMF. Xi Jinping's

The Governance of China (Beijing: Foreign Languages Press, 2014) contains the current leader of China's main statements on foreign-policy issues, most given while he was attending international conferences or on bilateral visits. For a discussion of Chinese environmental issues, see Judith Shapiro, *China's Environmental Challenges* (Cambridge: Polity Press, 2012). On China being either a revisionist or status-quo power, see Aaron L. Friedberg, *A Contest for Supremacy: China, America, and the Struggle for Mastery in Asia* (New York: W. W. Norton, 2010). Lastly, my *The New Emperors: Power and the Princelings in China* (London: I.B.Tauris, 2014) has an overview in the fourth chapter of the post-2012 leadership and its role in the world.

3   CHINA AND THE UNITED STATES: THE ULTIMATE LOVE–HATE RELATIONSHIP

John J. Mearsheimer's *The Tragedy of Great Power Politics* (New York: W. W. Norton, 2001) is the classic and highly influential account of where conflict between an established and an emerging power might lead. *The China Challenge: Shaping the Choices of a Rising Power* (New York: W. W. Norton, 2015), by Thomas J. Christiansen, a former senior US Department of State official, is a lucid and readable account of where United States–China relations were in 2015. For the official US account of the outcomes of the 2015 US–China Strategic and Economic Dialogue on the economic track see https://www.treasury.gov/press-center/press-releases/Pages/jl0092.aspx. Former Australian prime minister Kevin Rudd's report, 'The future of US–China relations under Xi Jinping: toward a new framework of constructive realism for a common purpose' (summary available at http://belfercenter.ksg.harvard.edu/publication/25237/summary_report.html), offers a characteristically immodest view on the current and future status of the relationship between the two countries.

4 ZONE TWO: THE ASIA REGION

On policy players within China on the South and East China Sea disputes, see Linda Jakobson, 'China's unpredictable maritime security actors' (Sydney: Lowy Institute, 2014), available at http://www.lowy-institute.org/files/chinas-unpredictable-maritime-security-actors_3.pdf. For China–Japan relations and the role of the Chinese public, see James Reilly, *Strong Society, Smart State: The Rise of Public Opinion in China's Japan Policy* (New York: Columbia University Press, 2011). To get the background and recent status of the South and East China Sea disputes, see Bill Hayton, *The South China Sea: The Struggle for Power in Asia* (New Haven, CT: Yale University Press, 2014). China–Pakistan relations are dealt with in an excellent and highly readable study by Andrew Small, *The China–Pakistan Axis: Asia's New Geopolitics* (New York and London: Hurst, 2015). For the Belt Road Initiative and its complex possible meanings, see Timothy Summers, 'What exactly is "one belt, one road"?', *The World Today* 71 (5) (September 2015), at https://www.chathamhouse.org/publication/twt/what-exactly-one-belt-one-road. The formal Chinese government statement on this initiative, 'Action plan on the belt and road initiative', is to be found on the website of the Chinese State Council, at http://english.gov.cn/archive/publications/2015/03/30/content_281475080249035.htm. Relations between China, Japan and India are covered by Bill Emmott in *Rivals: How the Power Struggle Between China, India and Japan will Shape Our Next Decade* (Boston, MA: Houghton Mifflin Harcourt, 2009).

5 ZONE THREE: THE EU AND CHINA – CIVILIZED PARTNERS TALKING PAST EACH OTHER

Robert Ross, Øystein Tunsjø and Zhang Tuosheng's *US–China–EU Relations: Managing the New World Order* (London: Routledge,

2010), particularly chapter 2, Hanns Maull's 'The EU as a civilian power: aspirations, potential and achievement', is an excellent overview of the cognitive difference between the EU and China, and the causes of this. The Chinese government's two articulations of officials' views on the EU can be seen in 'China's policy paper on the EU: deepen the China–EU Comprehensive Strategic Partnership for mutual benefit and win–win cooperation', State Council (Beijing, 2014), available at http://www.fmprc.gov.cn/mfa_eng/wjdt_665385/wjzcs/t1143406.shtml and 'China's EU policy paper', State Council (Beijing, 2003), available at http://en.people.cn/200310/13/eng20031013_125906.shtml. On EU–China values and human rights dialogue, see Katrin Kinzelbach, *The EU's Human Rights Dialogue with China: Quiet Diplomacy and Its Limits* (London and New York: Routledge, 2014). See also Katrin Kinzelbach and Hatla Thelle, 'Talking human rights to China: an assessment of the EU's approach', *China Quarterly* 205 (March 2011), pp. 60–79.

6   ZONE FOUR: THE WIDER WORLD

On China in Africa, see Ian Taylor, *China's New Role in Africa* (Boulder, CO: Lynne Rienner Publishers, 2010), and Shaun Breslin and Ian Taylor, 'Explaining the rise of "human rights" in analyses of Sino–African relations', Warwick University (2010), available at http://wrap.warwick.ac.uk/283/1/WRAP_Breslin_roape-china-2.pdf. For China and the Middle East, see Kerry Brown, 'Mixed signals: China in the Middle East', Fride [policy brief] (December 2014), available at http://fride.org/download/PB_190_China_in_the_Middle_East.pdf. Finally, *China Engages Latin America: Tracing the Trajectory*, eds Adrian H. Hearn and José Luis León-Manríquez, (Boulder, CO: Lynne Rienner Publishers, 2011) is a good overview of China in South America.

INDEX

9/11 attacks 33, 132
2008 Beijing Olympics 91, 94, 179

Abbott, Tony 211
Abe, Shinzo 124
Africa 71–2, 173, 175, 176–83
aid 180, 181
AIIB *see* Asian Infrastructure
    Investment Bank
Albania 78
Algeria 177
Anderson, Perry 147
Antarctica 69, 173, 198–9
Araújo, Heriberto 196
Arctic 69, 173, 199–200
Art of War, The (Sun Tzu) 19–20, 101
Asia 113–14, 142–3; *see also*
    Association of Southeast Asian
    Nations
Asian Development Bank 103, 124
Asian Infrastructure Investment Bank
    (AIIB) 6, 102, 103–4, 124,
    161, 211
Association of Southeast Asian
    Nations (ASEAN) 70, 104,
    113–14, 133–7
Australia 4, 45, 104, 117, 198,
    210–11

banking 102–4
Barroso, José Manuel 156
Barthes, Roland 60
Bell, Daniel A. 31, 32

Belt Road Initiative (BRI) 6, 57, 70,
    113–14, 142–4
    and Central Asia 141
    and Middle East 191
    and Pakistan 132
Blackwill, Robert D. 99, 100
Botswana 179
Brazil 71–2, 195, 197
Brexit 148, 155, 171
BRI *see* Belt Road Initiative
BRICS (Brazil, Russia, India, China,
    South Africa) collective 72, 183
Britain *see* Great Britain
Buddhism 131
Burma *see* Myanmar
Bush, George H. W. 83–4
Bush, George W. 33, 130, 191

Cambodia 17, 134, 136
Cameron, David 149, 160, 161
capitalism 28, 88
Cardenal, Juan Pablo 196
Carter, Jimmy 81
CCP *see* Chinese Communist Party
Central Asia 140–2, 204
Central Military Commission
    (CMC) 46, 48–9
Central Party School 58
Chan, Stephen 179
Chang Wanquan 191
Chau, Donovan D. 177
Chiang Kai-shek 77, 113, 121
Chile 195

China 11–14, 112–13, 169–71,
    201–7, 208–9, 215–16
  and Africa 176–83
  and AIIB 102–4
  and ASEAN 134–7
  and Asia 113–14, 142–4
  and Australia 210–11
  and borders 15–17
  and Central Asia 140–2
  and citizens 60–2
  and containment 93–6
  and corruption 207–8
  and culture 28–31, 38–9
  and cyberespionage 97–8
  and democracy 31–2
  and Djibouti 1–2
  and domestic policy 35–6
  and economy 22–3, 33–5,
    107–10, 167–9
  and environmentalism 106–7
  and Europe 146–7, 148–58, 171–2
  and Five Principles 14–15
  and foreign investment 52–6
  and foreign policy 4–5, 6–9,
    24–5, 32–3, 43–4, 63–74
  and India 129–32
  and intellectuals 57–9
  and intelligence 49–50
  and investment 36–7, 165–7,
    209–10
  and Japan 119–24
  and Latin America 193–7
  and liberalism 91–2
  and maritime disputes 115–19
  and Middle East 183–93
  and modernization 25–8
  and North Korea 124–9
  and opacity 3–4
  and Pakistan 132–3
  and people movement 37–8
  and polar regions 198–200
  and provinces 44–6
  and Russia 137–40
  and society 40–1
  and Soviet Union 78–9
  and state enterprise 51–2
  and strategies 18–22, 23–4
  and Taiwan 175–6, 212, 213–15
  and Third World 173–5
  and Tibet 158–60, 161
  and trade 162–5
  and USA 75–8, 80–91, 99–102,
    105–6
  see also Chinese Communist Party;
    People's Liberation Army
China National Offshore Oil Corpor-
    ation (CNOOC) 52–3, 178, 191
China–Arab States Cooperation
    Forum (CASCF) 184–5, 186
Chinese Communist Party (CCP) 3,
    12, 21, 25, 88, 204–5
  and Deng Xiaoping 84–6
  and non-state companies 55–6
  and North Korea 126–7
  and Sino-Japanese War 120, 121
  and USA 111
Ci Xi, Empress 26
Clegg, Jeremy 166
climate change 6, 106–7, 110, 209
Clinton, Bill 90
Clinton, Hillary 99, 108
CMC see Central Military
    Commission
Coker, Christopher 97
Cold War 14, 19, 82
Colombia 195
colonialism 17
Comey, James B. 76
Communism 14; see also Chinese
    Communist Party
Confucius Institutes 29
Cooper, Robert 147
corruption 207–8
Costa Rica 197
Cuba 69, 194
Cultural Revolution 4, 20, 29, 76–7
culture 29–31, 38–9
cyberespionage 50, 76, 97–8

Dai Bingguo 35
Dalai Lama 129, 149, 158, 159,
    160, 161

De Gucht, Karel 162, 164
Dehqan, Hossein 191
democracy 88, 105
Democratic Republic of the Congo 179
Deng Xiaoping 18–19, 28, 46, 84–5, 122, 174
  and USA 70, 82, 83, 175
Ding Xuexiang 65
Djibouti 1, 2, 38, 96, 181–2
DPRK *see* North Korea
Dulles, John Forster 78
Dutarte, Rodrigo 118

East China Sea 36, 49, 62, 89, 95, 114
  and disputes 115–19, 123
economics 22–3, 33–4, 106, 168–9
  and Central Asia 140–1
  and China 102–3
  and Europe 151–2, 155–6
  and India 130–1
  and Middle East 191
  and USA 88, 89, 100–1, 107–9
EEC–China Trade and Economic Cooperation Agreement 150
Egypt 184, 185, 189, 190, 192–3
energy 116–17, 185, 187, 190–1
environmentalism 106–7, 196; *see also* climate change
espionage 49–50, 76, 97–8
European Union (EU) 71, 133, 148–58, 171–2
  and culture 145–8
  and economy 34, 167–9
  and governance 170, 171
  and investment 165–7
  and rights 160–1
  and Tibet 158–60
  and trade 162–5

Fan Jinghui 188
Fei Xiaotong 40
financial crises 89, 155
Five Principles of Peaceful Coexistence 14–15, 25

Forum on China–Africa Cooperation (FOCAC) 177
Four Modernizations 26
Freedman, Lawrence 20–1
freedoms 89
French, Howard 178
Friedberg, Aaron 92
Friedman, Thomas 59
Fujian 45–6

Gang of Four 150
Gao Hucheng 155
gas 117, 138
Germany 147, 163, 166
Ghana 177
GlaxoSmithKline (GSK) 207
Goodhart, David 147
Gorbachev, Mikhail 82
Governance of China, The (Xi Jinping) 64
Great Britain 35, 42–3, 103, 166–7, 206–7
  and Brexit 148, 171
  and Hong Kong 11, 14, 213
  and telecoms 53, 54
  and Tibet 158–9, 160, 161
Greenland 200
Guangdong 45
Guevara, Che 194
Gulf Cooperation Council 185, 186

Habermas, Jürgen 147
Han Fei 3, 20
Hollande, François 160, 161
Hong Kong 11, 14, 25, 78, 98, 213–14
Hong Lei 1
Hope, Bob 82
Hu Jintao 22, 23, 64, 170–1
  and Africa 180
  and Japan 123
  and North Korea 125
  and Pakistan 133
  and Russia 138
  and Taiwan 176
Huang Hua 4

Huawei 53–4, 165, 166, 173, 211
human rights 15, 154, 161, 179, 189
Huntsman, Jon 92

Iceland 70, 104, 200
India 14, 16, 49, 96, 129–32
Indonesia 71, 115, 116, 117, 134
industry 26
infrastructure 103–4
Inner Mongolia 45, 170
intelligence 49–50
International Monetary Fund (IMF) 102–3
internet 67, 91
Iran 6, 71–2, 185, 190
 and nuclear deal 110, 191–2, 209
Iraq 95, 186
iron ore 55, 63, 72, 117
ISIS (Daesh) 188, 190
Israel 189

Jang Song-thaek 126, 127
Japan 12–13, 24, 61–2, 103, 143
 and Australia 211
 and China 119–24
 and East China Sea 116
Jasmine Revolution 92, 186, 189
Jiang Qing 80
Jiang Zemin 16, 33, 64, 139, 201
Juncker, Jean-Claude 156

Kang Youwei 25–6
Kazakhstan 140
Kerry, John 127
Kim Il-sung 14
Kim Jong-il 125, 128
Kim Yong-un 125, 126, 128
Kissinger, Henry 20, 42, 80–1, 132
Koizumi, Junichiro 122–3
Korea see North Korea; South Korea
Korean War 77, 124
Kurlantzick, Joshua 134, 196
Kyrgyzstan 140

Laos 17, 69, 135
Latin America 71–2, 173, 175, 193–7
Leading Small Group on Foreign Affairs 44
League of Arab States 185
Lee Kuan Yew 120
Leonard, Mark 147, 151–2, 170
Lewis, Mark Edward 113
Li Keqiang 90, 102, 156, 163
 and Africa 177–8, 180
 and Europe 172
 and Latin America 173, 195, 197
Liang Qichao 25–6
Liberia 179
Libya 189–90
Lin Biao 80
Lisbon Treaty 156
Liu Guijin 179
Liu He 65, 90
Liu Huaqing 116
Liu Xiaobo 92, 94, 159, 200
Liu Yuan, Lt Col 47–8
Liu Yunshan 30

Ma, Jack (Ma Yun) 55
Ma Xiaotian 48
Ma Ying-jeou 176, 197, 212
Malaysia 71, 115, 116
Manchurians 27
manufacturing 88, 131, 205
Mao Zedong 2, 12, 26, 28, 150
 and Cuba 194
 and foreign policy 41–2
 and Japan 121–2
 and Soviet Union 78–9
 and Third World 174, 175
 and USA 77, 80–1
Marxism 28
May Fourth Movement 26
Mearsheimer, John 92, 105
Merkel, Angela 159, 162–3
Middle East 6, 38, 63–4, 71–2, 173, 183–93
military assets 38, 95–6, 106
Ming dynasty 17

Ministry of Foreign Affairs (MFA) 1, 43–4, 117–18
Ministry of State Security (MSS) 49–50
Modi, Narendra 130, 131, 132
Mongolia 27, 93, 204; *see also* Inner Mongolia
Monnet, Jean 147
MSS *see* Ministry of State Security
Mugabe, Robert 180–1
Myanmar 16, 17, 93–4, 134
and China 45, 135, 136

National Endowment for Democracy 91
nationalists *see* Chiang Kai-shek; Taiwan
Nehru, Jawaharlal 14
Nixon, Richard 16, 81, 209
North Korea 14, 34, 69, 94, 124–9, 192
North Pole *see* Arctic
Norway 159, 200
nuclear power stations 167
nuclear weapons 6, 79, 125, 126, 127–8

Obama, Barack 70, 75, 87, 99, 136
and China visit 92
and climate change 106
oil 2, 182, 187, 190–1
Opening Up the West initiative 140–1
Opium Wars 11
oppression 12–13
Osborne, George 161

Pakistan 42, 132–3
Palestine 189
Paul Tsai China Center 91
People's Liberation Army (PLA) 23, 46–9, 75–7, 79, 97, 132
People's Republic of China (PRC) *see* China
Peru 195, 196

PetroChina 52, 178, 191
pharmaceuticals 207–8
Philippines, the 116, 118, 134
piracy 2, 182
PLA *see* People's Liberation Army
pollution 106–7
Polo, Marco 113
Putin, Vladimir 16, 137–8

Qianlong, Emperor 51
Qing dynasty 11–12, 25–6

Ramo, Joshua Cooper 31, 32
Red Star Over China (Snow) 80
Regler, Klaus 155
religion 89, 99, 131
Ren Zhenfei 53
renminbi (RMB) 106, 108
Republic of China *see* Taiwan
Rio Tinto 208
Ross, Robert S. 5, 83
Rudd, Kevin 210–11
Russia 16, 137–40; *see also* Soviet Union
Ryckmans, Pierre 60

Sarkozy, Nicolas 159
Saudi Arabia 71–2, 185, 190, 192
Senegal 178
Shanghai 45
Shanghai Cooperation Organization (SCO) 70, 104
Shirk, Susan 23
Siberia 138–9
Silk Road 112–13
Singapore 32, 71, 134
Sino–Japanese War 12–13, 26, 119–22
Sinopec 52, 178, 191
Snow, Edgar 80
Snowden, Edward 98
social media 91
socialism 26, 28
soft power 29
solar panels 162, 163, 164
Song dynasty 17

South Africa 179
South America *see* Latin America
South China Sea 36, 49, 62, 114, 135
  and disputes 115–19
  and USA 89, 95, 99
South Korea 14, 125, 127
South Pole *see* Antarctica
sovereignty 14, 16–17, 133–4
Soviet Union (USSR) 5, 19, 28, 47, 137, 204
  and borders 16
  and China 14, 78–9
  and Gorbachev 82
  and North Korea 124, 128
steel 164–5
Strategic and Economic Dialogue 86, 105–6
Studwell, Joe 197
Sudan 179
Sun Tzu 19, 20, 21, 24, 101
Switzerland 104
Syria 6, 185, 189–90

Taiping uprising 11
Taiwan 15, 25, 30, 35, 49, 204
  and China 212, 213–15
  and the EU 154
  and Fujian 45–6
  and maritime disputes 115, 116
  and recognition 175–6, 189, 193, 197
  and USA 76, 77, 93, 109–10
Tanaka, Kakuei 121
Tang dynasty 113
Tanzania 177
technology 26, 53–4
telecoms 53–4, 165, 166
Tellis, Ashley J. 99, 100
terrorism 89, 188, 190
Thailand 134
Thatcher, Margaret 82
think tanks 58–9
Third World 174–5
Tiananmen Square uprising 47, 83, 84–5

Tibet 11, 15, 35, 91, 140, 170
  and the EU 154, 158–60, 161
  and Middle East 189
tourism 37, 60–1, 62, 146
trade 2, 4, 11, 88, 89
  and Asia 114
  and deals 104
  and Europe 148, 150, 157, 162–5
  and Japan 122–3
  and Latin America 195, 197
  and Middle East 186, 188
Trans-Pacific Partnership 104
Trump, Donald 7, 35, 64, 76, 89, 95
  and China 109–10, 203–4
Tsai Ing-wen 76, 109–10, 197
Turkey 185
Turkmenistan 140
Tusk, Donald 156

Uighurs 91
United Kingdom *see* Great Britain
United Nations (UN) 15, 23, 34–5, 80, 81
  and China 177
  and Convention on the Law of the Sea (UNCLOS) 116, 117, 118
United States of America (USA) 2, 3, 93–9, 175
  and AIIB 103–4
  and Antarctica 198
  and Australia 210, 211
  and CCP 111
  and China 7, 8, 9, 14, 32, 33, 70, 75–8, 80–91, 99–102, 104–6, 203–4
  and climate change 6
  and economy 34, 107–9
  and energy 52–3
  and environmentalism 106–7
  and espionage 50
  and India 130
  and Mao Zedong 41–2
  and maritime disputes 117–18
  and Middle East 190, 191–2
  and Pakistan 132

and PLA 48, 49
and Soviet Union 16
and Taiwan 214
and telecoms 54
and Trump 109–10
and Xi Jinping 207
universities 57, 58–9
USSR *see* Soviet Union
Uzbekistan 140

Van Rompuy, Herman 156
Vietnam 2, 16, 45, 69, 94
and China 134–5
and maritime disputes 116
Vietnam War 77
Volvo 165
Voss, Hinrich 166

Wade, Abdoulaye 178
Wang Hui 93
Wang Huning 44, 65, 90
Wang Jisi 57
Wang Xiaodong 62, 94
Wang Yi 44, 127, 186, 188, 192
warlords 26
wealth levels 168–9
Wedeman, Andrew 208
Wen Jiabao 123, 155, 156, 167,
172, 180
Westphalian treaty 16–17
World Bank 103
World is Flat, The (Friedman) 59
World Trade Organization (WTO)
7, 33–4, 52, 90, 122–3
World War I 26, 143, 171
World War II 12, 24, 97, 124, 171
Wu Bangguo 160

Xi Jinping 5, 6, 7, 9, 202
and Africa 180
and Australia 211
and Belt Road Initiative 113–14
and CCP 21, 204–5
and Central Asia 140, 141
and China 25, 208–9, 212–13
and culture 29

and environmentalism 106
and espionage 50
and Europe 145–6
and foreign policy 64, 65–9, 72, 73
and foreign travel 206–7
and history 12–13, 201
and India 130, 132
and Japan 123–4
and Latin America 173, 194–5
and maritime disputes 115
and Middle East 183–4, 185, 188
and North Korea 127, 128
and PLA 46
and polar regions 198
and Russia 138, 139
and Taiwan 214
and USA 70, 75, 87, 90, 175
Xi'an 112–13
Xinjiang 11, 15, 35, 140, 141, 170
and terrorism 188
Xiong Guangkai 47–8
Xu Caihou 48
Xu Zhiyong 91

Yan Xuetong 30–1, 57
Yang Jiechi 44, 135
Yang Yi 49
Yoshida, Shigeru 122
Yunnan 45

Zambia 179
Zhang Chunqiao 150
Zhang Dejiang 125
Zhang Gaoli 54
Zhang Ruimin 56
Zhejiang 45, 66–7
Zheng, Admiral 17
Zheng Bijian 22–3, 58
Zhou Enlai 41–2, 78, 80, 81
Zhou Yongkang 127
Zhu Guofeng 65
Zhu Rongji 88
Zimbabwe 179, 180–1
Zoellick, Robert 34, 103